"With clarity and erudition, Peter Kaufman provides an illustrative study of Augustine's views on leadership both within the Church and the *res publica*. In *Augustine's Leaders*, Kaufman offers to both student and scholar an insightful study of how Augustine confronted the challenges of his age and viewed the roles of those in authority. *Augustine's Leaders*, therefore, presents Kaufman's compelling analysis while advancing the dialogue of Augustinian interpretation among today's historians and theologians."

—MICHAEL J. S. BRUNO, St. Joseph's Seminary, Dunwoodie, NY

AUGUSTINE'S LEADERS

AUGUSTINE'S LEADERS

Peter Iver Kaufman

CASCADE *Books* · Eugene, Oregon

AUGUSTINE'S LEADERS

Copyright © 2017 Peter Iver Kaufman. All rights reserved. Except for brief quotations in critical publications or reviews, no part of this book may be reproduced in any manner without prior written permission from the publisher. Write: Permissions, Wipf and Stock Publishers, 199 W. 8th Ave., Suite 3, Eugene, OR 97401.

Cascade Books
An Imprint of Wipf and Stock Publishers
199 W. 8th Ave., Suite 3
Eugene, OR 97401

www.wipfandstock.com

PAPERBACK ISBN: 978-1-62564-202-8
HARDCOVER ISBN: 978-1-4982-8674-9
EBOOK ISBN: 978-1-5326-1565-8

Cataloguing-in-Publication data:

Names: Kaufman, Peter Iver

Title: Augustine's leaders / Peter Iver Kaufman.

Description: Eugene, OR: Cascade Books, 2017 | Includes bibliographical references and index.

Identifiers: ISBN 978-1-62564-202-8 (paperback) | ISBN 978-1-4982-8674-9 (hardcover) | ISBN 978 1 5326 1565-8 (ebook)

Subjects: LCSH: Augustine, Saint, Bishop of Hippo. | Africa—Church history. | Church history—Primitive and early church, ca. 30–600.

Classification: BR65.A9 K36 2017 (print) | BR65.A9 K36 (ebook)

Manufactured in the U.S.A.   MARCH 21, 2017

Contents

Acknowledgments ix
Introduction 1
1: Augustine's Emperors 7
    Wealth, Glory, and Domination 7
    Emperors and Donatists 15
    Theodosius 23
2: Augustine's Bishops 36
    On Becoming Bishop 36
    Polemics: Manichees and Donatists 46
    Paganism 52
    Excesses 58
    The Bishop's Court 63
    Measuring Success 71
3: Augustine's Pastors 75
    Motives and Emotions 75
    The Uncharitable 81
    Pelagians 88
    Promises 102
    Distress and Discipline 110
4: Augustine's Statesmen 117
    The Business of Babylon 117
    Marcellinus 132
    Counseling Statesmen 145
    No Angels 152
Conclusion 161
Bibliography 169
Index 181

Acknowledgments

Bob Dodaro, Eric Gregory, and Chuck Mathewes: I have been lucky to count them among my colleagues and friends. I never cease to learn from their interpretations of Augustine and political theology. Given their patience and goodwill, I have learned as well to articulate my alternatives to their views more cogently. The summer conferences on Augustine they organized in Charlottesville (2014) and Princeton (2016) kept me thinking about Augustine's times and his timeless appeal in the company of thoughtful, generous scholars, *inter alia*, Michael Bruno, Joseph Clair, Miles Hollingworth, Kristin Deede Johnson, Gregory Lee, and Jim Wetzel.

This is the second of my three volumes on Augustine's political pessimism and radical political theology. The first put the former in biographical context; the third will present the latter alongside the work of Hannah Arendt and Giorgio Agamben. This book answers one of the most important questions raised by the first, a challenge that must be met before completing the third: what, if not programmatic reform of this wicked world, did Augustine expect of its leaders?

Fragments of what follows were first aired in lectures delivered at Fordham and Samford Universities, the University of North Carolina at Chapel Hill, and the University of Chicago. And, at the Jepson School, University of Richmond, I've been fortunate to have colleagues willing to humor an odd antiquarian. Dean Sandra Peart at Jepson keeps this hospitable, seaworthy vessel phenomenally friendly. I've gotten invaluable counsel from Jessica Flanigan and Terry Price, here, and—as always, on other projects—from Clark Gilpin, emeritus professor and dean at the University of Chicago's Divinity School. The confidence of my colleagues at Wipf and Stock and Cascade Books has been inspiring. My conversations in the margins with my remarkably perceptive and tactful copyeditor, Jacob Martin,

ACKNOWLEDGMENTS

made this a much better book. Jacob is the sort of professional interlocutor every author wants. I also owe insights and corrections to a number of anonymous referees whose skepticism about earlier discussions of the issues here prompted me to rethink and reformulate conclusions before they were presented in *History of Political Thought*, *Harvard Theological Review*, *Religions*, and *Journal of Late Antiquity*, as well as in several collections: Cambridge University Press's *Augustine's City of God: A Critical Guide*, edited by Jim Wetzel; Palgrave Macmillan's *Frontiers in Spiritual Leadership*; and the forthcoming proceedings of the Celtic Classics Conference, edited by Michael Williams and Eoghan Moloney.

Robert Pozen and I met in high school in Bridgeport, Connecticut. His extraordinary abilities led to formidable achievements in law, finance, and public service—in careers remote from mine. Yet it seems appropriate to dedicate this book about leadership to Bob—particularly so, because he continues to be an exceptional source of advice to current and would-be leaders and an exceptional friend to an historian who only writes about their predecessors. For more than half a century, Bob, Liz, and their family have welcomed me into their home, and although a battery of facts and figures fill Bob's books, in that setting—but also when we talk about the art of living well and usefully—he reminds me that another eminent jurist, Oliver Wendell Holmes Jr., was right: "Life is painting a picture, not doing a sum."

Introduction

THE CONTINUING RELEVANCE OF Aurelius Augustine, bishop of Hippo in North Africa from the late 390s to 430, has never been questioned, to my knowledge, although questions about the character of his contributions to religious as well as political thought and practice have inspired lively conversations. In her recent study of late medieval images of monastic identity, historian Anik Laferrière at Oxford gets it right: "Augustine has functioned as the archetypal Christian in various settings," yet his deployments or placements "reveal much more about the priorities of those theologians" who refer and defer to him than about his interests and predicaments during his tenure.[1]

Michael Bruno's recent, useful expositions of relatively modern interpretations of what he calls political Augustinianism suggest that the desire to establish "a common ethic" and to "ground social relationships"—a desire "central in political and ethical theory"—makes Augustine increasingly influential.[2] Although Augustine's colleague and first biographer, Bishop Possidius of Calama, intimated that his subject only grudgingly involved himself in the political life of his see and provinces, Numidia and Proconsular Africa, as Eva Elm reminds us (*nur ungern*), nearly all the the historians and ethicists Bruno interrogates believe Augustine's legacy ought to inspire "genuine engagement" with political initiatives.[3] It should become clear here, as it was to Bruno, that I, along with a few others, dissent

---

1. Laferrière, "Augustinian Heart," 492.
2. Bruno, *Political Augustinianism*, 276.
3. Compare Elm, *Die Macht der Weisheit*, 134, with the exposition in Bruno, *Political Augustinianism*, 207–8, which, in this instance, concentrates on Charles Mathewes' *Theology of Public Life*, but which corresponds with what his survey's chapter, "Recovering Augustine's Vision," claims for Eric Gregory's *Politics and the Order of Love* and Robert Dodaro's *Christ and the Just Society*.

from the appropriations or adaptations of Augustine that shuffle passages from his work into an endorsement of some wished-for modern merger of religious piety and politics.[4] But if Augustine had been more skeptical about the prospects for meaningful political change than those other appropriators suspect, critical questions remain for historians who find their interpretations implausible. What did Augustine see as the proper roles for political and religious leaders of his time? And inasmuch as Augustine explicitly repudiated Cicero's conclusion that justice was the aim and essence of statecraft and declared the opposite, that a lack of genuine justice (*vera justitia*) was the distinctive feature of all secular governments, what did Augustine expect from emperors and other statesmen?[5] Finally, given his understanding of the church as *permixta*, as an institution that could never be rid of the wicked in this wicked world, what was Augustine's hope for episcopal and pastoral leadership?[6] The chapters that follow attempt to answer these questions.

Such questions might have been raised differently had Augustine continued on the career path that led him from Africa to Rome, then Milan, where he found the western emperor's Court and became acquainted with the imposing Milanese bishop, Ambrose. Augustine envied him his friends. He had come to find clients and patrons among the affluent and influential in the circles where Ambrose was respected.[7] Yet he soon reconsidered; the beggars of Milan seemed happier than ambitious courtiers. He learned that orators at Court with his gifts failed to advance, unless they became adept at dissembling. Augustine was expected to stretch the truth. He was hired to invent or inflate the virtues of statesmen in eulogies delivered before those who knew he was exaggerating or lying. Political society, sooner rather than later, if we may trust the account he submitted ten years after—but certainly, later—appeared to be littered with lies and driven by lust. Courtiers coveted gold and prized power over honor. Augustine long remembered the hypocrisy and bribery in Rome and Milan. He also remembered the difficulties he had experienced giving up the corrupt and ultimately inconsequential (*nugae nugarum*) political play in which he once yearned to find

---

4. Kaufman, "Augustine's Dystopia," and Kaufman, "*Deposito Diademate*" were published after Bruno completed his presentation of my position in his *Political Augustinianism*, 160–64 and 230–42.

5. See Horn, "Politische Gerechtigkeit," 61, and Augustine, *De civitate Dei* 2.21.

6. Augustine, *De civitate Dei* 8.49: *in hoc saeculo maligno*.

7. Augustine, *Confessiones* 6.3,3.

Introduction

a part.[8] But once he surrendered his ambition, he and Alypius, his close friend from Africa, recrossed the Mediterranean. Within years, they were bishops. The religious and political crises in Africa they faced from the late 390s to their deaths in 430 shaped challenges that differed from those that tested Ambrose. And the challenges, of course, framed Augustine's sense of the hazards, limits, and opportunities associated with emperors', bishops', pastors', and statesmen's leadership.[9]

Arriving in Africa, Augustine and Alypius found Christianity there, as they had left it, divided. Donatist Christians, whom we will often meet in this study, outnumbered their Catholic Christian rivals, with whom the two soon affiliated. Augustine became their leading spokesman shortly after his ordination. He preferred to discuss the disunity and his differences with Donatist bishops away from crowds.[10] Perhaps he worried that the laity would find Donatists' fears about contamination more compelling than his conviction that the Christians' churches should become schools for sinners. Augustine—with some exaggeration, no doubt—charged that his rivals wanted to purge congregations of the improperly disposed and that they equated propriety with prelates' willingness to maintain the schism that originated in the early fourth century. Donatists thought they were the progeny of martyrs (*filii martyrum*), because they and their predecessors suffered for having seceded from bishops who allegedly had conspired with persecutors. The secessionists in Augustine's time justified their decision to remain apart and defiant by referring to the refusal of their rivals to repudiate those supposedly sinister church officials.[11]

After 410, Augustine confronted another, yet much smaller, company of Christians who further complicated efforts to achieve a unified Christian response to African paganism. In that controversy, his position also seemed to put him at a disadvantage in appealing to crowds, insofar as ordinary Christians counted on their efforts to improve morally to please their God and earn salvation. Pelagian theorists catered to such expectations. They relied on a vision reported in the New Testament's final book of revelations to predict optimistically that heaven was ready to accommodate an infinite

---

8. Ibid., 6.6,9; 6.10,16; 8.1,2; and 8.11,26.

9. Elm, *Die Macht der Weisheit*, 121.

10. Augustine, epistle 49.1. For Augustine's most conspicuous failure at crowd control, which was unrelated to the Donatist controversy, see Lakhlif, "Saint Augustin et l'incident de 411," 1102–4.

11. *Actes de la conférence* 3.116.

number of the morally upright. At first, Augustine's counter would have seemed counterintuitive. He argued that morality did not guarantee entry and that God's grace would determine which few from the terrestrial city would pass to the celestial.[12]

Of course, he developed his arguments, hoping to make them appear reasonable as well as biblical. Donatist and Pelagian adversaries accused him of inconsistency, yet he claimed that only fools would deny him the right to make progress in his understanding and exposition of the faith.[13] Still, I learned that little changed in Augustine's views about leadership after he became bishop. What follows accounts for the few subtle changes—notably, Pelagians' influence on how he conceived of pastoral leadership—yet the subject of this book seemed best served by adopting a topical rather than a chronological approach. That risked repetition, inasmuch as the Donatist controversy persisted, gave his call for bishops' and pastors' leadership urgency and shape, and inspired his appreciation for emperors' and other statesmen's leadership. What follows resists the temptation to reintroduce in each chapter the origin and outcomes of the Donatists' secession, yet some of their grievances and of Augustine's responses have been strategically placed wherever it seemed appropriate.

The subject also calls for some repetition, inasmuch as it would have been remiss to overlook Augustine's sense that emperors' humility and compassion were assets pastors could use to encourage ordinary parishioners, because the chapter on pastoral leadership followed the one that discussed Emperor Theodosius. Indeed, humility was a constant feature in Augustine's commendations. It molded his judgment about leadership at Court, in the provinces, and in the churches. It kept him from importuning statesmen to evangelize political culture and the social order—as did his sensitivity to civic corruptibility. Self-interest was pervasive. Clusters of civic leaders resembled dens of thieves. The politics of empire was piracy on a grand scale.[14] When Luke Bretherton presumes to glance at government through Augustine's eyes, he sees political practices—and every fellowship derived therefrom—"based on a false ordering of loves." Yet the bishop would not likely have been consoled by his confidence that the stakes were not nearly as high for Christians as they had been for those pagan political

---

12. For a discussion of relevant texts, comparing Rev 7:9 with Matt 7:14, see Salamito, *Les virtuoses et la multitude*, 275–76, and the third chapter that follows here.

13. Augustine, *De dono perseverentiae* 12.30.

14. Augustine, *De civitate Dei* 4.4.

theorists who believed that the polis was the principal context for human fulfillment.[15]

It should become increasingly clear as this study proceeds that to appraise Augustine's leadership and to sift his appraisals of and advice for religious and political leaders require us repeatedly to confront the difficulties he had trying to unify the church in Africa and to lay the foundations for doctrinal consensus. His sermons, treatises, and correspondence will enable us tenably to contextualize what he professed to be his irenic intent, his general pessimism about political culture, and his widely acknowledged polemical agility. His skills were considerable. Augustine was a trained, respected wordsmith before he disavowed his political ambitions, that is, before he traded his desire to serve the government and himself for a longing to be of use to his church and faith. He had a jingo journalist's nose for what made new news and could turn a single assault on a Catholic Christian bishop into a *cause célèbre*. He sensationalized Donatists' belligerence and made it seem as if most of his secessionist opponents were complicit with terrorists.[16]

Pelagian theorists probably figured they had an advantage, foregrounding humanity's apparent abilities to overcome most temptations and the obvious innocence of infants whom Augustine and his allies insisted on baptizing. Pelagians might have wagered that the emphasis their critics placed on human frailty from the cradle to the grave would come across as morbid and mournful (*funesta*) but were outmaneuvered when Augustine added accounts of evils that innocents suffered—and that touched nearly all families in an age of high infant mortality—to the passages from sacred literature lamenting much the same and making Pelagians seem recklessly overconfident.[17] Pelagius, Augustine admitted, was adept at talking his way around the absurdly upbeat statements about self-reliance or sinlessness he and his followers had written; Pelagius was an artful dodger who gave the impression of liking his chances of making the implausible seem reasonable and religious. Augustine plundered Pelagian treatises for statements that, rhetorically rearranged and garnished, could be made to sound outrageous and heretical.[18]

---

15. Bretherton, *Resurrecting Democracy*, 404 n. 74.
16. Augustine, *Contra Cresconium* 3.43,47, and Augustine, epistle 185.27.
17. Augustine, *Contra Julianum opus imperfectum* 3.61, citing Exod 20:5.
18. Augustine, *De gestis Pelagii* 2–4.

Both political optimism and Pelagian optimism were, to his mind, wholly inappropriate and eminently refutable. Augustine intimated that government and church leaders were correct to conduct their business uncomplaining, but he groused about what Charles Mathewes, purporting to channel the bishop's indignation, describes as "the whole expanse of the miserable necessities of human society." That Augustine would have leaders lead without whining about their chores should not lead us to suspect that he would have them disregard drawbacks. They should know, as he did, that the social order over which they presided was "a fragile thing, always vexed by miscommunication, inattention, and outright malfeasance" (Mathewes, again) and that their "tragic vocation" was to make time in time tolerable.[19]

Yet, in what follows, we will see that Augustine wanted something more from his emperors (but would find it in only one), bishops, pastors, and statesmen. He wanted trust in God's sovereignty and divine grace, exemplary humility, compassion, prudence, drams of pessimism about the chances of perfecting righteousness in this world, but a brand of optimism that, he thought, was always in season—optimism about the celestial fate of the faithful.

This is a study and a story of those expectations and of Augustine's frustrations.

---

19. Mathewes, *Republic of Grace*, 176–77.

1

Augustine's Emperors

Wealth, Glory, and Domination

Several of the Old Testament's leaders were known to sin scandalously. King David's lust for another's wife and his plan to eliminate her husband were perhaps the most memorable instances. Augustine's attention, however, had been drawn to the allegations against Moses made by the Manichees, with whom he was closely associated for nearly ten years in the late fourth century (until the mid-380s) and who claimed the Hebrews' liberator had sinned by pilfering the Egyptians' properties before leading his enslaved people to freedom. Augustine answered that God commanded Moses to relieve the idolaters on the Nile of the gold they were using to gild their idols. Yet Augustine's reply to the Manichees quickly got more involved, and one gets the impression that he was trying out alternative explanations for the theft. Might God have simply permitted rather than commanded the Hebrews to grab and go? Was Moses only relaying their license to steal? And "steal" might be too strong a word, Augustine went on, for God may have had the Jews appropriate the Egyptians' wealth as wages for the work they had done in bondage. Of course, had the authorization originated with Moses, departing with the Egyptian gold would have been sinful. And there was no exonerating the Hebrews for greed stirred by their leader's revelation that God would not have them leave empty-handed. They were no exceptions to the rule that was all too familiar to Augustine, who formulated it influentially: inordinate desires to acquire—cupidity or concupiscence—were stronger than restraints that conscience alone could impose. But Moses was exceptional; neither guile nor greed tainted his leadership. He had not coveted what his followers took from the Egyptians' coffers. Most important for Augustine, Moses had not disputed God's authority to punish the Egyptians and to provision the Hebrews they enslaved. The Manichees' mockery of the Old Testament's stories and protagonists betrayed a pernicious incredulity. Augustine left their company, in part, because they refused to accept what he subsequently would, without blinking, namely, that God's will was always to be obeyed, even if divine intent was not instantaneously comprehensible.[1]

Leaders in the New Testament were cut from different cloth. They were fishermen and tax collectors following a carpenter from Galilee, whereas Moses and David were to the manor bred. Augustine imagined that God assembled apostles from among the powerless to shame the powerful. That worked; several centuries later, princes came to Rome, believing they could learn something significant for their souls' salvation at the apostles' and martyrs' tombs.[2] Jesus could have circulated the good news to the Jews as an affluent, polished orator—as one of the temple's elite, Augustine continued; Jesus could have summoned celebrated, erudite teachers to retell his truths. Yet the fact that messengers and their messiah appeared so humbly left no doubt that God worked through the otherwise unimpressive to gain a victory vastly different from those accomplished by this world's powers. But by the early fourth century, God had given the persuasive and powerful—even emperors—critical parts in Christianity's mission. In effect, those elites conceded that God had first commissioned humble legates (and that humility and contempt for worldly honors was commendable) by setting aside their crowns (*deposito diademate*) as they came to Rome to repent at a fisherman's tomb.[3]

Their repentance signaled to Augustine—more keenly than to the princely penitents themselves, one may suppose—that the glory associated with conquest and imperial expansion was specious and far inferior to God's glory. Augustine featured that contrast between political achievement and God's performances in the early books of his compendious *City of God*,

---

1. Augustine, *Contra Faustum* 22.71–72. For the Manichees' promises and appeals, see Augustine, *De utilitate credenda* 1.2, and BeDuhn, *Augustine's Manichaean Dilemma*, 1:180–86.

2. Augustine, *Enarrationes in Psalmos* 86.8.

3. Ibid., 65.4.

which he wrote after Alaric had sacked the empire's old capital in 410—and featured it in subsequent books for the next fifteen years. He recalled that Rome's history started with fratricide. Its gods turned a blind eye to the carnage that attended the pursuit of honor and political power.[4] Augustine conceded that virtuous people must have recoiled from the atrocities committed during the wars that turned their city, republic, and then empire into a sprawling leviathan. But leaders and chroniclers claimed that Rome's reaching for more territory was always a reaction to its neighbors' aggressions; others' provocations led to Rome's expansions. It attacked to defend or to deter attack.[5] But, to Augustine, Rome's wars exhibited its leaders' lust to dominate. And that lust, along with the destruction and panic that resulted from it, could not be contained on the frontiers. Factions ruthlessly pursued power in Rome. Early in the first century BCE statesmanship gave way to savagery, which Augustine reported in considerable detail, noting that leaders of the late republic who had served in foreign wars and who had learned thereby how vengeance on the vanquished shored up victories then applied that lesson in Rome. Feuds left lasting scars on the body politic. But some who were spared the victors' vengeance during civil wars grew numb. Gratitude for their survival had swallowed up compassion for their friends-turned-casualties. Dehumanization as well as periodic depopulation characterized Rome's pre-Christian history—as reported by Augustine.[6]

Could it have been different, less grim? Might the Romans have resorted to appeasement more often than to force? Augustine concluded that, given their indomitable lust to dominate and their ignorance of what God required of them—as well as their persecution of the early Christians who had become aware of just that—Rome's pagan statesmen and soldiers could hardly change their stripes. They accumulated territories, established bases, and subjugated others to their rule. They conferred the title "empire" upon their acquisitions. They were insatiable, plunging ahead with impunity (*non adempta cupiditas, sed addita impunitas*). Augustine's withering analysis finished with a story about Alexander the Great that would have been familiar to Cicero's and Sallust's readers, who had learned from them about the Macedonians' savagery and about the breathtaking speed with which they swept into Persia and beyond. In the well-traveled tale, imperious

---

4. Augustine, *De civitate Dei* 3.6.
5. Ibid., 4.15.
6. Ibid., 3.28.

Alexander asked a pirate whom he had captured why he had taken to a life of larceny. The pirate deftly responded that he was no more a thief than was his captor. The only difference between the two was that terrorizing the seas with a single vessel was branded piracy or plunder, whereas doing much the same with a great navy was called "empire." That curt reply, historian Brian Harding submits, enabled Augustine discreetly to "reveal the criminality obscured by the rhetoric of *imperium* [and of] *pax romana*."[7]

Augustine's endorsement of the pirate's reply could well have been as unequivocal as Harding suggests. True, in his *City of God*, Augustine showed some respect for the pursuit of glory that led Romans to devote time, energy, and blood to secure their state, which secured their reputations as well. The territorial gains—then losses—were providentially plotted, Augustine believed, attributing the Romans' association of glory with sacrifice to his God's rule over history. But glory was undependable; Augustine explained that it was founded on the admiration of one's subjects, who could be quite fickle, and on the skill of one's publicists, who were known to fabricate or exaggerate. Moreover, even if leaders' conduct was irreproachable and even if they treated enemies honorably and preserved the peace and prosperity of their cities and empires for a time, the glory they received as a reward was far inferior to the glory that God bestowed on apostles, martyrs, and faithful Christians.[8]

And havoc nearly always preceded glory. Gloryhounds, nevertheless, were undaunted. Their craving for glory was irrepressible. They were driven to become illustrious and acclaimed. They were disinclined to hear that the reputations they coveted were of no importance (*nullius*)—were "weighty as smoke," Augustine remarked, without completely discounting their sacrifices and achievements. The grievances that led to their wars were often petty, yet the gloryhounds exhibited courage, endured hardships, and displayed single-minded, if often sinister, purpose. The glory they got was well earned, Augustine conceded; they received their reward, he said, paraphrasing the Gospel of Matthew (6:1–2). But the biblical context was telling, for Jesus had been signaling that those who paraded their piety, conspicuously offering alms for the sake of reputation, were rewarded with reputation—but got no reward from God. In Matthew's Gospel and in Augustine's *City*, peers' praises did not make the praised praiseworthy. They did not make the unrighteous righteous. "Heaven is as remote from the

---

7. Ibid., 4.4; Harding, "Use of Alexander the Great," 118–19, 127–28.
8. Augustine, *De civitate Dei* 5.14–16.

earth as . . . substantial glory [*solida gloria*] is distant from empty praises" received for courage or perseverance in the service of terrestrial cities and empires. Yet Augustine understood that the faithful could learn from the gloryhounds' sacrifices. If the latter committed so ardently to the pursuit of both material advantage and the good opinion of the public—if they relinquished so much to win temporal and, *sub specie aeternitatis*, relatively negligible rewards—then how much more should faithful Christians be ready to sacrifice for rewards that were everlasting, for spiritual solace and for God's good opinion?[9]

Augustine's analysis might have seemed particularly astute with the empire on the defensive. Emperor Theodosius I, we shall learn, recovered the initiative in the East, to some extent, shortly after the Goths decimated his predecessor's army in 378 at Adrianople, but his tenure and that of his sons, Arcadius (in Constantinople) and Honorius (in Rome and Ravenna), were plagued by betrayals and usurpers at Court as well as by Goths, Vandals, and others whose occasional alliances with either of the empire's halves always seemed unsturdy. Augustine's *City of God* could be called an extended epitaph for the empire that the Christians believed they had conquered when Emperor Constantine converted to their faith. One might think of the *City* as a not-so-fond farewell to glory, politically rather than theologically defined.

But Augustine demonstrated little interest in contemporary political predicaments. He was chiefly concerned that the emperors he most closely watched, Theodosius I and Honorius, continued to make what historian Peter Heather describes as "highly Christian noises." Although they were only occasionally effective in having their edicts against heresies and paganism enforced, they were, as we shall discover, "still able to exert a powerful pull on the allegiances and habits of the provinces," inasmuch as the empire's affluent knew that conforming to their emperors' religion was more advantageous than nonconformity or noticeable dissent.[10]

Augustine, as a bishop from the mid-390s to 430, could hardly have been indifferent to the advantages that privileged locals among his parishioners were seeking. Attachments to things of this world (to possessions, promotions, and reputations) were deeply rooted in their characters and

---

9. Ibid., 5.17: *cum illa civitas, in qua nobis regnare promissum est, tantum ab hac distet, quantum distat caelum a terra, a temporali laetitia vita aeterna, ab inanibus laudibus solida gloria.*

10. Heather, *Fall of the Roman Empire*, 126–28.

their culture. Only exceptional individuals set aside the desire to acquire. Augustine was well acquainted with that desire, having spent years—until his turnabout in Milan in 386—pursuing the grail of fame and influence. His sermons seem never to have referred to those years. Indeed, they berated Christians who talked about heaven yet were as preoccupied with temporal rewards as he once was.[11] So historian Peter Brown's intimations, while not wholly indefensible, make his man more tolerant than he was of such hypocrisy, specifically, Brown's statement that Augustine had "accept[ed] on a 'no questions asked' basis [the accumulation of wealth], provided that much of it was spent within the church."[12]

Unlike Bishop Ambrose, whose commerce with emperors and their retainers in Milan occasionally jeopardized his leadership and life, Augustine sifted the Court's hypocrisies and political rivalries from a distance. Oddly, however, his *Confessions* discloses nothing about his reactions to the imperial government's conflict with the church in Milan in 386, though he was there at the time; his mother was among those who helped Ambrose resist the regime's attempts to take over one of the city's basilicas. Returning to Africa and becoming bishop, Augustine did encounter a crisis that developed from Court intrigue. Eutropius, who served Emperor Arcadius in Constantinople, coaxed Gildo, commander of the African garrisons, to defy Arcadius' brother Honorius in the late 390s and to transfer his loyalty and several African provinces from West to East. Nearly a decade later, Augustine would remember Honorius as a faithful and pious emperor whose edicts favored Catholic Christianity to the disadvantage of its pagan as well as its heretical critics.[13] But he immediately and repeatedly exposed Gildo's association with Bishop Optatus of Thamugadi, the leading prelate among those who ostensibly seceded from African churches in communion with Christians around the Mediterranean in the early fourth century. Gildo and Optatus were swiftly defeated by troops dispatched by Honorius. Yet their rebellion gave Augustine a rhetorical edge. For implacable Donatists of his time protested that their ancestors had seceded because the wickedness of bishops who collaborated with the church's persecutors would contaminate every priest they ordained and every bishop they consecrated. Augustine was quick to draw the conclusion about contagion that appeared to follow

---

11. Augustine, *Enarrationes in Psalmos* 51.6: *in coelestibus verbis trahunt cor in terra*.

12. Brown, *Through the Eye of a Needle*, 379.

13. Augustine, epistle 92.2–3. For the context, see Di Berardino, "Rileggere il 410," 11–14.

from his rivals' ridiculous claims: Eutropius, the villain at Arcadius' Court, seduced Gildo, who seduced and contaminated dissident bishop Optatus, who defiled all who subscribed to his cause, turning Donatism into an infectious disease.[14]

Political mistakes and misalliances were less important to Augustine than were the Donatist dissidents' ongoing estrangement from the African churches he served as advocate, bishop, and pastor. And of greatest importance to him were Christians' personal difficulties overcoming obstacles to humility and faith—or, as he put it, difficulties leaving behind Babylon, that is, their passion for possessions.[15] In subsequent chapters we will learn how he addressed those issues and why, in his *Confessions*, he referred to streets of Babylon, as though he were describing sordid slums where he and other adolescents sought guilty pleasures. But he also referred to shameful practices at and around the Court in Milan, where, as an orator for hire, he tried to advance his career, lacing with lies the eulogies he composed and delivered to flatter the powerful while other ambitious place-seekers, knowing that he had lied, were nonetheless quick to praise him. They expected thereby to acquire a soon-to-be-influential patron.[16] In some sermons Babylon became a city (*civitas*) or state (*respublica*), so we may be excused for suspecting Augustine had civic service or provincial politics—or statesmanship—in mind as he preached about the business of Babylon.[17] His contempt sometimes extended and applied to the empire, which he perceived as aging and shriveling up (*vedetis senescere et minui*).[18] He knew that conquest and oppression had not started with the first Roman emperors. Assyrians were equally cruel and did comparable harm. God choreographed the domination of some by others, but neither divinity nor history exonerated headstrong rulers (or the hirelings who advised and eulogized them) for making domination their business—and the business of Babylon. Historian Gaetano Lettieri was quite right to assume Augustine associated Babylon with everything he despised about the late antique state.[19]

---

14. For example, see Augustine, *Contra litteras Petiliani* 2.28,65 and 2.101,232; *Contra Cresconium* 4.25,32; and epistle 87.4–5.

15. Augustine, *Enarrationes in Psalmos* 44.25.

16. Augustine, *Confessiones* 6.6,9 and, for *iter platearum Babyloniae*, *Confessiones* 2.3,8.

17. Augustine, *Enarrationes in Psalmos* 51.6: *Babyloniae negotia*.

18. Ibid., 26(2).18.

19. Augustine, *De civitate Dei* 18.2, and Lettieri, *Senso della storia*, 197–99.

There was no point in asking why God gave the Assyrians and Romans empires. The former never worshipped him. They and the latter persecuted those who did. God's ways with this world bewildered onlookers, but Augustine insisted that they were not unjust.[20] And when the time was right, in God's sight, God converted Emperor Constantine. But the few references to Constantine in Augustine's sermons and correspondence avoid celebration. For example, one long letter on the nature of faith holds that Romans who never left the empire's western parts need not see to believe Constantine founded Constantinople in the East, but Augustine neglected to mention what Constantine saw, the vision that brought him to the faith, dazzling him and dazzling generations of the faithful who dated their deliverance to that time. And, as the founder of Constantinople, Constantine came into Augustine's script only briefly as he explained that terrestrial cities, unlike God's celestial city, were not eternal.[21]

Augustine did introduce Emperor Constantine at slightly greater length in the *City of God*, yet only after discussing what qualified as virtuous rule: that rulers should be self-assured, not arrogant; unmoved by flattery; slow to punish; inclined to pardon; and more intent on being in command of themselves (restraining base passions) than on commanding others.[22] He mocked the idea that the empire's fourth-century setbacks were the revenge of the pagans' gods for Constantine's disaffection from them and affection for a new and jealous god. Surely if they had such control, Augustine continued, the old gods would have prevented previous misfortunes, for downturns in Roman history were not new. Besides, uplifting changes followed Constantine's conversion: expenditures on Rome's costliest spectacles were cut, crimes were fewer, brothels were not rebuilt, and the reprobate were no longer permitted to behave disgracefully with impunity and thereby to demonstrate their civilization's moral bankruptcy.[23]

---

20. Augustine, *De civitate Dei* 5.21.

21. Augustine, epistle 147.5; Augustine, sermon 105.12. Szidat suggests that Augustine improvised when he wrote about Constantinople, departing from his sources ("Constantin bei Augustin," 250–52).

22. Augustine, *De civitate Dei* 5.24.

23. Augustine, *sermones nuper reperti*, Dolbeau 6.13.

Emperors and Donatists

Notwithstanding this inventory of advances, Augustine valued Constantine most as the emperor who had acquitted African bishops Caecilian of Carthage and Felix of Apthugni, who were accused of having handed over the faith's sacred texts to the church's persecutors. Thereby, the government undermined dissidents' justification for secession. Initially, in 313, Constantine forwarded the depositions against Caecilian and Felix to Bishop Miltiades, who presided in Rome and who summoned his colleagues to a council there. That assembly as well as a subsequent one at Arles, in 314, found in favor of Caecilian and Felix. Dissidents were confident the emperor would overrule his bishops; instead, as Augustine often reported with satisfaction, Constantine and his proconsul in Africa tossed out the plaintiffs' complaints.[24] They only then expressed their contempt for the Court, which circulated edicts, attempting to restore the African church's unity, but to no avail. The *pars Donati* assembled congregations alongside those of the Caecilianists, whom we know as Catholic Christians, given their pitches for a universal church (*katholikos*) rather than an exclusive, regional, African Christian communion. For their part, the Donatist secessionists persisted and outnumbered Catholic Christians in Africa when Augustine arrived. He noted that, because they were unable to draw the government to their cause, Donatists used Christianity's underdog status in the past to malign Catholic Christians whom emperors supported during most of the fourth century and into the fifth.[25]

Donatists not only turned back the clock to times and troubles—Pilate had Jesus crucified; emperors' deputies martyred the apostles—to make governing authorities seem to be Christianity's inveterate and permanent enemies, but they also willfully failed to see the past and present as parts of a divine plan. To gain the proper perspective, they need only have read the Psalms, according to Augustine, who found both promise and prophecy therein—a promise that "the whole earth and all its peoples [would] hasten to hear about Christ and to believe in him." *Ante oculos vestros*, before your very eyes, Augustine told parishioners, the pagans' idols have been and are continuing to be dislodged and destroyed, much as the psalmist had

---

24. See, for example, Augustine, epistles 129.4 and 141.11. Augustine claimed that the Donatists, while falsely accusing Caecilian of betraying the faith, welcomed collaborators into their congregations (*Contra Cresconium* 3.33).

25. Augustine, epistle 105.10: *Defunctus est Constantinus, sed judicium Constantini contra vos vivit*.

predicted. Christianity's story was one of development.²⁶ But, if the Donatists' sense of the faith's requirements (as Augustine represented it) were correct, the development would have been arrested long before their time. For the Donatist secessionists supposedly claimed that the sacraments' effectiveness depended on the flawless character of the prelates presiding. And no human, Augustine countered, could reach that level of perfection. Desires for a filth-free church were understandable but not realistic. There should be standards for clerical conduct, Augustine conceded, yet the development that the Psalms forecast could never be realized unless churches made room for prelates whose faith occasionally flirted with doubt and who sometimes failed to resist temptations. The sacred texts had not stipulated precisely *when* the empire would turn to the new faith, only *that* it would turn, as Constantine did at God's prompting. God seized the Roman Empire.²⁷

The Donatists had a very different interpretation of the fourth century. In their view, the empire seized Christianity, compromised the clergy, and forced the faith to serve a few regimes' nefarious political purposes. But for a short spell, Augustine sardonically pointed out, Donatist secessionists enjoyed the support of Emperor Julian, who reigned for eighteen months in the early 360s. To encourage divisions within Christianity, Julian returned basilicas that had been taken from the African dissidents. The emperor was trying to revive Rome's old religions and—wickedly, from Augustine's perspective—to deprive all the faithful, whom he contemptuously called Galileans, of the advantages previous emperors allowed them. Augustine was—or feigned to be—appalled by the Donatists' lack of circumspection. Their churches would soon enough have been taken from them, and they as well as Catholic Christians would have been losers, had Julian lived. He was an apostate and threat; Constantine, a pioneer and hero. Augustine insisted that the Donatists had bet on the wrong horse. They charged Constantine with corruption and—tending to generalize—accused political leaders of having dirty hands and sinister intent, while applauding Julian's insight, welcoming his patronage, and appealing to his rescript as a vindication of their clarifications of the faith that their only acceptable emperor was trying to eradicate.²⁸ The caution already mentioned still applies: we depend

26. Augustine, *De consensu Evangelistarum* 1.21; Augustine, *Enarrationes in Psalmos* 62.1.

27. Augustine, *Contra epistolam Parmeniani* 2.35; Augustine, *Contra Cresconium* 4.6.

28. Augustine, *Contra litteras Petiliani* 2.97,224.

on Augustine for much of what we know about the labyrinthian religious controversies that divided the African churches, and his characterizations of adversaries' purported inconsistencies were hardly impartial. But his position on this count is unambiguous, if not altogether reliable: the Donatist dissidents countenanced Emperor Julian's projects to destroy the unity of the church without recognizing them as strategies to eviscerate Christianity.[29]

The feud with Donatists during the late 390s and into the next century was one of Augustine's principal preoccupations (and we shall have several occasions to return to it); nonetheless, the tide had turned against them long before. Emperor Gratian had ordered his proconsul for Africa to dismantle the altars of "heretics," undoubtedly referring to Donatists' shrines set up in places left to them after Julian died in 363.[30] Constantine was the first but by no means the last emperor in the West to recognize that the Catholic clergy provided an exceedingly useful "alternative infrastructure" to the civic elite in Latin Christendom.[31] Donatist dissidents predictably scolded the clergy collaborating. According to secessionists, collaborators connived in an ongoing persecution of the uncompromised and uncompromising Christians who elected to serve the Donatists' churches. Augustine shuffled Emperor Julian into this phase of his rejoinder to dissidents' charges as well. How could they argue so emphatically that collaboration with the government, in general, was absolutely off, after having cheerfully accepted churches and other privileges from Julian—from *vester Pontius*, from their Pontius Pilate? The Christianity that the Donatist and Catholic Christians shared, albeit with different estimates of its disrepair, prospered because Julian's tenure had been so brief, Augustine held, and because Constantine's purpose had been revived by emperors Jovian, Gratian, Valentinian, and Theodosius, whom Augustine, in the heat of controversy, came close to coupling with the Hebrews' kings. And a case could be made that he contemplated endorsing Eusebius of Caesarea's contention that Emperor Constantine could be regarded as *chef des chrétiens*.[32]

---

29. Augustine, epistle 105.9.

30. *Imperatoris Theodosii Codex* 16.5,4.

31. Drake, "Intolerance," 210, and Drake, *Constantine and the Bishops*, 184–91, for "alternative infrastructure."

32. Augustine, *Contra litteras Petiliani* 2.92,202–3. For Eusebius' *chef des chrétiens*, see Inglebert, "Universalité chrétienne," 454–56, 460–61.

Yet whenever Augustine approached that point, he stopped short. He considered the triumphalism associated with Eusebius unbecoming. Constantine was undeniably a benefactor; before he embraced their faith Christians were often compelled to hide. After that remarkable change, there was cause to celebrate. Within a century, descendants of the pagans from whom they were hiding looked for places to hide their idols from antagonistic authorities. Constantine, his sons, and their successors—save Emperor Julian—up to Augustine's time favored Christianity yet still ruled a sinful city (*civitas impia*). So Augustine was grateful for, yet not overly optimistic about, the sustained support from the government.[33] He was happy that emperors subscribed to his faith, but just prior to the sack or so-called fall of Rome in 410, he made it clear that Christ's kingdom could have no political coordinates or boundaries on earth. That "kingdom" or city of God was seated in the hearts of the faithful. The Hebrew Scriptures' political history had been affixed to Christianity's other sacred texts, Augustine explained, to impart two lessons. The first disclosed the opposition between the politics on this planet and the celestial city (*aliud regnum*), parts of which were on pilgrimage in history. To remain faithful to the latter, it had been necessary to endure patiently the animosity of all kingdoms of this earth.[34] And it would continue to be necessary, Augustine assumed, because even the emperors, who trusted the promises of their faith, ruled unreliably. Politics called mischief statecraft. The second lesson he had learned from reading the political reporting in the Old Testament and from noticing in the New the apostles' and gospels' remove from political power concerned continuity and sovereignty. He considered the empire, from Constantine to Theodosius and Honorius, as the fulfillment of God's promise to circulate the good news that the creator had not abandoned creation. Confirming as much, the Christianity of the fourth and fifth centuries was still the Christianity of the apostles; its good fortune, however, ought to make the faithful conscious of their place in history as members of a spiritual conspiracy (*consensio*).[35]

It must have been difficult to emphasize Christians' spiritual realm (*aliud regnum*) or celestial city so soon after the faithful had looked to inherit a terrestrial one. Emperor Constantine gave liberally. He had churches

---

33. Augustine, *sermones nuper reperti*, Dolbeau 4.8.

34. Augustine, *Contra Faustum* 22.76: *aliud regnum pro quo oportet omnium terrenorum regnorum adversitatem patientissime sustineri.*

35. Ibid., 13.7–14.

built at public expense. He gave the Christian clergy tax exemptions. His sons and heirs were equally generous. Temples were rededicated as churches. Emperor Constantius II attended the dedication of the great octagonal church in Antioch. The Christian presence in the empire's cities was more and more conspicuous as the decades passed.[36] Increasingly visible, and in places monumentally so, Christianity was blamed when fifth-century political and military setbacks mounted. Augustine replied to the critics of his religion that the proliferation of churches and sermons had not yet resulted in successful evangelization of the empire; Rome's old gods, therefore, had no cause for anger. In fact, Augustine said, the pagans' gods, if they existed, ought to have been consoled that so many Christians either condemned or ignored their pastors' and bishops' sermons.[37]

Augustine's sermons included hard words for those "many Christians." He thought that they were so intoxicated or mesmerized by imperial patronage that they grew deaf to the gospels' good news about a spiritual or celestial realm compared to which their material advantages and relatively new standing in the empire were all but insignificant. The faithful, one suspects, might have been as upset by his tone as were the pagans, because he crossly ordered Christians out of the theaters. He condoned neither conformity to the standards and expectations of this world-turned-kind-to-Christianity nor extreme opposition to them, which was characteristic of Donatist dissidents. Augustine explained that Christians of all stripes, rather than boasting of their religion's political successes and their emperors' largess, ought to obey the clerics urging them to repent and repudiate their desires to rise above others, shout them down, and dominate.[38]

Of the bishops' many challenges (which a subsequent chapter sifts), one that Augustine repeatedly reformulated was to undermine the pride that normally fueled those desires "to rise above ... and dominate." Such desires were, of course, common among statesmen aspiring to imperial power, the very persons whose protection bishops required to secure and maintain places where they could assist the faithful to combat arrogance, repent their complacence, acknowledge their other imperfections, and steadily progress and approach what God would have them be.[39] What protection meant differed as circumstances changed. Catholic Christian prelates in Africa asked

36. Hahn, *Gewalt und religiöser Konflikt*, 149.
37. Augustine, epistle 111.1–2.
38. Augustine, *sermones nuper reperti*, Dolbeau 2.23: *surgere, reboare, dominari*.
39. Augustine, *Enarrationes in Psalmos* 138.21: *proficiant ... quotidie accedant*.

Emperor Constantine to endorse their case against colleagues whom they cast as petulant and predatory secessionists. As we now know, he obliged, although, under the leadership of their most enterprising bishop, Donatus, they thrived during the fourth century. In the early fifth, Augustine and his African Catholic colleagues asked Emperor Honorius to back their efforts against followers of Pelagius. The chancery, then in Ravenna, issued an edict forbidding those nonconformists from promoting the outlandish, sinister (*scaevus*) notion that the sins of Adam and Eve had not been transmitted to their posterity.[40] Chances are that historian Robert Markus was right to think that African Catholic Christian bishops came to realize that their church "had to learn to receive" from its emperors "almost everything except its own peculiar saving message."[41]

When he expressed in general terms what he hoped to receive from emperors, Augustine asked for peace. But Emile Perreau-Saussine may be safe suggesting in his study of the *City of God* that "on a scale which goes from the chaos of civil war to the peace of the heart, *pax temporalis* is somewhere low, but important."[42] Nonetheless, we may infer from Augustine's correspondence and sermons that he believed he could calm parishioners' restless hearts more easily when government authorities preserved rather than disturbed the peace. The problem was that their initiatives too often stopped halfway. Emperors were often too prudent to be thorough. Constantine had made a good start in supporting Caecilianists—soon to be Catholic Christians—but confessional strife continued during the remainder of his reign and for well over a century because the enforcement in Africa of the emperor's and the two European church councils' pronouncements intended to end the schism was uneven. But in late antiquity peace seldom stayed when it surfaced—and seldom surfaced. According to Augustine's analysis, the expanse of empire stirred envy, within its territories as well as beyond it frontiers, and the belligerence born of envy occasioned one war after another. The slaughter seemed interminable. Confronted by invaders or usurpers, emperors could hardly afford to give such challenges a miss.

But Augustine deplored the staggering consequences (*quanta strage hominum, quanta effusione humani sanguinis*). He conceded that it was incumbent on Christian emperors to fight injustices and that even

---

40. Quoted in Marcos, "Anti-Pelagian Legislation," 342.
41. Markus, *Saeculum*, 163.
42. Perreau-Saussine, "Heaven as a Political Theme," 187.

well-intentioned combat bred cruelty. He pitied chroniclers tasked with reporting the results because their tasks either drove them to tears or—what was more pitiable—numbed them to the blood (*quanta effusione!*) and the wretchedness of this wicked world.[43] Although Augustine wanted peace, he acknowledged that Christianity, spreading as the Psalms promised, was a beneficiary of the empire's wars. He cautioned that wars were constants, which was another reason for the faithful, whose faith came with a fervent desire for peace, to remember they were passing through the terrestrial city to the celestial.[44]

From the time Constantine became a patron of their religion to—and after—the 390s when Emperor Theodosius I outlawed pagans' pageants, many Christians considered their terrestrial cities comfortable, despite their wars and confessional conflicts. Christian emperors were their trophies. To Augustine, comfortable Christians were only nominally Christian. Those not-so-faithful faithful proved to him that, although the emperors could remake laws and institutions to accommodate the coexistence of Christianity and empires, they could not remake their subjects' souls.[45]

And resistance to any refashioning, over which the church's leaders might have presided, surely developed in the wake of Rome's humiliation in 410. Augustine's *City of God* specifically addressed the crisis of confidence that followed the sack of the old capital that year. Promises in the Psalms that he repeated so often were still relevant, although political fulfillment of them could not be expected. The gospel would be preached globally, as the psalmist intimated; the year 410 was neither a turning point nor a stopping point. Certainly an autopsy of the Christian empire was premature. But Augustine believed that the severe setbacks were meant to test and reorient the faith of the faithful. Humanity was too poorly equipped to go further in trying to comprehend the creator's purposes. Why God conjured up the misfortunes would remain incomprehensible, and what God might make of them would remain unascertainable. What Christians should know (or rather, believe) was that pious emperors ostensibly committed to the public good were among God's gifts, but certainly not God's most precious gifts.[46]

43. Augustine, *De civitate Dei* 19.7.

44. Augustine, *Enarrationes in Psalmos* 94.6; Augustine, sermon 328.5.

45. Augustine, *Enarrationes in Psalmos* 94.2. Also see Lancel, "L'Antiquité tardive," ascertaining *la coexistence du christianisme et de l'Empire dans les institutions, sinon toujours dans les âmes* (238).

46. Augustine, *De civitate Dei* 4.7: *quis enim de hac re novit voluntatem Dei?* Also see Duval, "L'éloge de Théodose," 174–75.

Nor were they particularly dependable gifts. Co-emperor Licinius, who appeared to share Constantine's new faith for ten years and who issued with him an edict tolerating Christianity in 313, turned on Christians as well as on his imperial colleague.[47] Constantine was also inconstant. After he endorsed the Nicene christological formula at the church council in 325, he favored those opposing it, the anti-Nicene Arian partisans who had been disposed to compromise by their defeat at the council. The emperor switched sides several times, leaving eastern churches squabbling bitterly when he died.[48] On border security, which was particularly urgent in the late third and early fourth centuries, Constantine was compared unfavorably to Diocletian, his pagan predecessor.[49]

But that comparison was crafted by Zosimus, a pagan and a self-appointed defense expert who composed his analysis nearly two centuries after Constantine's death and who was pleased to put that emperor's neck in the noose. He also complained that Constantius II—the one son of Constantine to have survived the other two, reunited the empire, and ruled for nearly a quarter-century—left the frontiers unfortified.[50] Augustine would likely not have registered complaints similar to those of Zosimus. The western empire with which he was familiar was most troubled by tribes crossing the Danube and Rhine Rivers, far from the African provinces. Yet Constantius had been a consistent ally of the Arian Christians. Embarrassing circumstances forced him in 344 to end the persecution of the leading Nicene spokesman, Bishop Athanasius of Alexandria, yet the emperor was identified with the christological formula that Augustine found repulsive and called heretical. So Constantius was given only a cameo role in Augustine's discussion of the harassment of bishops, which addressed a dilemma that was only obliquely related to any emperor's competence, specifically, whether bishops hounded by religious or political antagonists should flee their sees or stay to serve the laity.[51]

---

47. Cristofoli, "Religione e strumentalizzazione politica," 160–63.

48. Barnes, *Constantine and Eusebius*, 224–44.

49. Zosimus, *Historia nova* 2.34.

50. Ibid., 2.51.

51. Augustine, epistle 228.6–11. For Athanasius' brief reprieve, see Galvão-Sobrinho, *Doctrine and Power*, 145.

Theodosius

Augustine hardly bothered with the other fourth-century emperors who supported the Arian clergy. He remembered that Emperor Valens' persecution of the pro-Nicene party had ravaged churches in the East (*vastavit*), but Bishop Ambrose of Milan went further, concluding that Valens' attachment to the Arians drew down God's wrath on the empire and, therefore, was responsible for the catastrophic defeat of Rome's forces by the Goths at Adrianople in 378.[52] To be sure, Ambrose had been more directly involved than Augustine in the christological disputes. When he first met Ambrose, the bishop was locked in a struggle with Milanese critics of Nicene Christianity, defying Empress Justina, who insisted that a church be reserved for Arian worship. Ambrose refused. His obstinacy, impressive lay support, and the threat that Magnus Maximus, a usurper in Trier, might come to Milan to impose his and the bishop's will on the Court ensured that what Gérard Nauroy calls "the war of nerves" ended in the Nicene faction's favor.[53] Ambrose was relatively successful, but Emperor Theodosius I, who succeeded Valens after Adrianople and who presided over the eastern half (and shortly thereafter, *de facto*, ruled the western as well), more decisively resolved the christological quarrels. First he swept west and defeated Maximus. He left Justina's young son, Valentinian II, at Court in Milan with several custodians who no doubt reported to him, and he returned to Thessalonica and Constantinople. There he enforced measures that put anti-Nicene prelates at a disadvantage. So when he turned west again to take direct control, Theodosius' pro-Nicene prelates were justified in thinking that they were witnessing what Neil McLynn now marks as the "inauguration of a new partnership" between the government and their party, although Theodosius found it necessary to make some accommodations to retain the services of Arian Christian soldiers in the squadrons that helped him retain power.[54]

---

52. Compare Augustine, *De civitate Dei* 18.52 with Ambrose, *De fide* 2.16,139. Potter counsels against taking what was said about Valens' anti-Nicene crusade too seriously (*Roman Empire at Bay*, 554). The "persecution" could have been little more than his having tipped contested episcopal elections in favor of Arian Christian candidates.

53. Nauroy, "Le fouet et le miel," 56.

54. McLynn, "Transformation of Imperial Churchgoing," 258–59. For Theodosius' accommodation, see Whitby, "Emperors and Armies," 177; and for the prohibition of public discussions of christological issues, see *Imperatoris Theodosii Codex* 16.4,2: *nulli egresso ad publicum . . . disceptandi de religione*.

Augustine's Leaders

Augustine was impressed by Theodosius' restraint, although not because the emperor waived the chance to purge Arian Christians from his legions. What struck Augustine was the emperor's departure for the East after having saved young Valentinian II, his co-emperor, from Magnus Maximus. Theodosius could have seized power in the West without difficulty.[55] This is not to claim Augustine was indifferent to Theodosius' edicts favoring the Nicene faction and the general, if not stem to stern, purge of Arian Christians from his company. Augustine declared his preference for the Nicene christological formula in no uncertain terms. The father and son, he preached, were consubstantial; by sending his son into flesh, God had not demoted him. God had not debased or degraded Jesus' divinity.[56] Augustine surely shared the enthusiasm of pro-Nicene colleagues who attributed to Theodosius the revival of their faction.[57] Yet scholars have learned to mistrust confessionally motivated attributions of that sort. Still, emphatic edicts against Arian "sacrilege" suggest that, although Augustine only once alluded to Theodosius' indefatigable efforts to undermine Arianism (*non quievit*), they were important elements in his regime's religio-political rhetoric, if not also emblematic, effective features of his policy.[58]

Augustine was also somewhat subdued about Theodosius' anti-pagan legislation, yet he could hardly pass over in silence what contemporaries (inaccurately) interpreted as Christianity's momentous suppression of a pagan insurrection at the river Frigidus in 394. The battle followed some complicated maneuvering after the death of Valentinian II. Arbogast, who commanded the armies in the West and into whose care the young emperor had been entrusted, feared that Theodosius would suspect him of regicide. The commander, therefore, saw to it that an influential Roman Christian, Eugenius, was named emperor. The two hoped that Theodosius would accept arrangements that perpetuated the dual rule of the empire. Theodosius' response was unambiguous. He named Honorius, his nine-year-old son, emperor in the West and readied his troops. Francesco Corsaro is no doubt right to think that Theodosius never planned to make dual rule a matter of policy. Quite likely, despite Augustine's praise for the emperor's

---

55. Augustine, *De civitate Dei* 5.26.
56. Augustine, sermon 135.2.
57. Groß-Albenhausen, *Imperator Christianissimus*, 16–21.
58. Augustine, *De civitate Dei* 5.26. Also see McLynn, "Genere Hispanus," 111.

restraint, Theodosius used Valentinian as a placeholder in the West while he consolidated power in the East.[59]

When Theodosius' intentions became clear, Arbogast and Eugenius had to improvise and create a following. Despite prohibitive legislation, many in the West remained fond of their cults, so, to win them to his cause, Eugenius relaxed the restrictions on pagan worship that Theodosius had imposed. The celebrations in Rome organized by Nicomachus Flavianus were so swaggering that Symmachus, the previous generation's paladin of Roman paganism, distanced himself from the delirium.[60] Eugenius also promoted pagans at his Court. Understandably, therefore, his and Arbogast's defeat at the Frigidus was patched into Christians' accounts as their faith's victory over the old Roman gods. The prayers of Emperor Theodosius were said to have summoned strong gusts that kept the weapons hurled by Eugenius' soldiers from reaching their targets. Augustine condensed the story but included the prayers and winds to document Theodosius' piety and his God's apparent response.[61]

Perhaps Augustine kept the Frigidus story short because he was intent on devoting his tribute in the *City of God* to Theodosius' character. Besides, the story and tribute were preceded by Augustine's caution that the faithful should not expect military miracles from their Christian emperors; if Christianity guaranteed Christian emperors' successes, emperors would convert for convenience, not from conviction. But Augustine might also have abbreviated his tale because the narratives emphasizing a pagan revival under Eugenius and a final victory for Christianity were hard to reconcile with the facts. Augustine might have been aware that Theodosius took roughly as many pagan troops into battle at the Frigidus as did his enemies.[62]

The theme would not have changed. God could have used blustery winds, Christian soldiers, or pagan troops as long as wars went terribly wrong for pagan higher-ups. Africa remained loyal to Theodosius, so Augustine, who had returned there years before the emperor had defeated Eugenius and Arbogast, had reason to suppose that Theodosius' heirs, Honorius and Arcadius, would not change course. Doubts about the ease

---

59. Corsaro, "Il trono e l'altare," 607.

60. For Flavianus and Symmachus, see Matthews, *Western Aristocracies*, 242–45.

61. Augustine, *De civitate Dei* 5.26; for Augustine's sources, see Courcelle, "Jugements de Rufin," 111–19.

62. Cameron, *Last Pagans of Rome*, 94–95, 122–23.

or speed with which the world might hear the gospel remained. Yet God had promised as much in the Psalms, Augustine often preached, explaining that the promise placed God in debt (*tenemus debitorem*). God being God, he went on, the debt would be paid—the promise fulfilled—by whatever means God chose.[63] The Christian emperors must have seemed to be the means. So possibly Augustine was tempted, as Robert Markus says, to think that Theodosius' reconquest of the West at the Frigidus signaled that politics had become "part of God's saving work."[64] Yet, conceivably at the time and most assuredly thereafter, he was far less exuberant than many of his contemporaries—particularly Prudentius and Rufinus, as we shall see. Then, after the empire's setbacks in the early fifth century, Augustine grew gloomy. He saw that Emperor Honorius' legislation against slave trafficking was ineffective and perhaps contributed to the problem when, deploring the brutality of the laws' prescribed punishments, he interceded to spare traffickers whom the churches had been unable to persuade to forego their trade.[65]

There were reasons for reserve during Theodosius' tenure as well. He was served not only by pagan soldiers but also by pagan proconsuls and consuls. He appointed Vettius Agorias Praetextatus, who had persuaded Emperor Valentinian I to allow nocturnal pagan sacrifices, as praetorian prefect. Augustine's tribute to Theodosius overlooked such pagans in public service. Possibly he surmised that highly placed pagans kept extremists of all stripes in check, extremists whose anti-pagan or, in Africa, anti-Christian and anti-Catholic Christian agitation disturbed the peace he so desired.[66] The consensus among historians seems correct: "Theodosius let himself be swayed far more by considerations of power and the future of his dynasty than by his religious beliefs."[67] When deputies were named to secure the East while the emperor went west to tackle Magnus Maximus or Eugenius, their competence mattered more than their religion. Evidence suggests that Theodosius was less interested in evangelizing the empire than in collecting taxes, paying troops, and defending frontiers. He seems to have been content that members of the aristocracy, who remained fond of the old cults

63. Augustine, *Enarrationes in Psalmos* 32(2).9; Augustine, sermon 22.4.
64. Markus, *Saeculum*, 30–31, and Markus, "*Tempora Christiana* Revisited," 201–2.
65. Augustine, sermon 10*.3–4.
66. See Ernesti, *Princeps Christianus*, 82–87, 476–77, for Theodosius as a brake on extremism.
67. Errington, *Roman Imperial Policy*, 258.

and resistant to Christianity, refrain from objecting publicly to his regime's opposition to pagan sacrifices.[68]

The poet Prudentius gave posterity a very different Theodosius. His emperor-turned-evangelist nearly threatened to torment subjects who refused to abandon Rome's old religions and trade up to Christianity. According to the poet, Theodosius delivered an oration to Romans in which he blamed pagans' poor judgment (presumably during the run-up to combat at the Frigidus) on dark spirits and black idols.[69] If the speech had been delivered, one can conjure up Theodosius linking pagans' poor political judgment—specifically, the support given to Eugenius and Arbogast—to their religious superstitions. Prudentius was not one to leave readers in suspense. He had his imperial orator imagine the enthusiasm that attended Constantine's conversion and proclaimed that all who heard Theodosius were called to Christ by his eloquence, fervor, and sincerity.[70]

Prudentius set the oration and its outcome as the culmination of Theodosius' reign; the emperor died soon after. Marianne Kah concludes that the poet also believed that the emperor's performance and his auditors' acquiescence sealed the partnership between Christianity and the government, making it "possible for his Christian subjects fully and finally to identify with the state" (*endlich voll*).[71] Augustine reported that pagans had been refuted (*confuti atque convicti*) during the tenure of Theodosius and that he had paused after his rout of Arbogast and Eugenius at the Frigidus to topple the statues of Jupiter they had erected in the Alps. But Augustine's tribute to Theodosius in his *City of God* says nothing about the speech reconstructed (or dreamed up) by Prudentius. Surely, if Theodosius' remarks were as effective as the poet suggested (or simply had been uttered at all), the occasion would have been newsworthy in Africa. Roman proprietors of Africa's great estates kept news as well as goods flowing across the Mediterranean. So, if Theodosius had unburdened himself as Prudentius indicated, Augustine's very general comment about the refutation of pagans seems strangely evasive. Hence, we may admire the poet's license or performance but doubt the details he supplied to add an impressive aftermath in Rome to the battle at the Frigidus. His story of the oration, however, acquired sturdy

---

68. Lippold, *Theodosius der Große*, 134; Leppin, *Theodosius der Große*, 187.

69. Prudentius, *Contra Symmachus* 1.423–24: *obscuras video tibi circumferrier umbras caeruleasque animas atque idola nigra volare*.

70. Ibid., 1.481–93 and 1.508–10.

71. Kah, *"Die Welt der Römer"*, 231.

legs. The sixth-century pagan historian Zosimus felt compelled to redraft it. He referred to the emperor's speech but asserted that the Romans refused to take Theodosius and his faith seriously, an assertion that corresponds better than Prudentius' kudos and Augustine's more ambiguous accolade with a consensus developing among historians that "paganism remained vibrant" among the Roman aristocracy "into the fifth century."[72]

Who, then, was Emperor Theodosius, and what did Augustine think of him? The answer to the second—our principal—question and concern will be less complicated than an answer to the first. But a few of those complications must be addressed if we are to gauge whether Augustine hijacked Theodosius, misrepresenting his religious and political sentiments, or tried to present a substantially accurate account of his leadership. The effusive praise that Theodosius received in the 380s was a far cry from Prudentius' rave review, but the emperor's apologists, at that earlier time, were replying to criticism of his armistice with the Goths who had defeated and killed his predecessor, Gratian. The critics at Gratian's Court were displeased that their emperor had summoned Theodosius from Spain to assist with the campaigns against tribes that were crossing the Danube. They would have preferred that Gratian promote one of their familiars. Theodosius seemed an imported emperor to them, and his readiness to settle for something less than a total, glorious victory over the Goths fueled their opposition. Themistius touted the truce. He was also taken by the Spanish import's apparent fondness and flair for philosophy, to which he attributed Theodosius' wise decision to negotiate. Themistius' Theodosius chose conversation over conflict and clemency over revenge. Those choices, the eulogist said, tamed the Goths.[73]

One suspects that Augustine, had he known about Themistius' judgments, might have approved of them and incorporated them into his *City*'s tribute to Theodosius. But Prudentius' more aggressive, uncompromising Theodosius seemed corroborated by his chancery's rescripts against pagans and anti-Nicene Christians, which found their way into the Codex Theodosianus. We have already noted the strong language that makes the emperor sound more messianic than moderate. Themistius' Theodosius seems to have disappeared. Did Prudentius' emperor swallow him up? Yet a contextually informed reading of the rescripts draws us to reconsider the contrasts

72. Zosimus, *Historia nova* 4.59; Salzman, *Making of a Christian Aristocracy*, 79–80.

73. Themistius, *Orationes* 14.182c (1:263); 16.210c–211b (1:301–2); and 17.213c–215a (1:306–7). Also see Ernesti, *Princeps Christianus*, 446–47.

between Themistius' moderate and Prudentius' militant. For the rescripts addressed local problems; undeniably, they put dissidents in jeopardy, but a case could be made that, even collectively, Theodosius' edicts made no "major contribution to the fortunes of orthodoxy." Intimidation rather than oppression looks to have been their aim.[74] They might have appeased militant prelates, especially Ambrose, who, as Hartmut Leppin attests, burrowed his way into Theodosius' inner circle, but the emperor's instructions swatted at dissent; no crushing blow appears to have been delivered. Theodosius' approaches to problems created by his empire's diverse and rival cults were pragmatic.[75]

Augustine, we now know, exhibited little excitement about the government's decrees, although, to his mind, they gestured appropriately. If emperors too often exposed confessional claws, there was no telling who would get bloodied. In the late fourth century, the pro-Nicene party fared poorly during Emperor Constantius' tenure. Julian did well by the Donatists. Very early in the fifth century, Augustine sounded a bit like Themistius. He pilloried politicians who loved temporal power and sought their glory in the subjugation of others. Soon after he lost Emperor Theodosius and a decade before he composed his screed on imperial politics in his *City of God*, Augustine was scowling at politically ambitious contemporaries who appeared weighed down by their inordinate affection for—and desire to acquire—status and power (*cupiditas*). Their claims to be protecting the church were bogus, he implied; their ambitions put their faith as well as the faithful in jeopardy.[76]

Augustine continued to deflate the residual optimism about the Christian empire in his *City*. As R. P. C. Hanson makes out, he lost his faith in Rome's fate. Surveying history, which included the republic's and the empire's multiple recoveries from setbacks and which illustrated the virtue of emperors' persistence, if not also their near invincibility, Augustine dug in his heels when he ceased looking back and started looking ahead, and above. *Sub specie aeternitatis*, if Hanson is right, Augustine concluded that "the empire must be condemned. It placed its whole hope and trust in success—*gloria*—and by that worldly standard it had at last failed."[77] Hanson's "at last" is important, because it locates Augustine's take on the government

---

74. Errington, "Christian Accounts," 423–35.
75. Leppin, *Theodosius der Große*, 156; Kah, "Die Welt der Römer", 126–27.
76. Augustine, *De catechizandis rudibus* 19.31.
77. Hanson, "Reaction of the Church," 276.

during the last two decades of his life. The question then was what could be redeemed—what could he redeem. And Augustine's answer: a Christian emperor's humility. That was valuable salvage, a lesson for every creature who, by nature, coveted honor, status, and power. And of all creatures, rulers would be most tempted to court fame and treasure titles. All the more precious, therefore, a humble Christian emperor, a celebrated statesman who prized piety rather than celebrity!⁷⁸

Theodosius was rare. With leadership came followers eager to please. Emperors would have to be exceedingly tactful to turn away from their ovations without either insulting them or seeming to feign humility to attract greater attention and adulation. Augustine counseled that emperors' contempt for glory ought to be concealed from their subjects. Emperors ought to take the praise on offer and not be seen to take it lightly (*parvipendere*). And they should publicly attribute the powers they possess to God's mercy, professing their unworthiness.⁷⁹ Augustine acknowledged that subjects would be genuinely surprised by such admissions of human frailty, but he trusted that shock would subside and that the perception of their leaders' humility would brew in their subjects an affection more lasting than any admiration occasioned by leaders' self-promotion. To ensure just that, emperors were advised to cultivate "a conception of themselves as repentant sinners" and to conduct themselves accordingly.⁸⁰

In his *City of God*, Augustine identified repentance as the "sacrifice" God expects and the bedrock of the faithful life. Repentance required that creatures recognize how far short of perfect righteousness they had fallen by presenting their contrite hearts as offerings (*sacrificium contriti cordis*). The psalmist had assured that God wanted no sacrifice, but Augustine explained that the veto referred to offering dead animals; the deity was not to be appeased in that way. Sacrifices of hearts bruised by self-accusation were necessary, however, to alert creatures to their dependence on their creator and redeemer, to assist them to develop and display self-discipline, to denounce self-deception, and to acknowledge that they were God's instruments. Augustine echoed the apostle: repentance confirmed that creatures were not conformed to this age.⁸¹

---

78. Augustine, *De Genesi contra Manichaeos* 2.16,24, and Augustine, *De civitate Dei* 5.18.

79. Augustine, *De civitate Dei* 5.19.

80. Dodaro, "Augustine's Revision of the Heroic Ideal," 153.

81. Augustine, *De civitate Dei* 10.5–6, referring to Psalm 50 and Romans 12.

No wonder, then, Augustine recounted Emperor Theodosius' public penance signaling his sorrow for a massacre in Macedonia. The *City of God*'s tribute to Theodosius, as we learned, mentions the emperor's victory at the Frigidus, anti-pagan initiatives, and support for the church, but it is capped with the penance required and orchestrated by Bishop Ambrose after Theodosius had ordered troops to slaughter an arena full of Thessalonians to avenge the death of the garrison commander there. Augustine dodged the details yet included a clause that somewhat exonerated the emperor and incriminated his bloody-minded subordinates. But the account starts with a blaring fanfare that drowns out excuses, extolling Theodosius' astounding humility. *Quid autem fuit . . . mirabilius!* What could be more marvelous than an emperor's self-abasement? Air, light, fertile soil, and the expanse of empire—as well as the glory for having expanded it—had been given by God to the virtuous and wicked in equal measure, Augustine proposed, but the devotion manifest in Theodosius' repentance and public penance was a gift reserved for the truly good and faithful. Augustine doctored what seemed particularly significant for Ambrose—the emperor's disrobing and setting aside the symbols of his power before his public penance—and then narratively deployed the exemplary expression of humility as a staging area for an editorial on rulers who elect to pursue power and glory rather than righteousness. Just as Theodosius divested himself, removing his crown to repent, he and all others who lead must leave their power and glory this side of the grave. But the righteous take their righteousness with them when they shuffle off this mortal coil.[82]

Ambrose was the chief protagonist of his account. Without discounting the difficulty of speaking truth to power, he pronounced that it was every priest's duty to confront even the most highly placed wrongdoers. God would almost certainly punish spineless priests and bishops. Yet Theodosius, Ambrose said, posed a special challenge. He was not only powerful but dangerously impulsive. If approached indelicately, his anger could ricochet around the realm and adversely affect churches far from Milan. Nonetheless, a bishop's pastoral duty was to impose penances. Ambrose's account of his courage and tact referred to the biblical tale of King David's crimes and correction, placing the Prophet Nathan's rebukes in the foreground and suggesting he was Theodosius' Nathan. Yet Ambrose was discreet. He saved

---

82. Compare Augustine, *De civitate Dei* 5.26 with Ambrose, *De obitu Theodosii* 34, but also see Ernesti, *Princeps Christianus*, 183–84.

that suggestion and comparison for his funeral oration for Theodosius.[83] Yet parts of Ambrose's harrowing tale circulated widely. Sozomen, for example, picked it up a generation later and dropped it in his ecclesiastical history. He misdated the massacre (and penance) and apparently drew on other sources to add gruesome details. For example, he either imagined or learned that Theodosius' soldiers had been given quotas of corpses to fill. But the staples of Ambrose's account resurfaced in Sozomen's—the bishop's courage as well as the penitent's humility, which was signaled by the emperor's appearance without his regalia.[84]

Ambrose's resolve—or, to be precise, his story of his resolve—has impressed onlookers, from his time to ours. At least one usually well-informed historian, Johannes Hahn, presumes that the bishop expressed "massive" Milanese indignation after the slaughter in the East.[85] But Peter Brown's take corresponds more closely with the bishop's report. Brown suggests that he "faced the awe-inspiring incarnation of the Roman order . . . as a spiritual guide," that Ambrose was more a philosopher instructing an imperious student on the devastating consequences of rage than an enraged prelate.[86] Neither the moral philosopher nor the church censor, however, made it into the account of Theodosius' penance in Augustine's *City* where "the church's discipline" brought the emperor to his knees. And Ambrose was missing as well when Augustine introduced the emperor into a sermon on penance, the point of which was to shame lesser mortals refusing to display contrition when their former emperor had stooped to the authority of the church.[87] Historian André Tuliere puts Augustine's omissions of Ambrose in perspective. To Tuliere, Theodosius and Ambrose participated in a coalition between the episcopal aristocracy and the government that was forged to hold in check the poor and middling sorts, the lesser mortals of Augustine's sermon. That sermon corresponds with what Tuliere considers a different approach *ad populum* taken by the prelates interested in reducing the spiritual distance between governed and governing. Arguably, Augustine accomplished exactly that by replacing Ambrose with

---

83. Ambrose, *De obitu Theodosii* 34.

84. Compare Sozomen, *Historia ecclesiastica* 7.25 (*NPNF*[2] 2:393) with Ambrose, *Epistula extra collectionem* 11.3–11.

85. Hahn, *Gewalt und religiöser Konflikt*, 88 n. 354.

86. Brown, *Power and Persuasion*, 110–11.

87. Augustine, sermon 392.3.

the discipline of the church as the catalyst for the emperor's admirable and imitable repentance.[88]

Theodosius died in 395. The emperor to whom Augustine and his African colleagues appealed and with whom they negotiated was Honorius, Theodosius' son who ruled the West after his father's death and until 423. Although served until 408 by Stilicho, a competent commander who had married Theodosius' niece and expeditiously put down an African insurgency, Honorius was rather unremarkable, and his record on border security was abysmal.[89] On his watch, Italy was overrun. He and his brother Arcadius in Constantinople never ventured far from the safety of their courts. The advice that the latter do so could be read as a complaint about both—a complaint that one can imagine circulating among provincials who would have agreed with Synesius of Cyrene, bishop of Ptolemais, that emperors with firsthand knowledge of war best knew how to preserve the peace.[90]

But Africa was remote from the frontiers where warlike emperors were wanted. African clerics, including Augustine, seem to have been unperturbed by Honorius' absence. Theodosius, too, had never visited. The Catholic Christian bishops there were satisfied to have had Honorius' supportive edicts in their battles against Donatist secessionists, Pelagians, and pagans. But it was important to Augustine to have the emperor's proconsuls in Proconsular Africa, the governors in Numidia, and the Court's other deputies—vicars, tribunes, and commanders, some of whom we shall meet in the chapter on statesmen—keep the peace. Peace in this wicked world (*malus est mundus*) was critical if the faithful were to position themselves for their victory yet to come.[91] Emperors and their deputies could ensure that the undisciplined, uncooperative, and heretical, threatened with dire consequences, not overwhelm the faithful, but they could not ensure that Christians lived untroubled by such "colleagues." So Augustine and the African Catholic Christian clergy faced challenges we must discuss in the next two chapters. The most galling critics of Catholic Christianity had to

---

88. Tuliere nonetheless suggests that Ambrose and Augustine were cut from the same cloth ("La politique de Théodose le Grand," 61–71). McLynn, reflecting on the collaboration between Ambrose and Theodosius, senses that "the weakness" of the latter's "political situation"—not the strength of his faith—brought the emperor to Ambrose, whose "ceremonial services" enabled him to save face ("Genere Hispanus," 107).

89. Leppin, *Theodosius der Große*, 234.

90. Synesius, *De regno* 16.

91. Augustine, *Enarrationes in Psalmos* 123.4; Augustine sermon 105.8–9.

be polemically put down, and the faithful in the pilgrim city would have to be inspired to retain hope in their ultimate victory, to restrain their base desires, and to practice compassion in the interim.[92]

It is worth thinking about what Augustine's Theodosius contributed to meeting a few of those challenges, specifically, to helping Augustine console and inspire the faithful after the sack of Rome in 410 and arming him against pagan critics who blamed their empire's humiliations on Christianity. Augustine's tribute to Theodosius in the *City of God* emphasized that power had not corrupted him; unlike his pagan predecessors, Theodosius had not been provoked by a passion for glory (*ardor gloriae*). Other idealizations of the emperor studied by Jörg Ernesti tugged him closer to figures around whom imperial cults formed or draped him with archaic Roman and republican virtues. The result, Ernesti confirmed, appealed to senators in late fourth-century Rome, who occasionally tilted toward paganism, by keeping Theodosius "slightly out of focus," having him trifle with matters of faith, yet nearly divinizing him.[93] Christian idealizations of the emperor were equally tendentious. Yet they seem to rest on incontestable observations that John Matthews itemizes: Theodosius, he says, gave devotees of his religion what they "most wanted: Christian piety, deference to bishops, Catholic legislation, and the suppression of paganism."[94] To that bundle Augustine's *City* adds felicity. Theodosius not only made Christians happy, but he was also truly happy as a Christian. Augustine claimed that the emperor did not bathe in his subjects' adoration and presume to possess all the virtues they ascribed to him. He knew he was a mere subject in the celestial city and an instrument of God's will in the terrestrial.[95] According to Augustine, Christian emperors were happier to have achieved self-discipline—happier to have mastered their less creditable desires than to bestride the Mediterranean and rule multiple tribes and territories. The section on happiness and especially the tribute to Theodosius in the final chapter of the *City of God*'s fifth book bring to a close the text's mixed review of the love of glory and the lust to dominate, both of which characterized and stigmatized Roman history as Augustine retold it. The statement that

92. See, for example, Augustine sermon 105.9: *O fidelis, noli corrumpere spem, noli amittere caritatem.*

93. Ernesti, *Princeps Christianus*, 349–50.

94. Matthews, *Western Aristocracies*, 252.

95. Augustine, *De civitate Dei* 5.24: *si inter lingues sublimiter honorantium et obsequia nimis humiliter salutantium non extolluntur et se homines esse meminerunt.*

most explicitly contrasts the felicity of the faithful to the delights that had accompanied conquests, affluence, and political influence expressed the *City*'s certainty that Theodosius was happier (*gaudebat*) standing in church than running the world.[96]

Augustine's training in Africa suggests that he aspired to be among statesmen running the world. He had mastered the cadences of praise that would have served him and influential clients well. But after spending time in Rome and especially in Milan, you now know, he came to regret and abandon political ambitions. He told us in his *Confessions* that he was good at inflating the virtues and concealing the vices of powerful figures but also that public relations was not good for him. Lying to and for those who knew he lied weighed on his conscience. He seems to have developed a busier conscience as he grew more serious about Christianity.[97] Augustine left that world behind, but so much of what he later wrote displayed his rhetorical and oratorical skills. His sermons, correspondence, and polemical treatises are superbly crafted, as were his *Confessions* and his *City of God*. His knack for subtlety and hyperbole comes across in his tributes to Rome's two most prominent Christian emperors. His capsule on Constantine seems rather clueless about that emperor's personality. After itemizing the traits that virtuous leaders ought to possess—traits that made them slow to punish, inclined to pardon; self-assured yet not arrogant; unmoved by flattery, devoted to self-discipline—Augustine linked Constantine with none of them. The *City* touts his reign—that it was long and prosperous—but not his rectitude.[98] The text's tribute to Theodosius is, in effect, a hymn to his humility. Yet Augustine was careful to avoid a "great danger" or "temptation" that he would associate with Pelagian optimism. Christian emperors were God's sign that promises of Christianity's global reach could be fulfilled, yet one must beware of glossing over the scandals that plagued politics. In the terrestrial city, they were unavoidable; Christianity's greater glory was to come in the faith's final, celestial victory.[99]

---

96. Augustine, *De civitate Dei* 5.26; Duval, "L'éloge de Théodose," 135–42.

97. Augustine, *Confessiones* 6.6,9

98. Compare Augustine, *De civitate Dei* 5.24 with 5.25. Also see Salamito, "Constantin vu par Augustin," 556–59.

99. Augustine, *De perfectione justitiae hominis* 15.35: *Non enim modo . . . in tantis opprobriis impiorum dicendum est eam esse gloriosam quia reges ei serviunt ubi est periculosior majorque temptatio, sed tunc potius gloriosa erit.*

2

Augustine's Bishops

On Becoming Bishop

AUGUSTINE WARNED THAT POLITICS were becoming too important. He thought that the faithful excessively trusted their Christian emperors. We shall find him ever so faintly nostalgic for the persecutions that inspired ordinary Christians and their clergy to contemplate consolations offered by their faith in troubled times. He missed martyrs. Specifically, he missed the martyrs' repudiations of successes measured materially. Such successes were spoiling Christianity. Christians were complacent, counting on favors from authorities, forming or perpetuating factions—feuding with each other, perhaps more virulently after Emperor Constantine and his successors ended their regimes' opposition to the faith. But by the time Augustine returned to Africa from Italy, Christians and pagans alike had been tutored—and chastened—by their legions' and emperors' inabilities to defend an empire once thought invincible. Augustine likely winced as he contemplated the insecurity, complacency, sectarian rivalries, and ruin. Many of his sermons as well as his correspondence and treatises explored administrative and pastoral challenges related to the unwelcome developments, to problems related to the little political leverage that churches could exert, and to the material successes too unreservedly welcomed by the faithful. This and the next chapter introduce and illustrate the issues Augustine identified and the ways he would have had his clerical colleagues resolve them.

He returned to Africa in 388. The cities he had known, Thagaste and Carthage—and the one he would soon come to know, Hippo Regius—appeared politically and economically stable, notwithstanding the increasing demands for taxes made by local and provincial agents of the central government. But those demands depleted funds that would otherwise have been earmarked for municipal improvements, according to Claude Lepelley (*gravement amputés*), who therefore sites the region in "a history of inexorable decline" from the 380s into the 430s.[1] He may be right, but the coastal city of Hippo seems to have been a bustling port and, from the late 390s, a place where Augustine, as bishop, was busy exchanging ideas as well as insults with polemicists of various stripes. His first stop was home, in Thagaste; he had not intended to take a leading part in Christianity's bouts with dissidents, secessionists, and pagans. The adrenaline that helped him excel in polemics seems not yet to have been surging. On his return to Africa, he looked to retire to his family estate with several like-minded friends.

In a sermon preached decades later Augustine explained that he had gone to Hippo to confer with a man who inquired about his small company of contemplatives in Thagaste. Perhaps he also hoped to encourage the faithful in Hippo to locate another contemplative collective there. He said he detested traveling. He worried that his reputation for insight and eloquence might tempt Christians to waylay him to fill a vacancy. But he figured he was safe in Hippo. The incumbent, Bishop Valerius, was very much alive and well respected. But at that time (391), Valerius was thinking ahead. He and his parishioners pressured Augustine to stay and be ordained. After several years Valerius nominated him as his coadjutor and successor.[2]

The image of Augustine very reluctantly but—finally—obligingly responding to Hippo and Valerius' overture seems the one he wanted to project. Bishop Possidius of Calama, which was roughly seventy-five kilometers from Hippo, wrote the first account of Augustine's career and reported that his subject consented to serve only after substantial pressure had been applied (*compulsus atque coactus succubuit*). But Augustine was likely the source for that story, which corresponds with the protests he subsequently expressed when he seemed to be fatigued by the chores and challenges related to his job (*negotium*), fondly recalling his leisurely conversations with

1. Lepelley, *Les cités de l'Afrique romaine*, 1:197 and 1:414.
2. Augustine, sermon 355.2.

learned friends at Cassiciacum or Thagaste (*otium*). Having left Ambrose and Milan, he appeared genuinely pleased to be out of politics, if we may trust the sentiments proffered ten years later in his *Confessions*. So, to repeat, despite the leadership he would exercise thereafter, Augustine looks to have had no interest in leading churches before Valerius and his parishioners in Hippo Regius drew or threw him into their trenches in 391.[3]

Socioeconomic interests attracted others to church leadership. From the time of Constantine, developments "open[ed] the church to the world," Werner Eck argues, and Hugo Brandenberg adds that a new view of church leadership (*einer neuen Führungsschicht*) spurred status seekers or social climbers to contemplate careers in their parishes and dioceses. But of the motives of would-be bishops and the parishioners who wooed them—motives that Eck usefully catalogues—only one seems to apply to Augustine: the desire to appease a respected current incumbent.[4] Augustine, after all, was known to have indignantly denounced colleagues who chased promotions. He was austere and expected austerity of the clergy. He emphasized the distinction between Christians' hopes for eternal rewards, which bishops ought to cultivate by preaching the promises in sacred texts, and the desires for temporal gains that so many pagans proudly exhibited, even after parts of their empire were in ruins.[5] Possidius, probably coached by Augustine, claimed that before becoming bishop, his subject counseled Christians to resist the temptations or seductions of this world (*illicebras*), recognizing that the repercussions of doing otherwise would disgrace them and their faith.[6]

But Augustine's emphases and distinctions did not incline him to forego the challenge of leading the faithful, although, as we mentioned, his admiration for Christianity's martyrs seemed more intense than his esteem for many of its churches' administrators. By the time he returned to Africa, the religion was generally accepted or, where paganism persisted, grudgingly indulged. The government and Catholic Christianity continued to harass the one faction there that revered martyrs' self-abandon, even to the point—if Augustine is to be trusted—of staging heart-stopping scenes

---

3. Possidius, *Sancti Augustini vita*, 8; Kaufman, *Incorrectly Political*, 33–34.

4. Eck, "Der Einfluß der konstantinischen Wende," 568–70, 576–80; Brandenburg, "Die Eroberung Roms," 263.

5. Augustine, epistle 209.6; Augustine, sermon 157.5.

6. Possidius, *Sancti Augustini vita* 3.

of their own suffering by defiance and violence that provoked reprisals.[7] Whereas he extolled the martyrs' sensibilities, Donatists idolized their self-sacrifices. Augustine extrapolated from texts that both Donatist dissidents and Catholic Christians held sacred that God was far less concerned with how the faithful left this world (*non qua occasione exeant*) than with how well they lived in it.[8]

Yet living in it chastely—living in but not of the world—did not necessarily preclude political maneuvering. Possidius' biography presumably reflected Augustine's view that the culmination of his career was the conduct and outcome of the Council of Carthage, specifically, the proscriptions against the Donatists confirmed by Marcellinus, the presiding tribune, in 411; all that good work, Possidius maintained, was begun and was brought to pass and perfection by Augustine.[9] So, despite his reluctance to countenance Christians measuring their successes in temporal terms, Augustine seems to have put great stock in concrete policy outcomes. At the Council, he convinced his Catholic colleagues to display moderation (*nostra mansuetudo*) and to advocate clemency, marking the contrast between them and intransigent Donatists, as he did in previous polemics. He persuaded Marcellinus and other government authorities that Catholic Christianity in Africa was poised to take advantage of the church's position—open to the world—and that Donatist dissidents undiplomatically were committed to keeping their sects exclusive, and hostile.[10]

Bishops' conferences in Africa appear to have met without government oversight. The Council of Carthage in 411 was an exception. It is hard to tell exactly what to make of Emperor Honorius' decree that Christianity's clerical community devote itself to prayer and turn a blind eye to vexatious concerns related to regional politics and commerce. Might the chancery have been addressing a singular situation in which the church's interference or influence had been destabilizing? Whatever prompted Honorius'

---

7. Augustine, *Contra Cresconium* 3.49,54 and Augustine, epistle 185.12, referring to Donatist extremists. Also consult Kriegbaum, *Kirche der Traditoren*, 152–54; Kaufman, "Donatism Revisited," 135–39; and, for the Donatist extremists' version of "suicide-by-cop," Shaw, *Sacred Violence*, 762–64.

8. Augustine, epistle 111.6.

9. Possidius, *Sancti Augustini vita*, 13 (*totum illius bonum coeptum et perfectum est*); for correspondences between Augustine's and Possidius' ideals of episcopal service, consult Elm, *Die Macht der Weisheit*, 143.

10. Augustine, *Contra Cresconium* 3.47,51; Augustine, epistle 88.7.

rescript, it was unrealistic.¹¹ Locally, Catholic Christian bishops and probably a few Donatist moderates were becoming prominent in civic affairs. Prelates often served alongside local *curiales*, helping maintain order and promote peace. Claudia Rapp notices that "the distinction between the episcopate and a civil magistracy could become blurry." Politically engaged bishops and their "audiences," about which we will soon hear much more, were surely symptoms of Catholic Christianity's churches' raised public profile.¹² Bishops were conspicuous civic patrons. To Augustine, their participation meant that the poor, who were victimized in most schemes to maximize tax revenues, could count on advocates. Opposition to exploitation surfaces often in his correspondence and sermons. When he learned that a landlord he had converted was behind a plan to extort money from tenants, he crossly explained to him that the suffering of the financially strapped was temporal—temporary—whereas the torments awaiting those who tormented the poor would be hellish and everlasting.¹³

The effectiveness of such "explanations" depended on offenders' fears concerning the afterlife, the sincerity of their faith, and their willingness to be instructed or intimidated. And conceivably Augustine's doubts about any or all of the above led him to approve the appointments of local ombudsmen to cope with commoners' complaints. Emperor Diocletian has been credited with improvising administrative arrangements that included the nomination of *defensores civitatum*, "defenders" or protectors of their municipalities. Their functions seem to have increased as did their independence from the town councils and *curiales* during the fourth century. Greater stress was put on their protection of the poor, although they also became responsible for the prohibition of pagan practices.¹⁴ There is evidence Augustine requested that a *defensor* address commoners' concerns during the liquidation of Donatist parishes in his diocese and to sift grievances against the young man he commissioned to deal with the fallout, Antoninus, to whom we will return in due course. But he also acknowledged he was powerless to place an ombudsman or *defensor* in the city of Hippo to ensure that commoners were neither defrauded nor otherwise bullied by

---

11. *Imperatoris Theodosii Codex* 16.2,40 (*Constitutiones Sirmondianae* 11).

12. Rapp, *Holy Bishops in Late Antiquity*, 172–73. For the distribution of bishops in Numidia and Proconsular Africa, see Dossey, *Peasant and Empire*, 127–29.

13. Augustine, epistle 247.1; for his related interventions, see Lepelley, "Le patronat épiscopal," 30–33.

14. *Imperatoris Theodosii Codex* 1.29,6 and 16.10,12, respectively.

more prominent and instrusive neighbors. The difficulties he reported may be related to those experienced elsewhere and often in the empire, difficulties in delivering what historian Robert Frakes calls "efficient justice" to the poor. Augustine regretted that bishops were unable to rid their dioceses of poverty; bishops and pastors could only commiserate.[15]

Precisely at the time Augustine articulated the need for respected, impartial ombudsmen the curial elites were polarized. They preferred any restructuring that would award them greater authority than less privileged colleagues on the curia had—and that would reduce the *defensores* to dwarfish bureaucrats. *Curiales*, in this instance, might have been reacting to what looks to have been their own demotion or decline. They were losing power to representatives of a reorganized, resurgent central or imperial government. According to Claudia Rapp, Augustine and other bishops—whether they were "operating in conjunction" with the *curiales*, with emperors' deputies, and with (or without) *defensores*—were never fully integrated into the administration of justice.[16]

Bishop Ambrose of Milan might seem to have been an exception. He cared about the fair distribution of local resources yet never shed his aristocratic biases. He looks to have had a large, loyal, local following but lavished time maintaining a regional, ecclesial network simultaneously cultivating friendships with secular authorities—all of which made his reach something of a marvel.[17] Emperors and their deputies used him as an emissary. He consulted with Emperor Gratian before becoming closely associated with Theodosius, although the stories about his immense influence at that emperor's Court in Milan are exaggerations. As Rita Lizzi reports, the rather inflated rhetoric in a few of his letters misled proponents of the church's claims to political authority to infer Ambrose and those close to the emperor were *equipollenti*, equally matched. Unquestionably the bishop had significant influence on Theodosius' religious self-presentation and almost certainly on some of his legislation. But relationships between bishops and emperors were incompletely theorized during the fourth century. And to argue that Augustine's *City of God*, in the fifth, yielded what predecessors had not, on that count, is problematic, insofar as efforts to tease a coherent

---

15. Compare Augustine, epistle 20*.29 (a *defensor* in the diocese) with Augustine, epistle 22*.2–4 (the need for *defensores*). Also see Sabw Kanyang, *Episcopus et plebs*, 280, and Frakes, "Contra Potentium Iniurias," 224–26.

16. Rapp, *Holy Bishops in Late Antiquity*, 287–88.

17. Compare Brown, *Through the Eye of a Needle*, 131–34, with McLynn, *Ambrose of Milan*, 248–51.

theory from that gargantuan, comprehensive text seldom, if ever, remain uncontroversial for more than a decade.¹⁸ Karl Leo Noethlichs, describing the distinct objectives of church and Court, characterizes the various partnerships into which the two entered as "contentious connections," which inclined each partner to protect its prerogatives and to try to limit the scope of the other's proclaimed purposes. Such self-protection obviously restricted the extent of cooperation.¹⁹

Augustine tried to avoid contention. His overtures to the powerful refrained from pitting his church's interests and needs against the responsibilities of local and provincial officials who were commited to *Realpolitik*. He never intimated that bishops possessed a superior perspective or position that entitled them to moral outrage. Counseling clemency, he wrote to the powerful as one Christian to another.²⁰ And, after having taken parishioners' problems to government officials, he reported—with more than a dram of self-pity but without recrimination—the petty humiliations to which he had been subjected when, on one occasion, he was kept waiting interminably and made to feel contemptibly insignificant.²¹ That highly placed prelates could expect some disrespect from African officials is not surprising. Many provincial and municipal magistrates resented the lost prestige of Rome's old religions. Yet within the church, bishops were their flock's foremen—their shepherds. They were in charge of congregations exposed to predation, despite the formal imperial decrees in their favor. Still, the great danger, Augustine continued, was the temptation to exploit their authority to feather their nests; bishops ought to take neither pleasure nor profit from their positions.²²

They were the apostles' successors, Augustine asserted; their leadership signaled that God had not forsaken the church when the apostles died. Just as the apostles replaced patriarchs and prophets, bishops replaced the apostles. Bishops became parishioners' "fathers"—as well as their foremen.²³ The needs they were consecrated to address were organizational and pastoral, although from our century's perspective (and, arguably, also from

18. Lizzi, "I vescovi e i potentes della terra," 96–97.
19. Noethlichs, "Materialien zum Bischofsbild," 54 (*Konfliktverbindungen*).
20. See, for example, Augustine, epistle 139.2, and Rebillard, "Augustin et le rituel épistolaire," 148–50.
21. Augustine, sermon 302.17.
22. Augustine, sermon 46.2.
23. Augustine, *Enarrationes in Psalmos* 44.32: *de prole tua tibi crevit paternitas*.

Augustine's) the line between the two keeps shifting. Pastoral necessities will surface in this chapter but will be addressed more comprehensively in the next. In Africa the principal organizational challenge was to silence what Augustine called contrary voices that caused contention. Only when all the flocks of God's sheep were fed the truth from the trough of their sacred literature interpreted by right-minded bishops would Christianity consolidate and stop presenting pagans and skeptics with an embarrassing spectacle.[24] To get to that point, bishops must forbid some of the ostensibly faithful (yet odd, often obstreperous theorists) to "touch" the Bible (*noli tangere*). Arian Christians, for example, should be kept from interpreting passages about the incarnation as if Jesus' birth diminished his divinity.[25] Augustine supposed that only unenlightened Christians insisted that statements about the deity's unity and Trinity were incompatible. The persistence of heretical doubts and heretics' resistance to mysteries reflected an inability to approach divinity through faith.[26] Bishops who drew and disseminated truths from sacred texts and urged the inquisitive to tolerate biblical ambiguities cleared obstacles to repentance for the laity. Augustine often warned, however, against self-importance. Winning and pressing to win the competition with heretical exegetes, bishops needed to be reminded of the virtue of humility so that, seeking to establish their moral and intellectual superiority to skeptics, Arians, Donatists, Pelagians, pagans, or Manichees, they might be fearful of overreaching when preaching obedience.[27]

The critics of Catholic Christianity commonly overreached, Augustine complained, accusing them of insolence and arrogance. He picked a psalm critical of insurgents to caution parishioners about their critics' antics. He depicted the bulls grazing in that text as pretentious rivals who babbled seductive nonsense (*vaniloqui*) to lead the herd, the faithful, away from their more perceptive shepherds (*intellegentiores*). He preached that the bulls' foolish doctrines tested not only the good sense and constancy of the laity but also the competence of Catholic Christianity's leadership. Heresy, Augustine intimated, was a God-given occasion for the *intellegentiores* to display their abilities to convey the truths of sacred literature and to uphold as preeminently important the unity or, where division had occurred,

24. Augustine, sermon 46.30; Elm, *Die Macht der Weisheit*, 141.
25. Augustine, sermon 244.4.
26. See Sieben, "Augustins Auseinandersetzung," 203–4.
27. Augustine, sermons 134.3 and 146.1.

the reunification of their churches. The bulls—heretics, skeptics, and secessionists—awakened the bishops they opposed. And once drowsiness was dispelled (*sopore discusso*), Catholic Christian executives could offer ever more compelling interpretations and applications of their faith to the laity. Equally to the point, heresy rewarded the best bishops with authority and a wholesome celebrity. They might otherwise have labored largely unnoticed. Too modest for the church's good, they would have avoided opportunities to exhibit their gifts. But, encountering the insolence and idiocy of bullish heretics, they acquitted themselves influentially, Augustine continued, and they showcased the power of their faith's truths. He noted that Catholic Christianity's congregations would never be free of predatory, fractious, heretical or sectarian preachers. The wicked were fixtures in the terrestrial city, and God's sheep attracted the wolves and bulls among them. But one of Augustine's consolations was that, opposing objectionable opinions, better bishops improved their dexterity by preaching polemically and proved their leadership of the Christian community.[28]

Late in his career, Augustine preached a short sermon in which he aired out his impatience with colleagues who seemed to have had no interest in becoming those better bishops. Despite the spate of attacks on Catholic Christian doctrine, as he presented it, a number of his colleagues were inattentive or forgetful that they were consecrated as overseers, ἐπίσκοποί, to discipline delinquents. The importance of that, Augustine said, should not be understated. Bishops were models for heads of households whose oversight enabled discipline to flourish. When he spoke of bishops' leadership, he considered their influence as well as the complexities of their calling without suggesting that the latter could be cited as excuses for failures.[29] A bishop's job, of course, had its pleasant moments. He clarified in another sermon that bishops need not be constant scolds and that it would be a mistake to discount their gratifications, conspicuous among which were the congratulations they deserved for creditable conduct and effective pastoral care. If all they did in their sermons and conversations was polemically to spar with sectarians or censure parishioners, their careers would have been terribly dreary. Their goodwill would soon fray. So, fortunately, uplifting results of their ministries leavened their lives. If supervision simply meant scolding—and seldom, if ever, seeing the good and satisfying in their

---

28. Augustine, *Enarrationes in Psalmos* 67.39.
29. Augustine, sermon 94: *operari magis quam excusare*.

congregations (*si nihil boni*)—bishops might be pardoned their occasional failures to be diligent and vigilant.[30]

In a sermon delivered in 425, on the anniversary of his ordination, Augustine explained why the burdens (*sarcinae*) bishops carried were heavier than those borne by the laity. He likely anticipated that his explanation would impress parishioners with their responsibilities to bishops as well as to God and would move them to repent their sins and correct their conduct. He started with what even the most muddleheaded, who missed or misperceived the alerts circulated by prophets, gospels, and apostles as insubstantial, ought to recognize as indisputable when their preachers called them to account, specifically, that creatures were bound to answer in the hereafter for any unrepented misbehavior here. What was less obvious yet true, according to Augustine, was that God would hold bishops responsible for their parishioners' slip-ups and backsliding. In the anniversary sermon the onus shifted from the laity to the episcopacy. Horrid punishments (*immanissima poena*) awaited bishops whose oversight was compromised by their pandering for the laity's praise, by their desires to be popular and not to be known for prying. God wasted no sorrow on bishops who pulled their punches, coddled whom they should have condemned, and let ungodliness go unrebuked. Augustine seemed to be channeling his God's condemnation, imagining the irretrievable commoners who could have been spared eternal torment had their bishops been more conscientious and emphatic moral monitors.[31]

His anniversary sermon exploits the parable in the nineteenth chapter of the Gospel of Luke, which reports a king's displeasure when one of his deputies handed over only the funds given him on his sovereign's departure. On the king's return, other stewards who invested and increased their treasure were rewarded. The steward who did not was reprimanded. The lesson Augustine imparted was that bishops should spread the truths entrusted to them and realize an appreciable return in self-aware, penitent souls. Bishops' affection for the faithful ought to motivate all who witnessed the returns on investments, particularly because their sacred texts' promises assured them that the repentance and goodwill bishops inspired among many of their parishioners would demonstrate God's readiness to forgive. The alternative was to have bishops hold back, as noted, and to endorse the reassuring yet mistaken declaration that God's grace or mercy covered a multitude

---

30. Augustine, *sermones nuper reperti*, Dolbeau 10.2.
31. Augustine, sermon 339.1–2.

of sins at no cost to the sinners. It could not have come as a shock to anyone attending Augustine's sermons on discipline that the bishops trading in that treacherously comforting notion were derelict and—worse—they were responsible for encouraging parishioners' reckless disregard for the necessity to repent. Augustine's anniversary sermon was scrupulous, stipulating to colleagues and to the laity just what bishops could and could not do. They could only—and should tirelessly—pronounce the truths of their faith scooped from scripture, the duty that all pastors shared, as we shall discover. Those truths emancipated the faithful, pronouncing God's judgments in advance and enabling bishops and pastors to put parishioners on notice so they could show contrition and recalibrate the courses of their lives. What kind of Christian would choose to be a disciplinarian with such awesome challenges? Augustine confided that he might have chosen differently had Jesus' directive ("feed my sheep") not frightened him (*terret me evangelium*). Fear led him to be vexatious, to risk falling foul of his friends. But the bishop would be botching his job, Augustine went on, if he left parishioners to wallow in their sins, to take their pleasures uncensored, and to hoard their possessions. He would be a bad bishop and terrible pastor if he asked to be left to enjoy his leisure, making no fuss over the morality and immortality of others' souls.[32]

Polemics: Manichees and Donatists

Augustine came to condemn the morality and intelligence of the specialists who led the Manichees, with whom he had been associated for nearly ten years in Africa and Italy. With some distortion, the specialists could be called Manichaean bishops. They were instructors dedicated to rationalizing religious doctrine, and their dedication and rationalizations fascinated Augustine. They were seers, of a sort, a breed set apart to impart wisdom about the origins of—and the conflict within—the cosmos and to liberate Light trapped in matter. Supposedly, they were distinguished from followers by their extraordinary resistance to temptations that typically overwhelmed ordinary others. Manichaean specialists—the elite of their sect or "school"—and their partisans honored Mani, a third-century Persian prophet, as founder. Some also subscribed to a blend of what passed as his ideas and what their specialists teased from Christianity's sacred texts. Augustine paid close attention from the late 370s into the 380s; Jason

32. Ibid., 2–4.

BeDuhn attributes his interest to a predilection for esotericism. But his doubts about the sect's elect followed from his conversations with Faustus, a specialist whose desire to impress Christians with Mani's wisdom brought him to Carthage to study with Augustine. Faustus' reputation for learning led Augustine eagerly to anticipate his arrival. Once there, however, Faustus disappointed. His erudition, insights, and conduct fell far short of what Augustine, the Manichee, expected.[33]

By the mid-380s, he regretted harboring hopes for enlightenment from the sect's specialists. He composed a series of caustic treatises against the Manichees—the first shortly after his baptism. He concentrated on Manichaean misinterpretations of the Hebrews' scriptures, although his complaints about their specialists' swagger and shameful behavior sprawl across the pages of his anti-Manichaean tracts. On becoming more committed to—and more knowledgeable about—Christianity, he learned to appreciate its bishops, who preached humility and shunned the kind of notoriety (*non amant propatula*) Manichaean elites coveted. He found that specialists only pretended to be austere but were insincere, promiscuous, and petulant. Some years after Augustine set his collision course with Faustus and became disenchanted with the Manichees' takes on Christianity, creation, and liberation, he professed that he had never met a specialist whose deportment was above suspicion. He seems to have been especially annoyed at the scabrous excuse that shameless specialists offered when they were caught in compromising positions: when their mischief and scandalous misbehavior became known, they told other Manichees that Judaism's and Christianity's heroes—from Adam to the Apostle Paul—were reputed to be egregious sinners yet were also commemorated as pillars of their faiths.[34]

What accounted for the Manichees' popularity? One could make the case that, despite generations of prelates drawing inferences about good and evil from biblical passages, not only intelligent Christians but also curious, intermittent, or fringe Christians—among whom Augustine should be numbered in the early 380s—experienced a crisis of intelligibility. Before he became a bishop, Augustine recalled that he had been frustrated; pastors proved to be uncooperative and uninsightful teachers. They fended off or

33. Augustine, *Confessiones* 3.10,18; 5.6,10–5.7,13; BeDuhn, *Augustine's Manichaean Dilemma*, 1:241–43. Decret probably exaggerates, but perhaps only slightly, when he depicts as "messianic" the expectations attached to Faustus' coming to Carthage (*Aspects du Manichéisme*, 58–59).

34. Augustine, *De moribus ecclesiae Catholicae et de moribus Manichaeorum* 2.19,68–2.19,72.

failed to answer satisfactorily his questions about the meaning of enigmatic passages in the Bible. As noted, he found that Faustus was no help. The highly touted Manichee seemed to him little better than a buffoon. Snippets of several other philosophies captivated him now and then, yet he could not decide what to profess and what finally to dismiss as superficial (*quid mihi tenendum, quid dimittendum esset*) until he heard Bishop Ambrose preach in Milan. By then, he had decided that the Manichaean specialists were grotesque, theatrically parading mystifications as clarifications of sacred literature. For Ambrose showed him how to make sense allegorically of obscure passages in the Hebrews' scriptures that seemed to stretch credulity and that—when he was under the influence of the Manichees—led him to despise as contemptible not just the biblical tales of Moses' marvels or of Jonah's ordeals but the Old Testament as a whole.[35] He continued to attack the Manichees, he said, because their specialists were so adept at spinning seductive promises. It fell to bishops to protect credulous Christians and others of the faithful caught in that crisis of intelligibility, to protect them from the Manichees' pestiferous explanations (*pestifera verba*), which, Augustine suggested, would not merely leave the laity in ignorance but would lead them to hell.[36]

Augustine was sure that the crisis of intelligibility could never be finally resolved for or by Manichees committed to putting mysteries of faith on a firm foundation of fact. Manichaean specialists followed the lead of their founder, Mani, who had overlooked human finitude and fallibility, Augustine claimed. The conceit that an informed mind could transcend limitations mobilized Mani's partisans, yet it could not rally them around a single theme that seemed to Augustine to have addressed conclusively the issues raised by the mysteries of creation and redemption. Manichees forgot they were mere men (*insipientes homines*) and—judging from Faustus—were woefully imperceptive.[37]

But Faustus was only one of the many specialists whose cosmologies appeared untenable. They could not resolve the crisis of intelligibility, in part, because of their plurality; Manichaean elites refused to settle on a single explanation of the origin of and purpose for creation. Rivalries among

35. Augustine, *De utilitate credendi* 8.20.

36. Augustine, *Contra epistulam Manichaei quam vocant Fundamenti* 11.12.

37. Augustine, *De moribus ecclesiae Catholicae et de moribus Manichaeorum* 1.7,11; Augustine, *Contra epistulam Manichaei quam vocant Fundamenti* 13.17; Augustine, *Confessiones* 5.7,13. As proof, he cited, inter alia, Faustus' failure to see that his immodesty and inelegance eroded Augustine's enthusiasm for Manichaeism.

specialists were common, and rivals, not knowing their "unknowing," as far as Augustine could tell, in effect normalized dissent. None could claim antiquity for his truths; therefore, the sect could not claim authority for its truths. But Christianity's bishops through the generations, following one another in succession—an apostolic succession—articulated a consensus handed down from those supremely solidly founded sees of the apostles.[38]

Generations of Christians debated whether bishops or sectarian specialists were more reliable sources of truth before Augustine closed ranks with colleagues. The *Acta Archelai*, an early anti-Manichaean script, records (or stages) two debates between Mani and the bishop of Carchar in Persia. In both confrontations, the bishop prevailed, and the prophet fled. Humiliation and flight punctuate an extremely unflattering account of Mani's life that accused him of having plagiarized. The *Acta* impugned his aptitude and honesty as well as his originality.[39] Augustine took a different tack in his *Confessions*. After reporting his discomfort and disappointment with Faustus, he reflected on the years he spent among the Manichees, angry with himself for having trusted the sect's elect and for having failed to ascertain how baseless their sense of superiority was. They posed as an aristocracy of virtue and intellect but were to be pitied, for they would never find what he had found in the Psalms and in the church—the antidote for arrogance, the antidote encouraging modesty yet giving him a sense of mission with which to approach his summons to take the lead in his faith's campaigns against putative perfectionists.[40]

Augustine presumed that Donatist secessionist leaders found no such antidote. They vilified rivals who prudently schooled rather than excluded sinners. Augustine exaggerated Donatists' pride when it suited his polemical purposes. He made it appear that they cast off somewhat sinful—yet generally sound—Christians as worthless shards. Probably most Donatist bishops' refusals to confer with him and listen to reason—to his reasons—stirred him to overstate their contempt and perfectionism.[41] But he welcomed those Donatists who elected to reconcile, and after the Council of Carthage adjourned in 411, he urged Catholic Christians to receive, as

---

38. Augustine, *Contra Faustum Manichaeum* 11.2: *ab ipsis fundatissimis sedibus apostolorum*.

39. Hegemonius, *Acta Archelai* 26.6.

40. Augustine, *Confessiones* 9.4, 8: *indignabar Manichaeis et miserabar eos rursus*.

41. Augustine, *Contra Cresconium* 2.1,1 (*nolunt nobiscus habere colloquium*); Hermanowicz, *Possidius of Calama*, 108–12.

"brothers," all who were ready to repudiate their exclusionist sect for an inclusive church.[42]

Donatism did not collapse in or immediately after 411, but the archaeological evidence from Augustine's Hippo suggests that Catholic Christianity during his tenure there enjoyed "a notable period of expansion"; new construction in the two churches over which he presided in the city enabled them to accommodate greater numbers than they had previously.[43] A sermon that he preached, either just before or soon after the Council of Carthage that year, stressed the bishop's (or shepherd's) obligation to recall and assimilate lost sheep. Augustine fretted about Donatists' resistance yet pledged to overcome it, to retrieve sheep that had strayed into dissident sects and that were perishing there, he said, for want of charity.[44] He believed as much because he considered that the Donatists' secession in the early fourth century and persistence in schism signaled a mean-spirited, unforgiving attitude toward the faithful in the churches they left. They seemed to have forgotten the directive in the Apostle Paul's first letter to Corinth, which placed charity or love above the other two theological virtues, faith and hope. Donatist bishops boasted of their predecessors' and partisans' willingness to die for their faith and to add to Christianity's stock of martyrs. But charity superseded faith in Paul's passage, on which Augustine elaborated: suffering and dying for the Christian faith was indeed admirable, he conceded, yet, if sacrifices were unaccompanied by love—by charitable dispositions—they were pointless.[45]

Augustine's charity was known to wear thin. Donatists' accusations—and what he perceived as their obstinacy—occasionally exhausted his goodwill. With some but not with complete confidence we can recreate the reasons he might have given. Earlier in the fourth century, two church councils across the Mediterranean—at Rome and Arles—judged African dissidents' charges against other bishops in their provinces to be unfounded. As we learned, Emperor Constantine followed their lead. Caecillianists were vindicated, but the Donatists refused to be reconciled. As a result, the African church was divided and, as Émilien Lamirande says,

---

42. Augustine sermons 296.12–14 and 357.4. Also consult Augustine, *Contra Cresconium* 1.3,4; Augustine, epistle 11*.25; and Schindler, "Vermitteln die neuentdeckten Augustin-Briefe," 117–21.

43. De Salvo, "Gli spazi del potere ecclesiastico," 1041–42.

44. Augustine, sermon 46.14.

45. Augustine, sermon 138.2, citing 1 Cor 13:1–3.

Caecillianists—or Catholic Christians—were "demoralized" for seven decades before Augustine returned from Italy.[46] Twenty years after he was ordained—years in which sectarians pressed their charges against Caecillian and subsequent Catholic Christian clergy—the Council of Carthage rejected the Donatists' accusations and evidence and, as noted, Marcellinus, on behalf of the government, sealed the verdict by proscribing the sect. But Donatism's leaders carried on. They complained that Marcellinus had been bribed. They spurned Augustine's offers to let them keep their positions in a reunified church. The conflict continued; details of the proceedings of the Carthaginian council were circulated to document that Marcellinus had been even-handed during the deliberations and benevolent afterward, although he formulated measures to protect prelates facing danger from the disappointed and enraged Donatists. Although some capitulated, joined the Catholic Christians, and retained their sees—or were appointed to others—a number of the secessionists returned to their dioceses unreconciled, leaving Augustine and his colleagues with more polemical work and in some peril.[47]

The polemic against the Donatists must have seemed never-ending, yet Augustine and Catholic Christianity were also confronted with an additional disagreeable challenge when an apparently small set of refugees from Italy arrived in Africa promoting a "new heresy," which was popular in some Roman circles and which required bishops to defend their position as the churches' gatekeepers monitoring the approach to eternal life. The partisans of Pelagius who circulated his and their treatises during the fifth century's second decade were probably pleased to have found their likely rivals in Africa in opposing camps. Without relinquishing his effort to refute Donatist arguments and to retrieve Donatists, however, Augustine took the lead in anti-Pelagian polemics, to which we will return in the next chapter. Opposing both Pelagians and Donatists, however, he came to believe he was defending the authentic church of the martyrs.[48]

Augustine argued that to patch the suffering of Christianity's martyrs into a brief for the Donatists' courage and persistence was to dignify secessionists' stubbornness and to dishonor the memory of the martyrs;

---

46. Lamirande, "Aux origines du dialogue interconfessionnel," 224–25.

47. Augustine, epistles 139.4 and 141.1–7.

48. See Augustine, *Contra Cresconium* 4.3,3; Augustine, *De peccatorum meritis, et remissione et de baptismo parvulorum* 26; Augustine, *Retractiones* 2.33 (*novam haeresim*); and Barreteau-Revel, "Faire l'unité," 236–37.

in effect, Donatism transformed martyrs whose ordeals inspired Catholic Christian solidarity into an eccentric troop of self-assured individualists.[49] Pelagians appeared to Augustine to be using martyrs' perseverance as evidence of humanity's virtuosity rather than as a testament to God's will and goodwill.[50] At just this juncture, Elena Zocca points out, polemical and institutional concerns dovetailed in Augustine's work; they were, she maintains, *in perfetta consonanza*. He and his colleagues had suffered as martyrs for the truth. Bruised by the slanders of their critics, Catholic Christianity's bishops coupled their commitments to suffer for the faith with those of its first-century heroes (and casualties). For, as we learned, Augustine pictured bishops as the apostles' heirs.[51]

Paganism

Christophe Hugoniot surmises that municipal officials in Hippo, *haut du pavé*, were Donatists when Augustine became bishop there in the late 390s. Hugoniot's evidence is hardly overwhelming, but if secessionists outnumbered Catholic Christians and were advantageously positioned, Augustine's failure to start meaningful discussions with Donatist Bishop Proculeian would make sense. Unsurprisingly, Proculeian, who became bishop two years before Augustine, would hardly risk his sect's enviable status sparring with a polished orator.[52] Paganism in Hippo presented a very different challenge. Despite authorities' prohibitions, their spectacles were often staged. They seem to have interested a number of Christians who Augustine hoped would have outgrown the pageantries' attractions. He hoped all Christians had been persuaded that their faith possessed the truth and that paganism was wilting. He hoped the faithful would resist temptation, drawing pagan neighbors to church rather than crossing the line between their religion and those neighbors' beguiling mysteries and cults.[53] But the line between paganism and Christianity was not as clear as Augustine would have liked. He was emphatic: pagans could not cross and enjoy the benefits reserved for

---

49. Augustine, sermon 276.1–2.
50. Augustine, *De praedestinatione sanctorum* 31.
51. Zocca, "La figura del santo vescovo," 478–80.
52. Augustine, epistle 33.1–4; Hugoniot, "Les légats du proconsul d'Afrique," 2083–84.
53. Augustine, *sermones nuper reperti*, Dolbeau 26.58: *per vos fieri potest, convictos ad salutem lucremini*. Also see Lepelley, *Les cités de l'Afrique romaine*, 1:365–66, 379–81, and Galvão-Sobrinho, *Doctrine and Power*, 76–77.

the faithful as long as they worshipped idols. Celestial consolations for the miseries of this life were unavailable to idolaters. Yet many pagans persisted in lobbying local officials for privileges and prerogatives they enjoyed before Emperor Theodosius' chancery set limits and circulated prohibitions. In many African cities and villages pagans lost the buildings that housed their idols, but, Augustine pointed out, they kept idols in their hearts.[54]

They never abandoned their gods and were quick to blame Christians for having done so when natural and military catastrophes befell the empire. Pagans let on that the gods were angry for having had their worship suppressed. Augustine complained that the pagan elites knew better yet goaded the more superstitious to interpret every setback as the gods' vengeance—particularly after Goths invaded Italy early in the fifth century.[55] Yet, even before Rome was sacked in 410, a pagan pogrom left sixty Christians dead in Africa after the cult image of Hercules in Sufes was destroyed. Augustine was irate; he believed local authorities connived with the mob and were thus responsible for the slaughter. Their Hercules would be restored, Augustine said, offering to have him resculpted as soon as the pagan townsfolk and their leaders resuscitated the Christians they had murdered.[56] Nine years later, in 408, pagans rioted in Calama when Christians pressed local officials to enforce an edict prohibiting their processions through the city. They stoned the basilica and killed a priest. Bishop Possidius left for Ravenna to petition Emperor Honorius to assess extravagant punitive damages. Augustine became involved when Nectarius, a local notable, asked him, at the behest of the Calama pagans, to help ensure that penalties not bankrupt them and fuel the animosity that already existed. Nectarius' clients or constituents had no objection to compensating the Christian community for losses, yet they apparently feared that Possidius would use the riot to put pagans at a permanent economic disadvantage. Nectarius imagined that Augustine would want to settle affairs in a way that encouraged Christians and pagans to coexist.[57]

---

54. Augustine, epistles 232.1–4 and 263.4; Augustine, *Retractiones* 2.43,1.

55. Augustine, *De civitate dei* 2.3.

56. Augustine, epistle 50. Also see Lepelley, *Les cités de l'Afrique romaine*, 1:355–57, 2:307, and Shaw, *Sacred Violence*, 249–51.

57. For Nectarius' overture, see Augustine, epistle 90. Hermanowicz suspects that Nectarius was a Christian ("Catholic Bishops and Appeals," 497–98); Shaw endorses the consensus that he was a pagan somehow connected with the Calama elites (*Sacred Violence*, 252).

Augustine sent his barbed responses to Sufes, 275 kilometers from Hippo, but traveled the seventy-five kilometers to Calama to speak with the pagans. He learned on site that it was difficult to determine guilt and innocence. Many pagans had refrained from attacking their Christian neighbors yet offered no assistance to the injured. And some Christians, milling about, saw the confusion as an opportunity to loot. Certainly, the savage deserved punishment, but he was disinclined to deprive them of life or limb. He had no reservations about taking from them the resources that they had used to gild their idols. What especially disconcerted him, however, was that the pagans asked of him what they dared not ask of his God, known to be merciful. A bishop's duty was not just to soothe all souls but to use all occasions doggedly to draw souls to God—and to draw to a close the history of paganism in Calama.[58]

Nectarius was having none of that. He trusted that celestial rewards were independent of confessional affiliation. His second letter to Augustine suggested they were reserved for all who were devoted to civic service. He imagined that the safety of this world's cities was dear to God, sufficiently so to have the deity want those who secured it close to him for eternity.[59] Augustine replied with something of a disclaimer that nonetheless kept up his attack on paganism. No probe could discover from history whom God had rewarded—and predict whom God would reward—for services to this world's cities and causes. Perhaps, Augustine speculated, God would desist and grant pagans the immunity they and Nectarius sought, leaving them unpunished in the present yet deferring punishment to the hereafter. God might take that tack, but bishops must presume otherwise and avoid complicity in the pagans' eternal torment. They should explain that divine mercy sometimes appeared in history as punishment, which led to the remorse and reform of pagans, directing them, with bishops assisting, to repent and find refuge in God's grace and to possess celestial rewards. Nectarius would have shown greater affection for his Calama clients, Augustine volunteered, if he had advocated punishment, even to the point of impoverishing the pagans—if he had accepted the possibility that God was an opportunist, using the crisis and their calamity to coax them to repent and responding to their repentance and conversion by absolving them of their sins and

---

58. Augustine, epistle 91.9–10.
59. Augustine, epistle 103.2.

holding a place for them in heaven. Bishops ought to welcome the chance to be complicit in that grim yet ultimately beneficial process.[60]

But Augustine was also known to link God's saving work with pardons as well as with punishments. He argued in 413 that bishops were responsible for obtaining amnesties, for staying executions and giving offenders opportunities to repent their sins. Macedonius, vicar of Africa at that time, was skeptical (*vehementer ambigo*); he believed that the practice of having bishops appeal to set aside the verdicts of secular magistrates thrust religion into policy, undermining political authority and inviting recidivism.[61] Augustine answered that God's compassion was nearly inexhaustible and that select villains could become its beneficiaries, if rescued from the stake.[62] He conceded that their release could have regrettable consequences, but he argued that reprieves would result in far more good than harm; magistrates, counseled by bishops, ought to keep in mind the good effects. Clemency gave the church time to save souls. Augustine's correspondence with Macedonius, composed several years after he had written to Nectarius, repeated an observation he made after the Calama riots: punishments were meant to safeguard society. The Apostle Paul, after all, recognized that secular magistrates wielded their "swords" as God's deputies. But while writing Macedonius about reprieves for Donatists, Augustine was even more insistent that punishment and pardon (*plectendo et ignoscendo*) had places in the successful reclamation of offenders. Bishops could and should help magistrates determine when to indulge and when to indict.[63]

Incorrigible pagans, of course, posed a problem. Rather than opposing capital or corporal punishment, Augustine advised, bishops ought to back off. Pagans who foolishly and unalterably were unafraid of Augustine's God could only be kept in check by their fear of the government, by their expectation that offenses against the church would lead to destitution or worse. General amnesties would only fuel their arrogance and embolden them to menace the faithful. Nectarius thought differently. He was worried pagans would come to hate Christianity more passionately if left with the sense that its bishops cared nothing about their fate.[64] Municipal reconciliation might follow if Augustine pitched for a comprehensive pardon, he

60. Augustine, epistle 104.11.
61. Augustine, epistle 152.2–3.
62. Augustine, epistle 153.8.
63. Ibid., 18–19.
64. Augustine, epistle 103.4.

suspected, yet he made no promises on that count. In response, Augustine suggested that Nectarius, perhaps purposefully, understated the probability that pagans would feign repentance, once they found their insincerity could win pardons. Besides, pagans' apologies and regrets would be wanting, Augustine argued, because, unlike the sorrow of the faithful who behaved badly during the Calama riots or simply withheld assistance from their assaulted coreligionists, pagans could not experience the faith in their hearts (*quod inest cordibus eorum fides*) that stirred Christians to reflect on the magnitude of their offense against a God who sacrificed his son for their salvation. Pagans' sorrows were prodded and informed by what the sorrowful could gain from—and should fear from—God. The Christians' remorse and repentance were more profound. Moved by that faith within, and by a conviction (and embarrassment) that their deportment betrayed their compassionate deity who would forego judgment, Christians' grief, from Augustine's perspective, was authentic. Pagan offenders had no sense of the infinite mercy of the celestial source of forgiveness, and so they had no sense of the magnitude of their offenses. Their grief was self-serving and therefore inauthentic.[65]

Augustine seems to have agreed with Nectarius that some punishments could leave scars, making it difficult, if not impossible, for pagans to forgive the Christians' failures to forgive and forbidding pagans from coming to terms with their fate, terms that would enable them peaceably to coexist with Calama's congregations. But Augustine, as visiting bishop, apparently cared less about the administration or settled state of terrestrial municipalities than about the city of God. He was intent on shifting the focus from short-term measures that might quiet Calama to long-term or permanent changes that would expand the company of Christians with faith in God's sovereignty and in the mercy that reconciled the repentant. Civic-spirited Nectarius looked to restore the *status quo ante*, a resolution that, he trusted, could be braced by the gratitude of Calama's pagan elites for the Christians' (for Augustine's) part in their reprieve. Augustine, however, considered the crisis in Calama what we might describe as a teachable moment, a chance to stipulate terms for repentance, which demanded nothing short of the pagans' conversion and which might lead to confessional solidarity rather than *détente*.[66]

---

65. Augustine, epistle 104.9: *fontem ipsum indulgentiae . . . agnoscere neglegunt*.
66. Augustine, epistle 91.7.

He was unrealistic. Confessional solidarity was hard enough to maintain among Christians. Pagans compelled to choose between destitution and conversion would unlikely reconcile themselves promptly and devoutly to their new faith. Numbers had left their cults decades before the Calama crisis yet continued to practice their rituals secretly where public performances were prohibited by law. And historian Claude Lepelley suspects that the secrecy increased the ardor of pagans' attachments to what Augustine termed superstitions and magic.[67] Other historians also find signs of a pagan revival at the end of the fourth century, despite the prohibitions issued by the imperial chancery. Éric Rebillard counts three or four pagan proconsuls of Africa during Augustine's tenure. Only five or six of the twenty-one can be identified as Christians. Others' confessional commitments remain unknown.[68] And Serge Lancel, inspecting the decorative arts in private homes, concludes that long after its public presence was forbidden, paganism stood on sturdy "cultural legs."[69]

Augustine worried about paganism's staying power. The few episodes of unruly pagans attacking African Christians were troubling, as was the memory of the widespread pagan revival during the eighteen-month reign of Emperor Julian in the early 360s. Augustine was still a preteen at the time, too young to remember specifics. But, if Claude Lepelley is correct, bishops at the end of the century still considered a repeat possible. They did not see "the sea change in the rhythm of civic life" that David Hunt associates with that century's end during which Christian festivities started to "displace pagan celebrations at the heart of public experience."[70] Bishops took some initiative, hastening the implementation of imperial legislation—or trying to—with their sermons against paganism. Yet, if Augustine's sermons are any indication of a general trend, the bishops worked pagans' funerary practices into their graveside rituals and merged what historian Peter Brown calls the "heroization" characteristic of paganism with Christianity's veneration of saints.[71] Augustine probably did so, in part, to reduce the shock pagans experienced after they converted to Christianity. But a

---

67. Lepelley, "L'aristocratie lettrée païenne," 336–37, commenting on Augustine, *sermones nuper reperti*, Dolbeau 26.28.

68. Rebillard, "Augustin et le rituel épistolaire," 150.

69. Lancel, "L'Antiquité tardive," 245.

70. Compare Hunt, "Church as Public Institution," 252, with Lepelley, "L'aristocratie lettrée païenne," 342.

71. Brown, *Cult of Saints*, 5–7, but also consult Markus, *End of Ancient Christianity*, 111–17, and Lizzi, "I vescovi e i potentes," 101–2.

principle he articulated in a letter to colleagues seems relevant: Augustine held that the results of punishing pagans or, for that matter, recalcitrant Christians were uncertain; one could not tell how much pagans would endure before they capitulated or whether their coerced conversions would be sincere and lasting. In his judgment, the crisis at Calama obviously called for punishment. But under other circumstances, it was wise, he said, within strict limits (*aliquantulum*) to adapt—rather than abrasively to object to—some practices from which the faithful would draw the unfaithful.[72]

Excesses

Bishops were not expected to develop workmanlike social programs, but Augustine's correspondence with Nectarius gives us a glimpse of what his might have looked like had he ever made the reform of terrestrial cities a priority. He anticipated that confessional solidarity would have led to municipal solidarity and civic responsibility. When idols in pagans' hearts had been smashed and when citizens worshipped together and possessed the truth, that common light dispelling humanity's ignorance about God, authorities would be better able to keep the peace.[73] And knowing what pleased God, the faithful would need but a nudge from a bishop's sermon to appreciate the uses to which their material success should be put; they would share rather than hoard. True, Augustine presumed that poverty—the penalty for their malevolence—would instruct the pagans of Calama, but a sermon he preached several years after that crisis instructed affluent Christians, addicted to their "delicacies" and "excesses," to see that insolvent neighbors were supplied with necessities.[74]

It was easier to battle excess—and to win—in the small company of clergy that Augustine gathered around him in Hippo. Elsewhere in that bustling port city, commerce trumped charity. Many of the faithful were preoccupied with profit. Fortunes were made, and some were offered as endowments to the church. Possidius, Augustine's first biographer, tells us that he took little interest in financial management, yet he was known to liquidate some of his church's assets to distribute alms to the poor.[75] The laity, he learned, suspected that bishops cared most for their basilicas, in-

---

72. Augustine, epistle 95.2–3.
73. Augustine, *In Evangelium Joannis tractatus* 35.9: *bene nobis fuit in luce communi*.
74. Augustine, sermon 61.11–13: *utere superfluis, da pauperibus necessaria*.
75. Possidius, *Sancti Augustini vita* 24; Brown, *Through the Eye of a Needle*, 181.

vesting in stone and perhaps lining their pockets with legacies. He replied that close inspection of his and of his colleagues' coffers would vindicate Christianity's leadership; nearly all bishops followed the example of Jesus and subsidized the poor. Augustine repeatedly urged the laity to do as much. Making that point in a sermon that answered complaints about clerical profiteering, he groused that the faithful seldom inquired strenuously about the fate of the less fortunate among them; as long as the poor were fed, the affluent overlooked their inadequate clothing and squalid shelter. The well-off were too busy amassing excesses to capitalize on opportunities to follow their savior's example. Charity could not take root in such terrible soil that was watered to no avail (*frustra irrigata*) by sermons brimming with the injunctions and instructions from their sacred texts. Their excuses were invalid: Augustine heard the miserly denounce their bishops for having been remiss but protested that he and clerical colleagues, much as Jesus, never ceased presenting the plight of the poor and emphasizing the need to provide for them.[76]

On one notable and somewhat controversial occasion—and when they seemed least to deserve his consideration—Augustine set about to defend his parishioners. Valerius Pinianus and his wife Melania, Roman refugees famed for their philanthropy, visited Hippo the year after their city's sack in 410. They were touring Africa on their way east. Some parishioners in Augustine's churches conspired to abduct Pinianus and have him ordained to keep his purse close, but he got wind of their intentions and promised to sprint from Africa if they came after him. To Augustine, the episode was embarrassing, yet he spun it slyly and refrained from rebuking his flock.[77] First, he plotted Pinianus' escape from the faithful in Hippo, who, he admitted, were becoming unruly as well as unreasonable. To calm them, he promised that Pinianus would stay, trusting the promise would dispose parishioners to drop their guard and give the couple a chance to get away. That done, however, he exonerated his congregation. When word of Hippo's "hospitality" reached Thagaste, where Pinianus' mother-in-law was staying, she wrote to scold Augustine, assuming he either had lost control of or had egged on his congregation. He replied, acknowledging that the prospect of a windfall likely tempted the agitators, yet he also characterized them as selfless; they merely wanted a magnanimous benefactor-in-residence to help the less fortunate in the diocese, he claimed, redefining

---

76. Augustine, *Enarrationes in Psalmos* 103(3).12. Also see Augustine, epistle 122.2.
77. See Lepelley, "Le patronat épiscopal," 24–26, for Augustine's embarrassment.

"windfall"—or, to be precise, redistributing it—and adding that the faithful in Hippo, even more laudably, wanted to make Pinianus their priest, not because they sought his money but because they hoped to have among them someone celebrated for contempt for money, someone whose generosity attested Christianity's contempt for temporal advantages. How should we interpret Augustine's explanation and exoneration? He apparently wrote to clear Hippo and himself. None, he said, disgracefully chased coin. To have responded otherwise would have impaired Augustine's ability to offer himself and his clergy as examples of the charitable dispositions and unselfish work he would have all parishioners do. The Pinianus problem moved him to defend congregants whose temperament and tactics he had so often criticized for excesses, but bishops who would have the laity listen to criticism and counsel needed to know how and when to excuse as well as when to accuse.[78]

Excusing and accusing fellow bishops posed different problems. For they were peers, whom primates or councils or popes might discipline but who, arguably, were out of reach of other highly placed prelates acting alone. In a sermon preached soon after his appointment as bishop, Augustine noted that high office tempted the best-intentioned to become self-important, even greedy. The antidote was transparency; while avoiding excess and trying to meet standards they set for parishioners' conduct, bishops should, above all, strenuously discountenance deceit. Their sanctity should not be a show. If they deceived their parishioners, they ought to anticipate being deceived by them.[79] Augustine later learned, however, that reckless colleagues who did not trouble to disguise their treachery could do as much damage as the deceptive.

He was responsible for the most conspicuous case of mismanagement in early fifth-century Africa. In 411, after the Council of Carthage, many Donatists in his diocese defected. Catholic Christian congregations grew. Augustine needed help, so he sliced a modest diocese from his own, proceeded to find a priest to promote, and deposited him in the town of Fussala. Bishop Silvanus of Summa, the primate of Numidia, came for the installation, but the nominee did not. Augustine improvised, and, on the basis of others' recommendation, he fast-tracked a young priest, Antoninus, just twenty years old and susceptible to temptations a more seasoned candidate would have resisted. He got swept up (*subvectus*) and puffed up

---

78. Augustine, epistles 125.1–2 and 126.3–8.

79. Augustine, *sermones nuper reperti*, Dolbeau 10.4.

by the arrogance of power (*insolentia dominationis inflatus*).⁸⁰ Bishops had authority to monitor priests' character and conduct and to depose delinquents, but Antoninus had catapulted into an office, technically beyond Augustine's reach, although the aggrieved and enraged Christians in the new diocese had turned to him.⁸¹ Flurries of complaints about their new bishop fell on Hippo. Augustine was told Antoninus leased the church's properties and spent the rents to furnish his private villa. To build it, he extorted funds from parishioners, pilfered timber and tiles, rustled their cattle, stole crops. He seems to have been guilty of what is now called racketeering—of what Augustine saw as lust, self-indulgence, and malevolent despotism.⁸² In his *Confessions*, he wrote about the craving to reign over others that overcame ordinary people (*principandi libidine*); in his treatise *On True Religion*, he allowed that even those who successfully resisted most temptations could be tempted to claim and, when chances came, to take tyrannical control.⁸³

Augustine conferred with colleagues. Parishioners' charges of sexual misconduct were dropped for lack of evidence, but Augustine, collaborating with Bishop Aurelius of Macomades, the new primate of Numidia, drastically reduced Antoninus' responsibilities, subdividing the diocese of Fussala. Antoninus, in effect, was unseated. He retained authority over only a few clerics and the small portion of his former parishioners who had not answered the primate's summons to assemble and select a new incumbent. Antoninus escaped excommunication by promising to make restitution to his victims and seemed content with the settlement (*adquievit*) as some bishops arrived to oversee the choice of his replacement. But Augustine, his annoyance evident, guessed that Antoninus had only paused to find ways to form factions, create frictions, and salvage his standing—and that he had contemplated an appeal to Rome even before the new incumbent arrived to be ordained.⁸⁴

Antoninus twice took his case to Rome where two consecutive bishops ordered inquiries. Their delegates almost certainly learned of Augustine's part in the controversies—his injudicious nomination of the young,

---

80. Augustine, epistles 20*.3–4 and 209.3.

81. See Noethlichs, "Materialien zum Bischofsbild," 37.

82. Augustine, epistle 20*.6.

83. Augustine, *Confessiones* 3.8,16; *De vera religione* 38.70–71.

84. Augustine, epistle 20*.8–9. Also see Dossey, *Peasant and Empire*, 137–38, and Evers, *Church, Cities, and People*, 254–55.

reckless bishop of Fussala and his forbearance when his nominee was first accused. Perhaps to forestall criticism, as rancorous depositions were taken and the disputes dragged on, Augustine tried to tranquilize his embittered, contentious nominee and colleague by tinkering with the initial settlement, offering to assign him additional estates, yielding one of his own properties, and continuing to search for ways to appease Antoninus.[85] The laity's objections seemed to count for little, because Augustine wanted to ward off a round of recriminations that would have attended efforts to get rid of Antoninus altogether. The overheated rhetoric that such efforts would no doubt have prompted would have given pagans and Donatists a scandal they could spin to the disadvantage of Catholic Christianity. But, from Augustine's correspondence, we can only infer his strategy of appeasement had failed.[86]

Citing pragmatic reasons for Augustine's attempts to place, then placate Antoninus gives him the benefit of our doubts. His letter to Pope Celestine, the second bishop of Rome to call for an inquiry, suggests he wanted to retain final jurisdiction over disciplinary matters for African bishops. They would be in a much better position to know when petitioners from their provinces were tampering with the truth. Indeed, he claimed the reports Antoninus had sent to Rome were misleading—that there were craters in the plaintiff's narrative only those close to the controversy could fill with facts damning to his cause. Augustine did not contest Rome's right to interrogate all parties to resolve personnel problems far from the empire's old capital. He cited precedents for papal involvement. After consulting knowledgeable African prelates, previous bishops of Rome had disciplined offenders, laicizing several of them.[87] Consultation was critical. And, Augustine alleged, Rome's role was to ratify what bishops in the provinces decided; third-century African bishops had recommended depriving colleagues, and the bishops of Rome acquiesced. Augustine and his colleagues in Numidia investigated Antoninus' excesses and deprived him of much of his power yet let him retain his rank. Ready to cede to Rome's

---

85. Augustine, epistle 20*.18.

86. See Lenski, "Evidence for the *Audientia Episcopalis*," 97, for Augustine's forbearance. Février is sure (*sans doute*) that Augustine's letters were composed to answer critics whose complaints have not survived ("Discours d'Église et réalité historique," 101–15).

87. Augustine, epistle 209.8.

final judgment, they expected its bishops to endorse rather than reverse decisions made on site.[88]

So Antoninus would remain a bishop, but with little more than a priest's power. From this distance, however, it is hard to see why. If Augustine's accounts are trustworthy, Antoninus was unpopular and continued to oppress the laity while his appeals were being heard. Augustine described what rattled Fussala parishioners in some detail, but he explained that they so feared retaliation that they insisted on anonymity.[89] Presuming Augustine was not cut from the same cloth as Antoninus, the latter's laity referred to the former as the author of their misfortune. He blamed himself, conceding he was imperceptive—wrong to give Fussala to Antoninus and blind to that incumbent's intense desires to reacquire the whole of his see, desires that lay behind Antoninus' dissembling during deliberations intended to relocate and rehabilitate him. And Antoninus' tenacity quite simply surprised him. Augustine owned up to errors in judgment: congregations "vilify me, and I deserve their censure."[90]

The Bishop's Court

As far as we can tell, he had followed procedures; after choosing poorly, assigning Fussala to Antoninus, and receiving parishioners' complaints, Augustine conferred with fellow bishops. He brought the accusations to the attention of the primate of Numidia. The crisis might thereby have been contained. The imperial chancery let bishops in the provinces be judged and, when appropriate, deposed by primates or by assemblies of their peers.[91] With reference to the Fussala affair, however, Augustine was in a fix; he was the chief contributing cause of all the unpleasantness. And that impression, which called his judgment into question, could only have impaired his ability to hold court for a time. As we shall learn, he was not fond of that function. He did not relish having the tawdry details of his parishioners' disputes with each other hauled into church, reminding him of the litigants' less than creditable affections. But Emperor Constantine

---

88. Compare Merdinger, *Rome and the African Church*, 170–77.

89. Augustine, epistles 209.4 (*de intolerabili dominatione*) and 20*.22.

90. Augustine, epistle 20*.23: *clamaverunt enim etiam de me ipso quae merebar audire quod ego auctor fuerim tanta calamitatis illorum*. Also consult Merdinger, *Rome and the African Church*, 162–63, and Lancel, "L'affaire d'Antoninus de Fussala," 283–84.

91. See Cimma, *L'episcopalis audientia*, 101–2.

had decreed that bishops preside over their courts or "audiences" and that they referee various civil disputes in their dioceses.⁹²

Subsequent legislation reconfirmed the courts' competence. Early in his pontificate, Augustine suspected that lawsuits would flood into the churches' courts. With a story about Alypius, his *Confessions* illustrated God's foresight, alerting bishops to the surge in litigation. Some strange sounds and curiosity drew his friend to the scene of a crime in Milan. When the officials sent by the silversmiths who were being robbed found him holding the hatchet that the thief had dropped, Alypius was falsely accused and nearly molested by a mob. An acquaintance intervened, the crook confessed, and Alypius learned a lesson that served him well when he was bishop of Thagaste. On Augustine's reading of the incident, Alypius learned in dramatic fashion about the injustices that follow when authorities fail to sift fact from fiction. His studies of legal precedents, Augustine implied, had not prepared Alypius for court duties as well as this ordeal had done.⁹³

Passing the story along, as the *Confessions* did, would have to suffice, for every bishop could not be similarly instructed. Rustic bishops would have to muddle through, providing, as best they could, what historians A. H. M. Jones and John Lamoreaux depict as "rough-and-ready" justice. The alternatives, secular courts in the provinces, Jones says, were served by judges who were not known for their learning. He accuses many of having prolonged proceedings for profit. Equally problematic, the interminable appeals in secular courts were costly; they left less affluent defendants at a considerable disadvantage. Clara Gebbia agrees with Jones and Lamoreaux that a bishop's court, reaching verdicts that could not be appealed or overturned (*effringi non possit . . . dissolvi non possit*), provided "speedier justice."⁹⁴ The range of matters that could be brought before a church court was reduced after Constantine. The chanceries of emperors Honorius and Arcadius scaled back the bishops' jurisdiction in 408; the audiences were left "halfway," Jean Gaudemet guesstimates, between the informality of early

---

92. For an analysis of Constantine's legislation, see Drake, *Constantine and the Bishops*, 323–29.

93. Augustine, *Confessiones* 6.9,14–15.

94. Augustine, *Enarrationes in Psalmos* 25(2).13; Jones, *Later Roman Empire*, 517; Lamoreaux, "Episcopal Courts," 152–53 and 159; and Gebbia, "Sant'Agostino e l'episcopalis audientia," 685–86, 693–94. Also see Vismara, *Episcopalis Audientia*, 46–47.

Christians' deliberations and the comprehensive applications of canon law in church courts during the Middle Ages.[95]

Bishops' courts could be taken as laboratories in which the laity were to practice what pastors and bishops preached—or, to be precise, as Augustine was, to avoid vices their sermons associated with litigation: perjury, fraud, and greed. He was sickened, however, by the laity's failure to appreciate the seriousness of their situation when they not only decided to cheat in court but also approached him for advice on how to cheat (and beat) the system. If Augustine was reporting and not inventing for effect, many Christians (*multi*) solicited his counsel to that end, looking to lie without seeming to lie. Even more appalling to him, those seeking to slither around the law expected he would be flattered to be treated as the expert (*putantes . . . placent nobis*). He professed that he would not have believed Christian litigants in civil suits could be so rapacious, audacious, and idiotic had they not solicited him so often for advice on how to dodge justice.[96] Umpiring disputes in his audience exhausted him. Responsibilities related to litigation stole time from his studies. He sometimes insinuated that he would have the courts permanently adjourned. He believed bishops ought to devote their time to doing the opposite of what the courts did—decisions in their audiences too often perpetuated quarrels rather than ended them, he said. Verdicts left litigants whose causes had been lost more hostile and less willing to be reconciled with their adversaries at the bidding of the very bishops who had passed judgment. Possidius of Calama, Augustine's biographer, furnished an airbrushed account of his subject in court, yet Augustine's remarks about arbitration suggest he was a doleful judge delighted to plead his advanced age as an excuse to appoint a subordinate to take over as his audience's presiding magistrate.[97]

Still, during his tenure, he conceded that the courts served a purpose. Parishes, after all, were populated by imperfect Christians, many of whom wanted wealth and prayed to obtain or retain it. Augustine was unnerved by the theatricality of their prayers for property; some fell to their knees,

---

95. Gaudemet, *L'Église dans l'empire romain*, 237; Cimma, *L'episcopalis audientia*, 87.

96. Augustine, sermon 137.14: *multi a nobis consilia mala petunt, consilia mentiendi, circumveniendi*.

97. For his retirement, see Augustine, epistle 213.5. Compare Possidius, *Sancti Augustini vita* 19 with Augustine, sermons 133.2 and 358.2; Augustine, *Enarrationes in Psalmos* 118(24).3; and Augustine, *De opere monachorum* 37. Lamoreaux introduces other bishops' biographers who mentioned their subjects' resentment of time spent in their audiences ("Episcopal Courts," 150–51).

thumping their heads on the ground and weeping copiously.[98] But as indecorous as such supplications were, they were not as shameful as the efforts of others who used the bishops' courts to launch lawsuits that strained relations with neighbors to the breaking point. The courts' continued existence showcased the failures of Augustine and his colleagues to persuade parishioners, promised a place in the celestial city, that they were foolish to make a spectacle of themselves passionately and abusively contending in court *pro rebus terrenis*. Defendants or plaintiffs, they proved their hearts or affections had not yet been uplifted by their faith's good news and blessings.[99]

Rather than turn to bishops for explanations of those blessings, too many parishioners, Augustine said, deferred to them for the wrong reasons, and they expected that their deference would win them favorable settlements in the churches' courts. Augustine often repeated that he and his colleagues were commissioned as pastors, and we shall see what that meant to him in the next chapter, yet it is worth noting here that he considered his colleagues and himself caretakers, looking after parishioners' souls and salvation. Only infrequently, if at all, should bishops be asked to look after the laity's estates, coin, and cattle—their congregations' worldly affairs (*negotia terrae suae*). Bishops should be in the business of salvation (*negotium salutis*).[100]

Augustine's distaste for litigation and his resentment at having to confront contentious Christians in his court occasionally surfaced in his polemical work against dissidents. Replying to Pelagians, who concluded that the faithful could achieve (and claim as their doing) admirable equanimity in the face of losses, he allowed that parishioners were permitted to sue, taking their claims to court to reacquire what rightly had been theirs (*repetit sua*), as long as those litigants attributed both their rights and their virtues to God's grace. But the implications were that tenacious litigants were morally inferior to Christians prepared to forfeit their rights to property and that litigants as yet unprepared to do so were only spared condemnation on account of their steadfast, conspicuously unpelagian faith in grace.[101] Augustine's criticisms of the Donatists' belligerence also afforded

---

98. Augustine, sermon 311.13.

99. Augustine, *Enarrationes in Psalmos* 80.21: *contendit . . . pro rebus terrenis amplius quam decet eum cui promissum est regnum coelorum.*

100. Augustine, epistle 33.5: *non de aura, non de argentis, non de fundis et pecoribus."* Also consult Vismara, *Episcopalis Audientia*, 113.

101. Augustine, *Contra duas epistolas Pelagianorum* 3.5,14.

him an opportunity to pour scorn on all Christians who strong-armed, squeezed, and sued others to get rich.[102] Dissidents and litigants, of course, could have appealed to sacred literature that reported disagreements and discord, of which Augustine was well aware. He might have cited the friction between apostles to let parishioners see how unsightly it was to take accusations public but instead praised the Apostle Peter, who had accepted his colleague's rebuke, as an example of marvelous humility, something to counter the urge to indict.[103]

Yet, ever since Emperor Constantine created the audiences and notwithstanding his successors' legislation restricting the jurisdiction of the churches' courts, they were sites at which diocesans developed their diplomatic skills. Staggered as he was by conflict that the faithful felt compelled to pursue in his court, Augustine had no choice. A bishop's authority depended on his service (*praesumus sed si prosumus*), and the government's edicts as well as parishioners' belligerence made court work part of that service.[104] In the late fourth and early fifth centuries, bishops were justices who, a few historians speculate, had a profound influence on the contours of social life. Kauko Raikas, for one, argues that Augustine welcomed his chance to shape policy and became something of a judicial activist, making new law as well as enforcing existing law.[105]

The best evidence for Augustine's judicial activism seems to be a letter he wrote to discover what prevailing law said about the status of slaves, specifically, about the rights of tenants, parents, children—and landlords to enslave. He might have been canvassing widely, but only one inquiry survives among the letters discovered by Johannes Divjak and published in the early 1980s. Augustine sent it to Eustochius, a Christian layman, apparently learned in law, and Claude Lepelley suggests that the questions he posed might have been related to a case pending before him.[106] But Augustine's questions range widely. He asked whether fathers could sell their sons into perpetual servitude. If fathers sold their sons' labor for a set period and died before that time expired, were the sons released from the terms of

102. Augustine, sermon 359.2: *forte pressit et oppressit, torsit et extorsit*.

103. Augustine, epistle 180.4. Also see Augustine, sermon 77.4–5 and Pietri, *Roma Christiana*, 2:1585.

104. Augustine, sermon 340(A).3; Lepelley, *Les cités de l'Afrique romaine*, 1:216–19.

105. Raikas, "*Audientia Episcopalis*," 476–77. Also see Gebbia, "Sant'Agostino," 686, and Lancel, *Saint Augustin*, 366–67, claiming that the courts *faisaient de l'évêque un acteur de premier plan dans le jeu social*.

106. Lepelley, "Liberté, colonat et esclavage," 340–42.

their fathers' agreements? Did masters of estates farmed by tenants have rights to the labor of their tenants' sons, despite the sale of same to others? Could estate owners reduce tenants or tenants' children to slavery (*servos facere*)? Augustine's volley of questions might signal that he planned to use his court to reform current—and what he considered corrupt—practices, for he confided to Eustochius that other rulings had been terribly inadequate. Hence, a case could be made that his appeal for help in ascertaining what the laws required as good as conceded that commending humility and frowning on greed would hardly resolve all problems parishioners brought before him.[107]

But a case could also be made that the letter to Eustochius was unrelated to problems surfacing in bishops' courts and more directly related to bishops' extrajudicial counsel. The pastoral epistle of Titus unequivocally obliged bishops to advise slaves to obey their masters; perhaps Augustine sought instruction from Eustochius to avoid urging submission on persons unjustly enslaved.[108] Arguably, if he presumed to do more, to propose new law, we would have caught him clawing at current practice. But instead of complaining about indentured servitude—or what we now call child labor laws—he protested that the Apostle Paul, having told the faithful to steer clear of government courts, in effect, complicated bishops' pastoral work. Constantine gave Christians ecclesiastical alternatives to secular magistrates, but Augustine came close to blaming Paul (*molestiis . . . affixit apostolus*) for drawing contentious Christians into the bishops' audiences and for giving them annoying puzzles to solve.[109]

Eustochius' answers, if ever sent, are lost to us. Yet another letter among those Divjak discovered suggests that—whatever his legal expert supplied in response to his questions about slaves' status—Augustine had little faith in laws shielding free men, women, and children from slavery and regulating the slave trade. In that other letter he expressed his distress to his friend and colleague Alypius, who was then bishop of Thagaste but who, as we learned, had trained as a lawyer. Augustine reported that people from the countryside had been kidnapped and hauled to his see, the port city of Hippo, to be shipped to Anatolia and elsewhere to be sold as slaves.

---

107. Augustine, epistle 24*.1. Augustine, sermon 356.4 implies that the church's court might have a part to play in the emancipation of persons unjustly enslaved, for which, see Szidat, "Zum Sklavenhandel," 366–71.

108. Augustine, epistle 24*.1 explicitly refers to Titus 2:9.

109. Augustine, *De opere monachorum* 29.37: *tumultuossimas perplexitates*.

Such criminal matters were beyond the jurisdiction of his court. Yet even if it had been empowered to enforce the new laws against trafficking Emperor Honorius' chancery had circulated in the 420s, he confided to Alypius that he would have found presiding altogether unpalatable, because those edicts stipulated that convicted traffickers be beaten so brutally their lives would be forfeit. And he wanted none of that yet wanted the dreadful (*metuendo*) deportations stopped.[110] So, without consulting veteran lawyers or magistrates, Augustine hatched a plan to free as many captives as possible before they disembarked. He had neighboring bishops forward the names of missing persons, and, when they were found in his diocese, he found ways to liberate them. He did not specify how, yet he explained that the churches were vigilant, he was diligent, and parishioners were charitable. Perhaps in reponse, traffickers concentrated on winning influential local friends to outmaneuver Augustine and the church, but we are left with the impression that they were not completely successful in shrugging off Augustine's efforts.[111]

Those efforts apparently were extralegal, informal. Augustine could not subpoena traffickers to appear in his audience. To be sure, on this front, he may not have been driven inexorably to the conclusion Frederik van der Meer ascribes to him, the judgment that the deliberations in the audience were "useless and time-wasting." (Van der Meer also stressed Augustine's supposed "ineradicable aversion" to the courts.)[112] But despite what Alypius or Eustochius might have written in response, Augustine thought some injustices were beyond his court's competence to redress. He held court, he said, because unlike the Apostle Paul, who had directed the faithful to hide their quarrels from unbelievers and so, in effect, instructed them to have bishops resolve their disputes in what would become the church audiences, he and clerical colleagues were settled on site. The apostle was an itinerant; his ministry kept him from staying in one place long enough to preside and arbitrate. Augustine was stationary. He was obliged to judge, yet did so *contre-couer*.[113]

Clara Gebbia points out that Augustine neither sidestepped the crisis slave trafficking created in Hippo nor explored strategies to put himself and

110. Augustine, epistle 10*.4.
111. Ibid., 10*.8.
112. Meer, *Augustine the Bishop*, 259.
113. Hugoniot, "Légats," 2067–68; for Augustine's remarks on the apostle's itinerancy, see his *De opere monachorum* 29.37.

his court in a more advantageous position to resolve it. He did not attempt to expand his jurisdiction. He did no more than—and technically "could do no more than [—] plead for a new norm" that would be "more consonant with the Christian ethic to hold in check such crimes" as kidnapping and the enslavement of the free. Claude Lepelley, however, sees Augustine looking to law and groping for ways to have his court address such problems. Neither Gebbia nor Lepelley presents overwhelming evidence, but Gebbia's position seems more defensible.[114] Even the civil cases that came before Augustine's audience, as we have seen, drove him to despair. He hated having Christians squabble in his court and having them depend on interventions that were sure to alienate one of the contending parties. Parishioners bound by inordinate desires, burdened by greed, and soured by sentiments incompatible with the dictates of their faith were pastoral problems that, in court, became administrative chores.[115] Augustine believed that lasting resolutions and reconciliations would have to result from litigants' renewed dedication to faith and love rather than from legal manuevering. One imagines him repeating the biblical tributes to charity in court or recycling the formulas that he derived from them, ignoring the details of litigants' claims, and explaining to claimants and combatants that virtue does not greedily grab for what others have.[116] And the image of Augustine preaching compassion to querulous Christians suggests that the border between bishops' administrative protocols and pastoral leadership is difficult to fix. We shall try to fix and cross that border in the next chapter, but it suffices here to recall that Augustine noted the importance of retaining the trust of all his parishioners and notified them that proceedings in his audience complicated such retention. Bishop Ambrose of Milan seems to have had fewer concerns about his court's effects on his ministry. According to Giulio Vismara, he imagined he was fulfilling his civic responsibility presiding in his court.[117] Perhaps he considered the churches' courts critical elements in what Harold Drake describes as Christianity's "alternative infrastructure," an alternative to the late antique imperial Court's network of courts. Yet Drake is interested in confrontation, especially Ambrose's face-off with

114. Compare Lepelley, "Liberté, colonat et esclavage," 331, with Gebbia, "Sant'Agostino," 690.

115. Augustine, *In Evangelium Joannis Tractatus* 34.8: *ligatis cupiditates suis . . . habens grandem sarcinam avaritiae.*

116. Augustine, *De diversis quaestionibus octoginta tribus* 36.3: *virtus autem non appetit quod in aliorum hominum potestate est.*

117. Vismara, "Ancora sulla *episcopalis audientia*," 56–57.

Empress Justina and her son, Valentinian II, which Augustine witnessed but did not mention in his *Confessions*.[118] He might have been silent because he valued Ambrose less as a political strategist and far more as one of the excellent stewards of the church who had warned against minimizing God's part in redeeming Christians and who, having done so, both anticipated and corrected the Pelagians' mistakes about grace and nature.[119]

Measuring Success

Conceivably, Augustine was tempted to retire from public life by watching Ambrose embroiled in political controversy. Even before Ambrose baptized him in 387, Augustine had retired to Cassiciacum to contemplate perennial philosophical questions. If his *Confessions* can be believed, he planned a semi-retirement of sorts for that purpose even earlier.[120] And after he was baptized, he and friends returned to Africa and withdrew to his family estate in Thagaste to continue their studies and conversations. Only later and reluctantly, as we know, was he drawn into the ministry. He had no objections to highly placed prelates becoming powerbrokers. He never wrote negatively about Ambrose's episode with Valentinian II or about his later sparring with Emperor Theodosius. From one of Augustine's sermons that commented more generally on affluence, influence, and others' esteem, one may infer that he expected bishops, who achieved a modicum of fortune and some celebrity to exploit both to serve their parishioners and to put their hope and faith in God. Doing otherwise would liken them to the Pharisees whom Jesus criticized publicly. So Christianity's prosperous prelates were ideally positioned to show just how little the righteous should care for what the world regarded as success. Augustine recommended that they live as pilgrims who spend their nights in stables (*viator in stabulo*). And they should rate their amply provided lives as precarious.[121]

This theme resurfaced whenever Augustine advised bishops how to measure successes. Rich or poor, they ought to consider that the biblical Ezekiel's "prophesy to the shepherds" was addressed to them. Shepherds

---

118. Drake, "Intolerance," 209–10.

119. Augustine, *Contra Julianum* 1.3,10 (*excellentem Dei dispensatorem quem veneror ut partum*), citing Ambrose's *Expositio Evangelii secundum Lucam* 4.67.

120. Augustine, *Confessiones* 6.14,24.

121. Augustine, *Enarrationes in Psalmos* 93.7: *vident enim periculose se vivere in hac vita, sentiunt se esse peregrinos.*

were prelates put in charge (*praepositi sumus*), commissioned, to feed God's sheep. Their responsibility was awesome, Augustine preached, professing that they would be held accountable if their sheep strayed.[122] Should their positions or commissions go to their heads, they must remember that Jesus started his ministry by recruiting the unpretentious to confound the powerful. With time, the powerful—as we discovered in the last chapter—as well as the learned and wealthy joined the humble to worship in Rome at the tomb of an unassuming fisherman. The lesson Augustine drew from that development must have seemed a little unusual to those Romans who measured success materially, the lesson that glory deriving from service to the faith surpassed the tottering, meaningless glory (*inanem . . . nutantem*) attached to reputation, conquest, and pedigree.[123]

But Augustine appreciated that the lesson was not self-evident to all highly placed prelates. Bishops easily became hostage to those they served and, taking the pulse of their parishes, they provided ministries that their not-so-faithful faithful wanted rather than the sermons and counsels they needed. Bishops were known to have indulged parishioners' bad habits, letting the laity feast and frolic in churches. Augustine admitted that license of that sort triggered the growth of some parishes by appealing to pagans' fondness for festivities and that growth meant credit and coin for bishops who accommodated parishioners' disgraceful behavior. Bishops worthy of their commissions would likely offend some; as a result, they would be likely to draw smaller crowds or congregations, but the course they set corresponded with Jesus' directives to his disciples, that they feed their sheep rather than themselves.[124]

In another sermon on the churches' "course," Augustine implied that his colleagues had been negligent in the late fourth century, having failed to call Christians' attention to either their temporal duties or their celestial rewards. He rehearsed the dangers that faced Africa—especially Catholic Christianity—at the time. The Donatists were gaining ground. Some of their bishops had befriended insurgents who shut off grain shipments to Rome. Emperor Honorius was compelled to send troops to the provinces. The faithful panicked. They hoarded rather than shared supplies. Augustine's account introduced nautical imagery. Local churches were ships in rough seas; without dependable leadership, the crews—the laity—were without

---

122. Augustine, sermon 46.2, citing Ezek 34:2.
123. Augustine, *Enarrationes in Psalmos* 65.4.
124. Augustine, sermon 46.8.

direction and hope.¹²⁵ Later, during the crises occasioned by invasions of Italy and Spain as well as by the floods of refugees into Africa, Augustine tried to keep informed about his parishioners' morale and mischief when business took him from Hippo. On receiving news that the comfortable among his congregation were less than forthcoming with aid to evacuees from Europe as well as to their neighbors, he relayed his displeasure with a reminder that citizens of the celestial city were pilgrims in this world. Certainly, when this world seemed to be falling apart, he suggested, his parishioners ought to have needed no coaxing to use their surplus to relieve strangers' and neighbors' suffering.[126]

Augustine seems to have traveled less than his prominent African colleagues. He never recrossed the Mediterranean after returning from Italy in the late 380s. Alypius and Possidius went to Rome and Ravenna to solicit or sustain the Court's support. Augustine was in demand closer to home, however, attending to diocesan business away from Hippo or attending church councils or consulting with Bishop Aurelius in Carthage. He was in Milevis in late 425 or early 426 to ensure the promotion of a candidate nominated by Severus, the recently deceased bishop there. The laity had been overlooked. The incumbent only spoke of his successor with the local clergy. Parishioners therefore protested. Augustine intervened, protests subsided, and the bishop-designate was consecrated. Augustine took no credit; God restored peace and order to Milevis.[127] Yet Severus' mistake taught him a valuable lesson. In 426, shortly after he returned to Hippo, he assembled his congregation to announce his plans to scale down his responsibilities and to present his nominee for the next bishop. He was confident that no objections to his candidate would be raised. Parishioners were well acquainted with Heraclius' intelligence and modesty. Nonetheless, a conference was called to test Augustine's prediction. He wanted confirmation and, if we may trust the scribes' account of the crowd's resounding endorsement, he got it.[128]

The account documenting Augustine's nomination and the congregation's reactions lodges with his other correspondence and reads like a transcript of the meeting. It shows that Augustine scrupulously avoided a dual episcopacy. In effect and, apparently, in name, he had been appointed

---

125. Augustine, sermon 75.5–7: *turbetur tentationem procellis haec navis*.
126. Augustine, epistle 122.2.
127. Augustine, epistle 213.1.
128. Ibid., 2.

co-bishop by Valerius in 391, only to learn much later that co-episcopacy had been forbidden earlier that century at the Council of Nicaea.[129] The rivalries between Donatist and Catholic Christian bishops in many African communities must have made him wary of such an arrangement, as did his miscalculation in subdividing his diocese and appointing Antoninus to a new see of Fussala. For whatever reasons, Augustine was careful to ensure that he could not be accused of dishonorably handling Heraclius' succession. He told parishioners that he was ready to retire and that Heraclius would thenceforth be assigned nearly all of his daily responsibilities; unsurprisingly, they included presiding in the church's court. As we now know, Augustine was eager to give away the gavel. During previous deliberations, he persuaded his congregation to let him reserve five days each week for study, freeing him from the mind-numbing work that young and less fortunate colleagues, who were involved (or mired) as he had been in the laity's worldly affairs, continued to undertake. Such freedom, he claimed, enabled him to provide his colleagues with authoritative exegeses of sacred texts to counter heretics' or pagans' criticisms. But Augustine also anticipated opposition. And he feared the intrusion of a bishop's ordinary distractions. He prepared for lay dissatisfaction that might develop, if and when the enthusiasm for Heraclius' appointment ebbed—and when the congregation came to think his leisure was an objectionable extravagance. For Augustine made sure to explain emphatically that his leisure (*meum otium*) was serious business (*magnum habet negotium*). Other bishops' success would depend on his success combing for and reinterpreting texts that could be used against Catholic Christianity's interests. Other pastors would appreciate what he would continue to do, though more prolifically than before, teasing from sacred texts the counsels that should define and improve pastoral leadership.[130]

129. Ibid., 4.
130. Ibid., 5–6.

3

Augustine's Pastors

Motives and Emotions

BISHOPS' ADMINISTRATIVE LEADERSHIP WAS sometimes difficult to distinguish from their pastoral leadership or guidance, so, as noted in this volume's introduction, some repetition is unavoidable here. But one distinction between the two most always held. Augustine generally took to pastoral care yet unenthusiastically undertook many of his administrative duties. When he complained about being overworked and distracted, he usually referred to presiding over his court, disciplining wayward clerical colleagues, or ensuring that priests were available to speak to parishioners in their local dialects in his large diocese. All that was routine, but it seemed to him much more onerous than interpreting sacred literature to instruct, inspire, and console his parishioners and advancing Catholic Christianity's interests by gaining polemical advantages over Manichees, Donatists, Arians, Pelagians, and pagans. Most were disrespectful on hearing him declare he could not satisfactorily answer all their complaints about enigmatic passages in the Bible. He nonetheless claimed that the faith over which he and its critics fought appealed to an understanding that had been reformed by a purified heart, one prepared to accept that some truths were incomprehensible. With respect to those within reach as well as those beyond the ability of finite minds to fathom, Augustine applied himself to correct misapprehensions, to scuttle pagans' and heretics' pretensions, and to confront practical and intellectual challenges, which could be called pastoral.

Historians who still watch him doing all of the above—some of them in spite of their opposition—usually share Giuseppe Ferraro's admiration for his virtuosity.[1]

While addressing critics, he was also intent on assisting colleagues who were muddling through the complexities of Christian doctrine. He was mindful of well-meaning curiosity, and pastoral leadership, in his estimation, required providing emotional support and encouragement to persons who had declared for the faith as well as transforming explanations into applications that improved life within their churches. André Mandouze rightly reminds us that the man who circulated for centuries in seminary classrooms as a master of doctrine was a minister who took pastoral care as seriously as any, and more seriously than most.[2]

Conditions of life varied in his diocese. Hippo was a prosperous port. He preached there and in Carthage to relatively Romanized, affluent, and influential Christians. To the plains south of Hippo and into the mountains, rustics had different concerns. Perhaps they seemed overzealous to their coastal cousins. Donatists were popular in the backcountry, and, as historian Brent Shaw illustrates with the case of Bishop Gaudentius, their resistance to government efforts to enforce the edicts issued after the Council of Carthage was more determined.[3] Generally, leadership in rural and urban parishes required pastors to help congregations to cope with, if not fully to comprehend, God's ways with creation and, as important for Augustine, to provoke parishioners to pay God's love forward in their compassion for others.

Obstacles were formidable. Although emperors had converted to Christianity, the devil, Augustine noted, had not. The devil trawled for souls among the faithful who therefore needed proper instruction, constant encouragement, and occasional consolation.[4] Yet Augustine had not committed quickly to addressing those needs. During his first years as a Catholic Christian, he "asserted on faith many things that," Jason Bedhun gathers, "were only rote recital to him."[5] On meeting Bishop Ambrose, Augustine was moved to abandon his political ambitions, but he was uninterested in serving an apprenticeship in Milan. That he promptly "panted" for

---

1. Ferraro, "Lo Spirito Sancto," 84. Also see Heil, "Antiarianisches," 279–80.
2. Mandouze, *Avec et pour Augustin*, 521.
3. Shaw, *Sacred Violence*, 732–35.
4. Augustine, *Enarrationes in Psalmos* 93.19.
5. BeDuhn, *Augustine's Manichaean Dilemma*, 2:413.

the respect the Milanese gave their bishop, as Neil McLynn alleges, seems unlikely. Augustine seems to have been repelled by the crowds demanding Ambrose's attention, and, as we have seen, he withdrew from public life. If we may trust his *Confessions* and the works he composed beforehand, the Grail he chased had nothing to do with popular acclaim. He retired with friends to resume the soul-searching he had started before coming to Milan, to contemplate how to rein in his affections for the perishable—for reputation, position, even friendships—and to train himself to love God above all.[6] By the time he revealed as much, he was the bishop of Hippo. He knew that contemplatives were better off unburdened, that diocesan and parish responsibilities stole his time for study and self-inventory. Nonetheless, Augustine became committed to the cure of souls as well as to contemplation, to listening to others' confess and counseling them as they struggled to overcome their resistances to the faith and to the demands it placed on them. And, by then, he was devoted to helping Catholic Christian colleagues confront dangers. All told, from the 390s, Augustine was dedicated to making a difference, *foris*—outside.[7]

"Outside," however, pastors confronted battles raging in nearly all their parishioners. People seemed ill-equipped to prevail over their desires to acquire. Philosophy was little help. Philosophers tended to urge self-control—or, at least, an appearance of control—but temptations overtaxed the efforts of the ordinary to curb the flesh. Professing such control and boasting of extraordinary exertions to achieve it signaled to Augustine that self-assertion and arrogance would almost certainly make strenuous moral struggles interminable—unwinnable. Besides, parishioners' sense that they were losing control seemed an excellent place for pastors to begin their work. If Augustine had his way, they would disregard philosophers' claims that emotions were obstacles to self-realization. Pastors ought then to proceed to preach repentance, which, ideally, would replace parishioners' fear of punishment with a passion for righteousness.[8]

---

6. For the soul-searching reported in the fourth book of the *Confessions*, see Bowlin, "Augustine Counting Virtues," 296–97. McLynn concedes that Augustine "examined" Ambrose "from a distance" yet claims that he took the bishop of Milan as a "role model"—not as a foil ("Administrator: Augustine in His Diocese," 315). Kaufman argues otherwise (*Incorrectly Political*, 24–35).

7. Augustine, *Contra Faustum Manichaeum* 22.56: *honeste ambulans ad eos qui foris sunt.* Also see Capatano, "Leah and Rachel," 220–24; Mathewes, "Liberation of Questioning," 543; and Elm, *Die Macht der Weisheit*, 141.

8. For example, Augustine, sermon 154(A).1–3.

The emotions were soteriological assets. Augustine drew on sacred texts to argue that serenity undermines or, as Robert Dodaro aptly paraphrases, "numbs" believers' sensitivities, leaving them stoical and ignorant or indifferent to the need for grace.[9] Augustine's *City of God* savored the occasions on which Jesus expressed anger, grief, and joy. He found Jesus in tears for Lazarus in the Gospel of John (11:35); he cited Jesus' rage at the moneychangers in the temple in all canonical gospels. Incarnate, God was susceptible to passions that afflicted humanity because Adam and Eve had traded serenity for sin. The two creatures had been untroubled (*imperturbati*) where God originally put them. But, after their transgression, their heirs were prey to emotions, as was Jesus who condescended to live among them. But emotions that provoked agitation and anxiety were prompts for repentance. Whereas the philosophers advocated restraint, Christian theology, on Augustine's watch, countered that forbearance of that sort was unrealistic—and, worse, it perpetuated illusions that the power to defy temptation and to bridle inordinate desires could be developed without God's grace, the help that came before (and for) repentance. Hence, in effect, philosophers who had placed great stock in emotional control to the point that passions were ostensibly suppressed would have had followers forfeit their humanity to acquire a fleeting, false sense of wellbeing. Augustine argued as much, insisting that the dispassionate or unruffled (*durum*) not be confused with the righteous (*rectum*); pastors must advocate passion, he said, for if the faithful did not ardently sorrow for sin, they could hardly experience a remorse that led to repentance.[10] And they would be unlikely to overcome the impulse to excuse their behavior by citing the wickedness around them, particularly the misbehavior of their leaders (*praepositorum suorum malos mores*). Augustine admitted that the upright were neither as conspicuous nor as numerous as the unrighteous, but that sort of census and the philosophers who countenanced *apatheia*, he confirmed, should not divert the faithful's attention from Christianity's calls for their unfeigned repentance.[11]

He figured that feigned repentance was not uncommon. Undiscerning pastors could mistake counterfeit sorrow for genuine remorse, which developed, he maintained, only when sinners realized how deeply they had

---

9. Dodaro, *Christ and the Just Society*, 195. Also see Nisula, *Functions of Concupiscence*, 264–65.

10. Augustine, *De civitate Dei* 14.9–10; Augustine epistle 104.16.

11. Augustine, sermon 351.11.

offended their creator. Naturally, expectations that God would punish offenses stirred grief and regret, but Augustine asserted that repentance resulting from fear of reprisal was inauthentic. Only the faithful who trusted God's mercy and assurance of pardon exhibited the sincere, profound sorrow that led to genuine repentance. They did not repent to impress this world's magistrates about to reprove them for illicit endeavors. Nor did they repent to appease a celestial magistrate who demanded propitiation. The faithful penitents knew they were forgiven and repented, Augustine explained, because they offended the Father, Creator, and Redeemer who sent his Son to atone and obtain their forgiveness on the cross.[12]

Pastors in their parishes had ample opportunities to sift penitents' motives. Familiarity with their congregations gave them advantages on that count. But when, in 408, Augustine was summoned to another diocese, to Calama, where we found him in the last chapter, he expressed skepticism about the sincerity of the remorse pagans professed for having stoned the church and attacked the clergy there. The offenders faced punitive damages that, according to their advocate Nectarius, would, if awarded, leave them destitute. Their poverty, he prophesied, and resentment would make peaceful coexistence with Christians impossible. But by making restitution, Nectarius said, they showed their contrition, and that remorse would lead to reconciliation. Administrative and pastoral objectives converged in Augustine's sense (and accusation) that pagans' contrition was counterfeit, that their remorse did not mount to the status of repentance, and that the rift in Calama was beyond easy repair. But severe punishment might turn the trick. In other words, if Nectarius had the Calama pagans' lasting and most profound interests at heart, Augustine counseled, he should press for forfeitures and sanctions, because prying pagans from their attachments to possessions would bring them closer to faith in celestial rewards—and closer to Christianity. Only within that faith was authentic repentance possible. Property and prosperity gave pagans a false sense of security. They could not feel the frailty and finitude of their earthly existence. So Augustine redefined civic service for Nectarius: to serve his clients' interests and to see their city flourish (*florentem patriam*), Nectarius must help them discover the route from punishments to piety and explain to them the relative values of earthbound successes, benefits, and comforts, on the one hand, and celestial efflorescence, on the other.[13]

12. Augustine, epistle 104.9.
13. Augustine, epistles 90; 91.2–6 and 9–10; and 104.11.

Augustine's Leaders

Crises of Calama proportions in Africa were few and far between during Augustine's tenure, yet pastoral care—counseling and leadership—addressed the needs of parishioners with ordinary sins to repent. The faithful, for example, read and heard that they must not covet yet were unable to avoid sabotaging friendships by wanting what belonged to others. They had been instructed to respect their parents, yet family relations too often deteriorated when daughters and sons were insolent. That much and so many more of the faithful's failures may be inferred from Augustine's sermons and correspondence. He preached and wrote to persuade the covetous and insolent to repent, to acknowledge that God had remitted their sins and to concede God's role in fashioning their best intentions. Responsibility for behavioral reform fell to pastors, penitents, and their God, but, of course, for Augustine, God always had top billing.[14]

Few consequences of that reform were as important to Augustine as penitents' recoil from theatrical civic spectacles. He thought that African Christians and many refugees from Rome, who joined them after 410, were too fond of staged immoralities. He was ashamed of parishioners' apparent addictions to lewd displays, to the coarse, salacious nonsense that even Cicero had despised. Augustine was demonstrably ambivalent about Cicero, accepting some of his sentiments and rejecting others, but he thought the famed orator had been right to complain about the vulgar conduct ascribed to the gods by poets and dramatists. The enduring popularity of their fictions contributed to Augustine's conviction that efforts to dissuade the faithful from taking pleasure with the pagans ought to be fundamental features of pastoral leadership.[15]

Augustine introduced other reasons for Christians to avoid pagans' festivities and entertainments. Their presence, he said, derailed efforts to have the faithful participate in attracting unbelievers and the religiously indifferent to church. Christianity's virulent critics would capitalize on the presence of the faithful at the theater and among pagan neighbors at festivals, which retained elements of the provinces' pagan past. Christians dining with pagans near the altars to, and statues of, their deities showed solidarity with friends whom they should be trying to enlighten. Augustine suspected that compliant crowds at civic celebrations, together with

---

14. Augustine, sermon 251.8,7. Also consult Augustine, epistle 153.6 for assurances that penitent offenders would see to their own scourging. Discussion of God's share in prompting repentance and righteousness continues later in this chapter when we encounter the pastoral implications of Augustine's polemics against the Pelagians.

15. Augustine, *De civitate Dei* 1.32, 1.35 and 4.26.

the seductive powers of cleverly crafted idols, might just make the faithful forgetful of that duty, if not also forgetful of their faith. He acknowledged that some Christians might not yet be prepared to aggressively present their faith and convert their neighbors, yet their absences from civic celebrations that retained pagan features and thus the dwindling, disappointing attendance would shame—and conceivably win over—pagans who disregarded bishops' and pastors' direct overtures.[16]

To address what some of the faithful may have experienced as a vacuum when their participation in civic celebrations had been discouraged, Augustine's colleagues, Richard Lim says, "beef[ed] up" the Christian calendar of commemorations, promoting cults of martyrs "to respond to the culture of public spectacles." Lim concludes that "the emerging Christian ritual culture" competed with municipal pageantry to "control hearts and minds" in late antiquity.[17] And that competition was complicated by another—as Augustine doubtless knew only too well, and as we learned in the previous chapter—for Donatists would have had distinct advantages in the making of martyr cults. They paid the accustomed honors to the earliest Christians whose sacrifices were honored as well by Africa's Catholic Christians. Yet Donatists also had recent martyrs to remember, dead dissidents of the fourth century. Historian Cécile Barreteau-Revel proposes that Donatist secessionists, whom Augustine tirelessly tried to reconcile to his more comprehensive, compromising church, had been "nourished on heroic intransigence."[18] The Donatists commemorated defiance; Augustine countered by redefining martyrdom to include enduring trials and temptations in the conquest of one's infirmities.[19]

The Uncharitable

The Donatists' defiance and their maintenance of separate churches and a separate hierarchy posed *administrative* problems. But Augustine considered Donatists' refusal to reconcile with the tolerant, comprehensive

---

16. Augustine, sermon 62.10–11. For the power of compliant crowds (*auctoritate... obsequientum... turbarum*) and seductive idols, see Augustine, *Enarrationes in Psalmos* 113(2).3.

17. Lim, "Augustine and Roman Public Spectacles," 148–49.

18. Barreteau-Revel, "Faire l'unité dans l'église d'Afrique," 251–52, 258–59.

19. Augustine, *sermones nuper reperti*, Dolbeau 18.8: *scias ergo temptari te ... ut habeas animum martyris*.

church in Africa also—perhaps, primarily—a pastoral problem. For even moderates among the refuseniks, from Augustine's perspective, discounted challenges to their practices presented by the Bible's commendations of love or charity. Moderates and extremists alike seemed to Augustine to prefer to set aside such guidance and defend the schism by recycling arguments about alleged infractions that had been sifted long before, allegations that drove their forbears—and that kept them—from Catholic Christianity.[20] Soon after he was made bishop, Augustine was confident he could talk the secessionists into Catholic Christianity. He was wrong. They would not agree that the continued existence of their rival churches reflected their lack of charity. So, as we know, he grudgingly came to endorse the use of coercion. He no longer thought that his Catholic colleagues were overreaching when they proposed to have the government intervene and punish nonconformity. Augustine supposed that punishments (fines, confiscation, incarceration, and exile) along with the fear of punishment might give those within Donatist congregations incentive to reconsider the rationale for their enmity and disunity, ultimately kindling a love for others of the faith that could reunify African Christendom. But, unsurprisingly, the Donatists saw nothing charitable or loving in Augustine's lesson for pastors who entertained reservations about strong-arm tactics: if they found that their flocks were drawn away, he said, they were to flog those tempted and attempting to stray.[21]

Augustine knew that no critical matters of faith separated the Donatist secessionists from their Catholic Christian rivals, but he continued to think that an emphasis on charity, so central to pastors' vocations, was in short supply in sectarian circles.[22] To him, their conduct confirmed as much. They turned their antagonisms against long-dead prelates into indictments against pastors who could not share their disaffection. They hurled unfounded accusations against them—against Augustine as well as others who proposed that charity not only commended but commanded that rivals reconcile. The dissidents would not abide by decisions reached at the Council of Carthage in 411, which vindicated the prelates they vilified. In a sermon preached a few years after that council adjourned, and while many secessionists remained unreconciled, Augustine wondered whether he, other Catholic Christian bishops, and the government had exhausted

20. Augustine, *Gesta collationis Carthaginiensis* 3.56.
21. Augustine, epistle 93.5: *pastorem flagella ad gregem pecora errantia revocare*.
22. Ibid., 52–53.

every earthly approach to the problem; maybe only God—directly—could overcome Donatist rejections of efforts to restore order and peace.[23]

The premise was that charity issues in forgiveness. As we know, in the early fourth century, Caecilian and his colleagues were acquitted of the charges that Donatists registered against them. Had the accused been found guilty, the seriousness of their malfeasance, arguably, would have placed them beyond pardon. But Donatists of the late fourth and early fifth centuries accused their Catholic Christian rivals, generations removed from the Caecilianists, of failing to subscribe to opinions that had been discredited—specifically, in Augustine's mind, of continuing to perform their clerical tasks. Augustine considered those accusations mean-spirited. And to the extent that they divided the African church, those Donatist bishops and pastors who made them were unworthy of their vocations (*non sunt pastores*). Their scripture, calling for charity, would never have sanctioned such enduring acrimony.[24] Augustine believed that Christian fellowship depended on the affection of friends not only for the truths of their faith but for each other. Such affection sustained him during his vocational crises in Italy. Companies of like-minded friends, Jean-François Petit notices, "nourished" Augustine's ideals and dreams of extending similar conditions to others.[25] On his return to Africa, however, he found that the church there was deeply troubled. Undeniably, he read the situation tendentiously, but we must cope with his reading, because it influenced his understanding of leadership and made dissident Donatists villains. He complained that they filled their parishioners with malice, disfiguring what he described as beautiful (*pulchra*), the love within—and the unity of—the faith's churches. The secessionists had changed what should have been lovely into something ugly. They split the African church into two warring parties, and the proliferation of Donatist sects continued to defile the faith.[26]

Augustine spotted what he considered a telling inconsistency. Donatists refused to admit Catholic Christians into their company unless they submitted to rebaptism by Donatist prelates. The prerequisite signaled the secessionists' conviction that Catholic Christianity was not a proper church. Yet, troubled by the proliferation of sects splintering their movement, they welcomed the apostates who wished to return to their mainstream without

---

23. Augustine, sermon 46.17.
24. Ibid., 33.
25. Petit, "Sur le phénomène amical," 53–55.
26. Augustine, sermon 46.37.

requiring that they be rebaptized. For example, Christians baptized by Maximianus, a deacon who had been excommunicated by the Donatists, were not rebaptized when they left his sect for theirs, although Maximianus had dared to call upon bishops to condemn those who condemned him. *Pro unitatis vincula*, for the sake of unity, Donatists reintegrated their strays without repeating the initiation ritual. They claimed that the Maximianists had never been expelled from their churches. But Augustine possessed records that proved otherwise, and, to his mind, the evidence demonstrated how unprincipled as well as inconsistent Donatists were, for they steadfastly refused to reconcile with Catholic Christians whose congregations they had torn apart while pardoning renegades who had seceded from them.[27] Augustine, of course, was all for forgiveness. Pastors should alert Christians of all stripes both to scandalous behavior around them and to the need for patience and training in forgiveness. The Catholic Christian polemicists' job was to mark the secessionists' intramural squabbles as well as the tendency of schisms to beget schisms and sects. And when polemicists preached as pastors, they should mark the need charitably to extend forgiveness and to include sinners in a comprehensive or universal church—to win them with love, have them aspire to improve, and prompt them to repay God's love for them in their compassion for neighbors, broadly conceived.[28]

If we may trust Augustine, predatory secessionist polemicists deliberately mistook that Catholic Christian position as permissiveness, claiming that he and his colleagues were soft on crime. Donatists, that is, deliberately misconstrued the emphasis on charity and reconciliation as a measure of Catholic Christian pastors' tolerance of—and complicity in—their parishioners' sins. Augustine argued that sins were pervasive and that ordinary sins did not disgrace Christianity; life in time was training, and sage pastors, as wise coaches, expected missteps. Comprehensive churches were *permixta*, places where the good, bad, and better mingled—and where the missteps of some were occasions for them and for others, instructed (or coached) by pastors, to learn to be more graceful.[29]

From Augustine's perspective, the Donatists were perfectionists, and their intolerance of imperfection forfeited pastoral opportunities to instruct the faithful and displayed an unbecoming arrogance that discredited their

---

27. Augustine, epistle 51.2, and Augustine, *Enarrationes in Psalmos* 36(2).19–23. Also see García Mac Gaw, *Le problème du baptême*, 273–74.

28. Augustine, sermons 81.7 and 83.3–4; Augustine, *Enarrationes in Psalmos* 33(2).10.

29. Zocca, "L'identità Cristiana," 117–18; Di Berardino, "Rileggere il 410," 25–27.

Christianity. No doubt, for polemical advantages, he exaggerated his adversaries' perfectionism, yet their refusal to reconcile with Catholic Christians appeared to substantiate his charges that they pretentiously supposed they alone had powers to ascertain who was worthy (and unworthy) of the gospels' good news. Had Donatists been authorized to create exclusive churches, Augustine asked, or were they thereby preempting God's judgments? Their contentions, as Augustine relayed them, were that the eviction of sinners decontaminated their churches and that separation from Catholic Christianity kept Donatist congregations from the infection that somehow spread from some early fourth-century bishops through generations, invalidating the sacraments over which Augustine and his associates presided. To Augustine, Donatist secessionists were trying to create a terrestrial paradise, embracing the here and now rather than seeking an other-than-temporal felicity in the hereafter (*amplectendam terram*), making them no different from pagans who expected temporal successes would crown their efforts.[30] But what Donatist evictions did create was dissension. Secession proved contagious. Anthony Dupont and Matthew Alan Gaumer plausibly argue that Donatist divisions, especially "the intra-Donatist Maximian schism ... propagated several lucrative polemical footholds for Catholic leaders to exploit" by the time Augustine was consecrated bishop, whereas previously the dissidents' numerical superiority in Africa braced their resolve to avoid theological debates with their more cosmopolitan critics.[31]

Anxious to obscure, if not end, intramural squabbles and to restore unanimity and unity, Donatists forgave apostates willing to return and, without rebaptizing them, reincorporated them in their congregations. Ostensibly, forgiveness exhibited a charitable disposition, but Augustine believed that secessionists' apparent preemption of God's prerogatives as well as their premises made them resolutely uncharitable. They not only shunned Catholic Christians; their claims (1) that they alone could discern the integrity of pastors and bishops presiding over the faith's liturgies and, therefore, (2) that they alone could guarantee the effectiveness of the sacraments misled laypersons who, had they listened to Augustine, would have known that God—not clerics—was responsible for pouring grace through sacramental portals into congregations. What struck Augustine was Donatists' failures to learn from their experiences with intra-confessional strife to seek reconciliation with Catholic Christians and to appreciate that pride

---

30. Augustine, sermon 296.9.
31. Dupont and Gaumer, "*Gratia Dei, Gratia Sacramenti*," 311.

procured dissension and disunity, whereas charity promoted unity. To his mind, the dissident prelates were terribly poor pastors.³²

The Apostle Paul, Augustine's model for pastoral leadership, was charitable and humble, yet he could never be justly accused of having been soft on crime. He could have turned a blind eye to delinquency or indifference; nothing would have pleased the delinquent and indifferent more than being told that their faith was sufficient to bring them good fortune and celestial reward. Sinners among the faithful would have heaped honors on the apostle had he been uncritical, but honors had not interested him. He flinched when praised, Augustine guessed, adding that Paul had no use for the popularity some pastors prized and purchased by flattering parishioners. The challenge Paul had accepted was to underscore the importance of charity and unity without ceasing to be censorious when the quality of Christians' lives called for censure.³³ Pastors ought to learn from him that they must lead, censure, and discipline as servants and not as masters. Parishioners' infirmities or imperfections, Augustine was emphatic, must not tempt pastors to forget that humility, not superiority, was the distinctive feature of their profession.³⁴

At first blush, Augustine's counsel seems absurd. Pastoral authority and church discipline seemed to depend on their pastors' standing. The humble and self-effacing might be disregarded. Unless pastors leveraged their superior insight, they would have difficulty dealing with laity who were drawn into their comprehensive churches but who continued to savor illicit pleasures or to shrink from challenges that their faith, which required restraint, imposed on them. With pastoral care, pastors' patience, and, of course, God's help, preferences for celestial pleasures could take root, yet, upholding their end, pastors must pronounce (and warn of) judgments that might carry little weight unless they did. Still, Augustine was persuaded that pastors should lead, as apostles had, from among—rather than from above—and could effectively help parishioners make proper choices, manage temporal goods charitably, and avoid neglecting spiritual objectives.³⁵

---

32. Augustine, epistle 53.3; Augustine, sermon 46.18: *si superbia parit discissionem, caritas unitatem*.

33. Augustine, sermons 46.7 and 131.3 (*Deus superbis resistit, humilibus autem dat gratiam*).

34. Augustine, sermon 340(A).1.

35. Augustine, epistle 140.4.

Augustine charged that Donatists—poor pastors, indeed—pursued terrestrial objectives to the neglect of the spiritual. They lost sight of the cardinal Christian virtue as they grew more and more uncharitable both to sinners among their faithful and to Catholic Christian bishops trying to reunify the African Christian church. Donatists pursued perfection in time, making claims about their founders that history could not corroborate and claims about the virtues of their current bishops to which Catholic Christians' experiences gave the lie. Moreover, Augustine said, the claims offended all those who imagined that humility, alongside charity, was their faith's *sine qua non*. Donatists, he went on, had put their clergy in a place reserved for Jesus when they insisted that the effectiveness of sacraments depended on the pastors and bishops presiding; arrogance of that sort made them vile.[36]

Donatists' responses no doubt complicated the pastoral challenge of preaching humility and charity, specifically, as we learned, when they equated Catholic Christianity's emphasis on charity with permissiveness. But Augustine's appeals for charity and forgiveness were further complicated and likelier to go unheeded when the faithful saw that the faithless, arrogant, and miserly prospered. When misfortune depleted the assets husbanded by the faithful, they were predictably and mightily vexed (*maxime moventur*) and, to Augustine's displeasure, reluctant—and often outright opposed—if asked to contribute from their coffers to address their neighbors' needs.[37]

His response seems caustic and contemptuous. One can only guess at parishioners' reactions when he reminded them that God never promised prosperity to the righteous. *Non enim tibi promisit nisi se*; God promised himself, Augustine said, concluding that Christians—pilgrims in time—deprived of other possessions would always possess faith and expectations of a celestial homecoming. The pilgrims possessed God, so they could never be accounted poor.[38] How well did Augustine think that sermon would sell? Could he have presumed that pastors would inspire benevolence with explanations and exhortations of that sort when, as we discovered in the last chapter, he had encountered such malevolence? Litigious Christians in the bishops' court must have seemed to have forgotten that they were pilgrims. They sued and countersued, as if they loved their terrestrial city and its

---

36. For example, see Augustine, *sermones nuper reperti*, Dolbeau 26.55.
37. Augustine, sermon 25(A).1.
38. Augustine, sermon 137.10.

returns far more than the celestial, although their tenure in the former was brief and their preserve in the latter, should they but sieze on the remedies to anger—charity and forgiveness—would be eternal. Pastoral leadership, therefore, required fighting the current, specifically, acknowledging the tug of unrighteousness; conceding that the righteous would necessarily sin, nurse grievances, and envy others' good fortune; and seasoning one's counsel, consolations, and sermons with encouragement that, ideally, persuaded parishioners whose anger and envy might otherwise have developed into hatred. Augustine would have pastors preach salvation by expectation to offset resentments they would harbor and likely inspire in others.[39]

Hate and resentment stirred the uncharitable and vengeful to thrust forward with threats (*exsero comminationes*) rather than to reach out to rivals and appeal for reconciliation, whereas compassion stirred the charitable to pay God's love forward to rivals who were hostage to their hatred and to neighbors in need.[40] Pastors should preach the counsels of perfection drawn from sacred texts, Augustine advised, but the faithful should not be expected to sell all they have and give the proceeds to the poor. Better to ask the faithful to renounce this world in spirit and to be as prepared to lose their property as martyrs were to lose their lives. Such magnanimity signaled that one's priorities or loves were properly ordered, Augustine said, defining "virtue" as properly ordered loves.[41] Overcoming greed and ordering love, he knew, required God's assistance. That was given with faith, as grace, which—with pastors' encouragement—convinced Christians they were undeserving of what they possessed and—with pastors' pedagogy, as we shall see in the following chapter—explained to Christians what it meant to be possessed by God's grace.[42]

Pelagians

That need for instruction acquired greater urgency during the early fifth century when Pelagian literature started circulating in Africa, where

---

39. Augustine, *Enarrationes in Psalmos* 77.39–41. Also see Augustine, sermons 211.1 and 359.1, as well as Curbelié, *La justice dans "La cité de Dieu"*, 395–97, and Byers, *Perception*, 102 and 116.

40. Augustine, sermon 63.2.

41. Augustine, *De civitate Dei* 15.22; Augustine, epistle 157.33–36.

42. Augustine, *De vera religione* 28.51; Augustine, *De Genesi contra Manichaeos* 2.9,12.

Catholic Christians were still grappling with the problems posed by Donatist dissidents. Even after 411, when the Council of Carthage decisively found in favor of Augustine and his Catholic Christian colleagues, many secessionists held their ground. They defied government authorities and continued to quarrel with Augustine's reading of the church's nature and extent—specifically, its tolerance of character flaws among the laity and clergy. They thought Catholic Christianity's interpretation of universality as its defining virtue beneath contempt. Augustine held his ground as well, mixing his appeals for reconciliation with arguments against arrogance and against sectarians' apparent insensitivity and isolationism. Augustine also and increasingly attended to the claims made in the Pelagians' favorite texts that circulated in Africa after 410, as did the refugees from Italy who had been impressed with—and hoped to popularize—the ascetic strain of Christianity associated with Pelagius. Pelagius was teaching in Rome during the 380s when Augustine visited, but the two seem not to have met. They corresponded cordially until 416, although, before then, Pelagius' Sicilian disciples acquainted Augustine with what he took to be their astonishingly poor judgment—specifically, their ultra-optimistic views about human nature's purity and powers, views he subsequently attributed to their master and tirelessly tried to undermine.[43]

Soon after his last casual and cordial letter to Pelagius, Augustine collaborated with Alypius to retrieve two refugees who seemed enamored of Pelagius' ideas. They wrote to Juliana, a widow, whose daughter Demetrias had recently taken vows of chastity. Pelagius had encouraged her to do so. Augustine and Alypius approved Demetrias' decision yet were concerned that Pelagius had given her the wrong impression. By then, he was known to have attributed chastity to the chaste rather than to God. Augustine, by contrast, had learned from his struggles to be virtuous how hard it was to be continent, how lust confounded every human effort to resist temptations, and how much relief came with the knowledge that resistance and continence were gifts from God.[44] That relief was a source of humility as well as of comfort, and the humble, Augustine said, must recoil from claims in the Pelagians' literature that the virtuous deserve praise for their virtues, as if strenuous effort on their part had not been prompted, aided, and brought to completion by God. The letter from Augustine and Alypius

---

43. Ebbeler, *Disciplining Christians*, 12–13.
44. Augustine, epistle 188.3; Augustine, *Confessiones* 8.7,16–18; Augustine, *De civitate Dei* 14.23.

conceded that choice played a small part in Demetrias' resolve, but they insisted that God's part was considerably greater and all but overwhelming. To think otherwise was to show ingratitude for God's gift. Augustine and Alypius urged Juliana to have her daughter cease reading Pelagian literature and confess she was gifted because God gave her both a resolve to be chaste and strength to persevere. Her resolve and perseverance would become widely known; Augustine feared that, as her continence was celebrated, fame might go to her head.[45]

That message was too important to consign to a single letter. His insistence on divine presence in—and God's empowerment of—the righteous was common fare both in his polemics against the Pelagians and in his advice to pastors. His treatise on virginity, however, bears the closest resemblance to his letter to Juliana concerning Demetrias. Augustine unsparingly praised the chaste yet warned them to be humble. Bragging about their determination, in effect, ruined their reputation among the faithful, who must expect humility as well as restraint from the clergy and leading laity alike. And the faithful ought to expect the truth, which, Augustine maintained, was that the self-control of the celibate would have been impossible without God's work in and for them. Without God's help, they would have hastened to excuse their sins and probably would have remained intemperate. With it, they accused themselves and embraced chastity.[46]

Pelagians, Augustine complained, offered contrary counsel to the fortunate few who chose continence. Pelagians infuriated him by claiming that Christians making such choices possessed righteousness as a right rather than as a gift—a reward that led to celestial rewards, celestial dividends on their investments of effort. As noted, Augustine often prevailed on pastors to emphasize how little the faithful deserved God's assistance as well as the satisfactions it made possible. Pelagians apparently trusted that life after death was the time to settle up, as Jean-Marie Salamito suggests, a time for God to distribute returns on their righteousness practiced in this wicked world. Augustine thought differently about *post-mortem* settlements. He was convinced that there were no returns on investments Christianity's pastors or Pelagians could calculate in advance.[47] There were no back channels under the sun (*sub isto sole in hujus vitae vanitate*) through which pastors might get reliable information to distinguish between the righteous and

---

45. Augustine, epistle 188.9.
46. Augustine, *De sancta virginitate* 42–43.
47. Salamito, *Les virtuoses et la multitude*, 58–60.

the wicked with confidence. Unlike Pelagius and his admirers, Augustine believed that finite minds could not fathom how God measured merit. Christians who thought themselves righteous and deserving could be in for surprises. Judgments in the next life would probably be very different from the verdicts that mortals passed on each other in this one.[48]

To Augustine, the Pelagians' pugnacious style—much as their inflated estimate of what human nature could do with the grace they received in baptism and with only the law to guide them thereafter—could intimidate Christianity's pastors and tempt them to become little more than monitors overseeing moral instruction. Perhaps the Pelagians appeased some pastors by granting that baptism was important in the run-up to redemption. Yet, Augustine argued, the concession was a ruse; Pelagians put nearly all their faith in human nature. Their Christianity, therefore, was less Christocentric than that of the gospels or the apostles. And the significance they assigned strenuous effort showed how little they regarded the difficulties that the faithful encountered when they tried to refuse consent to the evil inhabiting them. Pastors must not be deceived, Augustine warned; their parishioners required explanations from sacred literature that consoled as well as informed. They also required constant infusions of grace. Pelagius apparently thought any emphasis on pastors' leadership let parishioners off too lightly. Augustine responded that Pelagius' partisans expected too much from human nature's unexceptional capabilities, as if continence and poverty could be embraced naturally or with minimal encouragement. He knew from experience that the former was a gift, as was the contempt for possessions that prompted charity and church solidarity.[49]

Such prompting was critical. Augustine imagined that he and his colleagues were less likely to experience church solidarity and Christians' compassion, if Pelagians convinced the faithful that talk of their enduring sinfulness was nonsense and talk of repentance meaningless. Anthony Dupont sees that Augustine, on that count, paired Pelagians with Donatists, inasmuch as the former's course from sin to salvation and what Augustine took to be the latter's demand for a sinless clergy rested on the flawed assumption that humanity, in time, could be free from sin.[50] The Pelagians'

---

48. Augustine, *De civitate Dei* 20.27: *erit judicium quale numquam fuit*.

49. Augustine, epistle 186.31–35. Also consult Salamito, *Les virtuoses et la multitude*, 97–98, 126–29; Nisula, *Functions of Concupiscence*, 301–2; Lam, "Menschwerdung des Gottessohnes," 233–34; and Ziolkowski, "*Tolle Lege*," 5–6.

50. Dupont, "Prayer Theme," 381.

propositions culminated by equating divine grace with God's other gifts, Augustine said with some exaggeration; they confused grace with the creator's provision of the human will and with the precepts of the law, neither of which could free parishioners from their captivity to concupiscence. Augustine cited the Apostle Paul's explanation of the law's purposes. Paul, he recalled, passionately and relentlessly (*valde enim assidue*) stressed that God had given the laws to the Hebrews to show how far short their efforts to obey them would fall. Whereas Pelagians looked to inspire confidence, God's laws inspired humility.[51]

When the defense of divine sovereignty and the definition of grace were not at stake, Augustine, as pastor, also sought to shore up or renew confidence; he wrote to a widow who came to Africa after 410 with other refugees from Italy and counseled her that courageously living for others—for her family, which included Juliana and chaste Demetrias—would merit eternal life.[52] Yet when the significance of divine grace needed reasserting, he emphatically defended it as the source of all merit. Pelagians took the commandment to avoid temptation as the opportunity to earn merit and as proof that humans naturally possessed the wherewithal to do so. Augustine, Alypius, and two other African bishops sent a rejoinder to Rome, where Pelagius had been influential, protesting that Christians' prayers for the power to avoid evil or temptation unmistakably acknowledged that success in such endeavors attested both the presence and power of God's grace. Augustine and his colleagues figured that their confirmation of exactly that merely echoed the distinctions between grace and nature (as well as between gospel and law) that the Apostle Paul established to help pastors explain the faith to the faithful.[53]

Why did Pelagians think so little of those distinctions? Why would they coach Christians to rely on what Augustine considered humanity's dreadfully impaired natural resources to please God? Did the Pelagians intend to cater to human nature's understandable—yet soteriologically dangerous, if not fatal—desires to be independent and deserving? Much of Augustine's *City of God* could be taken as a commentary on comparable desires to be in control of destiny. Pride stoked them and kept pagans (and the Christians who subscribed to the pagans' view and who succumbed to

---

51. Augustine sermon 156.4, citing Rom 5:20 and Gal 3:19.

52. Augustine, epistle 130.14: *neque enim in tempore utiliter vivitur, nisi comparandum meritum quo in aeternitate vivatur.*

53. Augustine, epistle 177.5.

the pagans' pride) lusting for glory and domination. From early republican Rome to the late empire, Peter Brown remarks, attributing the appraisal to Augustine, "an omnipotent denial of dependence characterize[d] the attitude of the earthly city." With what Brown sees as "exceptional savagery," Augustine's *City of God* "demolish[es] the whole of the ancient ethical tradition" that reassured starry-eyed Romans ungrateful for what they were given and permitted to achieve as well as unprepared for the miseries that followed when their lusts were paired with losses.[54] Augustine was sure that the Pelagians repeated such errors, recoiling from dependence and exhibiting ingratitude, although, unlike the pagans, they were inexcusable. They professed to be Christian and had not only witnessed Rome's decline but also read their sacred texts' passages about the extent of human nature's corruption. They were clever; their treatises documented their skills. But they also seemed to be thick-headed, unreachable, unteachable (*indociles*), blind to God's light and deaf to God's voice. Notwithstanding, Augustine also intimated that they knew the truth yet were ready to sacrifice it for popularity—eager to craft doctrine to appease, please, and proselytize.[55]

Whatever analysis seemed right to him at the moment, Augustine consistently was sure the Pelagians lacked the discernment pastoral leadership required. They grossly underestimated the intense pressures concupiscence exerted on the faithful. They missed what he took to be the fundamental, pedagogical purpose of divine law—specifically, the way in which law revealed to parishioners their predicament, their inability to obey the prescriptions or prohibitions inscribed in law. Augustine explained that the law's dos and don'ts were to be repeated often by pastors to expose the inextinguishable appetites and impulses pressing to take possession of souls dedicated to God in baptism. The grace they received in that sacrament was only a start. A baptized soul had not swapped its human for an angelic nature. The faithful were "fragile and wounded," requiring special assistance.[56] Concupiscence held on, making human life a series of struggles for virtue. Pastoral care and leadership spurred Christians confronting temptations and coping with afflictions to mount a robust resistance, capitalizing on the grace received in the church's sacraments and in answer to their prayers.

---

54. Brown, *Augustine*, 326.

55. Augustine, *De gratia et libero arbitrio* 11.23: *contra lucem Dei caeci et contra vocem Dei surdi*. Also see D'Agostino, "L'antigiuridismo di S. Agostino," 40–41, and Karfíková, *Grace and the Will*, 188–90.

56. Augustine, *De gestis Pelagii* 7.20: *fragili vitiataeque naturae*. Also see Lemmens, *Foi chrétienne*, 290.

Inasmuch as Pelagians' confidence was contagious, Augustine would have polemicists and pastors among the faithful reiterate that concupiscence survived, if not in full force at any given moment, in waiting. He compared it to an affliction that might be latent for a time yet inevitably and scandalously (*turpius*; *procacius*) would break out, even among the aged and impotent. Baptism robbed a Christian's unconscionable desires of much of their power, but the desires were permanent features of the human condition, keeping all persons tipping toward envy, cupidity, and shameless behavior—and keeping them in need of grace and pastoral care.[57]

The most comprehensive case to the contrary survives in Augustine's responses to his most persistent Pelagian critic, Julian of Eclanum, who argued that divine law was sufficient to prompt the faithful to muster their resistances. Only a cruel God, Julian objected, would issue a commandment or law that creatures could not obey—and then have prophets threaten disobedient worshippers with punishments. Augustine scolded Julian for presuming that moral standards for kindness or cruelty could be applied to God. Regardless of obedience, some were—and would be—saved, others were and would not. Still, cruelty must never be ascribed to God. The rationale for God's judgments was beyond the capacity of finite minds. Augustine counseled Christians not to approach their pastors or God with demands but to pray as supplicants, caps in hands, as it were, without losing faith that outcomes would conform to their deity's inscrutable, benevolent purposes. The lengths to which Pelagians seemed willing to go to have God's judgments seem comprehensible and benevolent made Augustine shudder (*exhorret*).[58] He could be content to have them stew, as though they were cheated of answers or explanations they had never been promised, as long as they refrained from assuming they had the answers that allowed them to transform the *ordo salutis*, the way to salvation, into a meritocracy. Augustine charged Julian with impertinence for posting routes to redemption. Pastors among the faithful should preach forbearance and, Augustine advised, encourage even their most cunning parishioners to quit questioning and accept the evidence of experience, notably, that concupiscence burned in all youth and alternately smoldered and blazed thereafter. It was not the

---

57. Augustine, *De peccatorum meritis et remissione* 1.39,70; Augustine, *De nuptiis et concupiscentia* 1.28–29.

58. Augustine, *De dono perseverentiae* 31.

part of piety to ask why. Rather, pastors ought to define piety as, in part, grateful acceptance of the strength that grace offers nature.[59]

Of course, that provision could be formulated because the right-minded had asked the right questions of their scripture. The function of the law, as just discussed, was no mystery to Augustine—law disclosed humanity's inability to please God without God's grace—because his study of sacred literature yielded answers. Augustine's criticisms of the Pelagians' (as well as pagans') impertinence, however, surged from his sense that they were pressing their inquiries disingenuously to gain polemical advantages. Inquiry was not, per se, presumptuous or wicked; Augustine's sermons are often punctuated with questions. Yet he was not probing to prove that his faith was intelligible. He believed that interrogating the faith and himself in public sermons served to encourage humility. What mattered most to him was that a pastor's preaching exhibit the limits of humanity's negligible powers (*viribus tantillis et paene nullis*).[60] In a sermon of doubtful date, Augustine contended that creatures would always remain uncertain about their neighbors' motives. He illustrated the point, citing his misgivings as he watched parishioners pray. Their posture might suggest piety, but he could not tell what they prayed for. Were they asking for deliverance from sin, a redemption to which the liturgy referred, or for deliverance from their creditors? Were they praying to express gratitude for God's love, promising to pay forward God's love in their love for others, or were they praying to acquire others' properties and to improve their families' financial positions?[61] If human motives were so obscure, how could one ascertain—and confidently convey—God's intentions in creating and redeeming? Yet probing sermons were integral to pastoral leadership, as they registered the distances between what finite minds could grasp and express this side of the grave and what would be revealed to the faithful, humble, and charitable on the other.

But Augustine replied unreservedly when he judged that a correspondent earnestly asked for answers. He was very testy—even resentful—when he sensed insincerity, as when Dioscorus, a Greek student preparing to wrap up his studies in Carthage and to return home in 411, wrote him with a set of questions. Augustine at first thought the would-be pastor was dishonest and only wanted to appear to be informed. Did Dioscorus think Augustine

---

59. Augustine, *Contra Julianum opus imperfectum* 2.235 and 3.26-27.
60. Augustine, *In Evangelium Joannis tractatus* 38.9; Alici, "Interrogatio mea," 386-87.
61. Augustine, sermon 22(A).1.

was idle and at leisure to help indolent pastors keep up appearances (*vacantem otiosumque credisti*)?[62] Eventually Augustine conceded Dioscorus' commitment to Christianity, but counseled him to ensure that his conduct as well as his intelligence won friends for the faith. He then settled to his task, supplying Dioscorus with the learning meant to avoid what the new pastor feared, that his first blunders might incline parishioners to think him capable of nothing more than ill-formulated exhortations.[63]

Parishioners' doubts about pastors' competence could render pastors all but ineffective. Doubts, planted and watered by pagan and dissident Donatist critics, could capsize the ministries of Catholic Christianity's most astute, resourceful pastors. Other critics abounded: Arian (or anti-Nicene) Christians, Manichees, and Pelagians. All would be eager to encourage parishioners' skepticism about what pastors who criticized them upheld—that is, about pastors' sermons and counsel that conformed to the positions on ecclesiology, soteriology, Christology, and piety that Augustine staked out.[64] Hence, Christian Tornau observes, Augustine's duty to demonstrate as well as to promote pastoral leadership ordinarily trumped the desire for privacy he occasionally registered. His reluctance to take up a cause or inform a conversation was no match for his fears of leaving his faith undefended or defended by poorly prepared pastors. So he regularly renewed efforts to equip the clergy with lessons from sacred literature that would provide them polemical leverage and, to a point, answer parishioners' questions.[65]

Some passages were of particular concern, passages that the opposition to Catholic Christianity might exploit or stories that too obscurely conveyed consolations.[66] One episode from the Hebrews' wars might be missed or misconstrued as testimony to humanity's strengths and merits. For when Moses raised his arms, imploring God's help against the Amalekites, the Israelites prevailed. But when, fatigued, he dropped his arms, the Amalekites looked as if they would win the battle. Moses' companions, noticing the difference, supported his arms, and the Israelites finished off their enemies. For Augustine, the companions were stand-ins for God's grace. The story should be read as reassurance that God never let the faith-

---

62. Augustine, epistle 118.2–5.
63. Ibid., 11.
64. Ibid., 12.
65. Tornau, *Zwischen Rhetorik und Philosophie*, 51–57.
66. Augustine, *Enarrationes in Psalmos* 18(2).4: *sed nonulla verba Scriptarum obscuritate sua hoc profuerunt, quod multas intelligentias pepererunt.*

ful lose strength and purpose for long, notwithstanding the weakness and wavering of nature.[67]

No passage in the Pentateuch, prophets, or Psalms, as far as Augustine could tell, suggested that the Hebrews had earned or merited God's assistance. Creatures, he concluded, irrepressibly took stock of their virtues; their confidence that God did so as well and rewarded their efforts billowed when fortune smiled on them. Pelagians capitalized on that misconception. Augustine had insisted in his *Confessions*, even before confronting the Pelagians, that Christians' inventories of virtues and their tallies of fortunate results were actually lists of God's gifts.[68] He knew as much from experience—yet also understood that humanity instinctively valued virtuosity. Submission and, for that matter, humility did not come naturally. The Pelagians were unpracticed in the latter, Augustine never tired of repeating, and they stridently opposed pastors' advocacy of the former, although submission was the proper posture for repentance. The faithful were to leave boasting behind, become less self-confident, grow more self-critical, and restrain their curiosity, leaving some mysteries mysterious.[69]

The faith of the faithful marked submission and was the only route to understanding the little that it was possible to understand, in time, about God's plans and pleasure. Faith was also an incentive for pleasing God—for doing God's work in the world, Augustine explained in his sermons on the Gospel of John—for faith was an undeserved gift that stirred both gratitude and the ardent desire to pay forward God's love in recipients' love for neighbors. Faith was required of Christians, he added, yet was also given to them.[70] As we now know, Augustine, countering the Pelagians, would insist that neither faith nor love doused inordinate desires; the faithful must accept, as he did, that they would be rattled—*ballottée*, Gérard Rémy says— yet they were supplied with pastors to create (and to satisfy) their needs for leadership, consolation, inspiration, and interpretation.[71] To meet that last "need," pastors and parishioners had not only the benefit of Augustine's exegesis and judgment but also an advantage that God had bestowed on humanity's damnably damaged nature. Augustine was referring to reason.

---

67. Augustine, sermon 352.6, commenting on Exod 17:8–13.

68. Augustine, *Confessiones* 9.13,34.

69. Augustine, *De vera religione* 45.84–85.

70. Augustine, *In Evangelium Joannis tractatus* 29.6: *non inveniat quod exigat, nisi donaverit quod inveniat*.

71. Rémy, "La notion de *medietas*," 213-16.

As he concluded his *City of God*, he acknowledged reason's contribution. Their minds helped Christians and pagans alike acquire the virtues of prudence and fortitude. Among proofs of what the keen mind could do, Augustine offered the ingenuity (*magna ingenia*) with which philosophers and heretics—was he thinking of the Pelagians?—formulated and adroitly defended their errors.[72]

Reason, therefore, could be deployed usefully or improperly. When the latter occurred, one could be fairly sure that God's gifts would issue in neither rectitude nor gratitude. Pelagians were a prime example. As for pagan philosophers, they seemed to Augustine more excited about creating than about solving puzzles. He was taken with them early in his career, the philosophers and puzzles. He preferred thoughtful pagans to the seemingly incurious and somewhat hysterical devotees of religious cults, including some Christians. But when he heard that Zeno and others had told their students there was little to choose between wisdom and ignorance, Augustine declared that the disciples had every right to curse their masters.[73]

Pagan philosophy came to perplex him. Interminable questioning was not to his taste. Augustine was also impatient with Christians who relied too confidently on reason, supposing their theology revealed everything about their faith: how and why God had created; why God redeemed some and not others; why bad things happened to good people. Augustine countered that God's creativity and governance surpassed anything creatures could conjure. He mocked his colleagues who pictured a clever, brawny craftsman (*fabrum magnum*) who had adroitly worked massive materials into shapes familiar to them. He ridiculed colleagues who posited a celestial ultra-emperor who controlled terrestrial affairs by fiat.[74] God's attributes, skills, and purposes were unfathomable; it was unreasonable to think reason would comprehend them. The Apostle Paul's approach seemed sound to Augustine: one should assume that there could be no shoddy workmanship—and no unfairness—on God's part. Hence, it was for creatures to wonder at the majesty and order of God's creation, to accept how justice was rendered and how mercy was tendered, and to waste no time passing off their conjectures as conclusive explanations of the mysteries that were and would forever remain impenetrable (*investigabilia*).[75] What might be

---

72. Augustine, *De civitate Dei* 22.24.
73. Augustine, *Contra academicos* 3.9,18–19.
74. Augustine, sermon 223(A).5.
75. Augustine, sermon 27.6–7.

known—and what the genuinely penitent should know—about divinity had nothing to do with the deity's tricks or traits, and everything to do with the gratuity of God's grace. Faith mediated the "knowledge" Augustine valued because it gave the faithful a vocation and commended humility and compassion as preeminent Christian virtues.[76]

By 416, he identified Pelagius as the source of what appeared to be the fraying consensus among Italian Christians about the Apostle Paul's insistence on the gratuity of God's grace. That year, he and Alypius sent Bishop Paulinus of Nola a dossier of Pelagian mistakes, showering him with passages to document the Bible's support for their claim that no human initiative deserved a reward; grace was gratuitous (*neque ibi praecedunt merita gratiam*).[77] Paulinus needed no persuading; Augustine and Alypius remembered that he had written about the reach of what humanity's parents had done, the sin that infected their progeny (*infecit*). The three agreed that there was much more of Adam than of Jesus in humanity and that the imbalance should shame all who professed hatred of iniquity yet remained in bondage to their base desires.[78] But pastors who preached shame were at a disadvantage. Pelagians' message was more uplifting. Augustine, Alypius, and Paulinus, however, provisioned pastors with supplemental resources that now ought to be familiar to us. The three began with the premise that constituted the staging area for all anti-Pelagian campaigns and that they culled from the Apostle Paul's letters to Corinth. Good works come from grace, they insisted; grace does not follow from good works.[79] Pastors should begin by shaming their parishioners, but the shame attested the presence (or gift) of grace. Grace inspired gratitude and humility, leading to repentance. And repentance, in turn, led to redemption and regeneration. The Pelagians could only compete, in Augustine's judgment, if they denied the need for grace, so he elsewhere asked auditors to imagine that Jesus had come to judge humanity and not to impart grace, *gratis*. Facing a just judge, the faithful could hardly escape punishment. But Jesus was sent with—and as—a reprieve. Christianity's pastors were commissioned to convey it. Augustine reassured them they were in good company. They echoed the good

---

76. Augustine, *Expositio quarundam propositionum ex epistola ad Romanos* 62; Drecoll, "Die Bedeutung der Gnadenlehre Augustins," 135; and Hombert, "Augustin, prédicateur de la grâce," 233–34.

77. Augustine, epistle 186.19.

78. Ibid., 40.

79. Ibid., 4: *opera ex gratia, non ex operibus gratia*, commenting on 1 Cor 4:7.

news anticipated by the psalmist, presented in the gospels, and celebrated by the apostles.[80]

So pastors had a well-defined role in promoting humility, a task that became increasingly critical and increasingly contentious when Pelagians' ideas circulated in Africa and, conceivably, caused some parishioners to lose their bearings. Pastors' sermons and counsel had to confirm the persistence of concupiscence and the gratuity of grace. Yet they had help. They—and the faithful—had an inward, intimate experience of grace and faith that deposited love in their hearts (*in corde*).[81] But with that help—the gift of grace and infusion of faith—came confusion, which pastors had to dispel. Augustine took the lead. He knew that the Paraclete, a comforting spirit, was promised in the Gospel of John to those who kept the faith. He knew that difficulties surfaced when Jesus' promise in that Gospel was set alongside Paul's explicit assurances to Roman Christians that God's Spirit and love already filled their hearts. Resolving what easily could have been taken as a contradiction and, in a sense, parsing—while categorically reasserting—the intimacy between redeemer and redeemed, Augustine concluded that the faithful experienced God's Spirit more abundantly (*amplius*) as the Paraclete after, although not as a reward for, love inspired by the Spirit that was possessed with faith (as God's gift).[82]

What could be called Augustine's inward turn has been attributed to his familiarity with Plato's various admirers and, as noted, occurred long before his encounter with Pelagius' ideas. Augustine's *Confessions*, composed ten years after the "facts" they reported had occurred, may be taken as evidence of his discovery of an otherness—a holy, wholly other within.[83] He admitted that his sense of divine immanence had been formed both by study of sacred texts (authority) and by what Platonists thought defensible (reason). The first was fundamental. He said he could not depart from it (*nusquam prorsus a Christi auctoritate discedere*) soon after he determined that a commitment to Christianity and continence suited him. He pledged he would thereupon forego foraging among philosophers and Manichaean

80. Augustine, *Enarrationes in Psalmos* 44.7.

81. Augustine, sermons 2.9 and 155.9.

82. Augustine, *In Evangelium Joannis tractatus* 74.2, discussing John 14:15–17 and Rom 5:5. The latter passage was often emphasized in the anti-Pelagian treatises. See, for example, Augustine, *De natura et gratia* 64.77.

83. Augustine, *Confessiones* 10.27,38, addressing God: *ecce intus eras*. For inwardness and alterity, consult Piccolo, *I processi di apprendimento*, 231–34. Cary relates "Platonist grace" to Augustine's inward turn (*Inner Grace*, 25–32).

specialists who formerly led him to suspect that the faith of the faithful was irrational. He anticipated that he would continue making sense of divine intimacy, by approaching it from two directions. He was confident that Platonism was compatible with Christianity (*non repugnet*). The revelation that grace placed a desire for the eternal in sinners who were trapped in the temporal seemed to Augustine to correspond with Platonism's views on virtue and interiority.[84] Preictably, with the arrival of the Pelagians in Africa, he emphasized what he earlier considered to be the more fundamental source for his thinking on inward grace. Because they inferred human nature's abilities to resist temptations and avoid sin from the fact that God was the author of human nature as well as from the Bible, he impugned Pelagians' interpretations of the latter, diving into the faithful's inner chamber to find God's love, grace, and Spirit—all of it preternatural. His conclusion from scripture, from his early struggles with all but unmanageable, discreditable desires, and from his study of sentiment was that the power to avoid sin, while there, within the faithful, was not theirs but God's.[85]

If we may trust his *Confessions*, Augustine, without sustained pastoral consultation, grew disenchanted with the flattery and foolishness that characterized the political career he traded for continence, Christianity, and—it would seem—contentment. He spoke with at least two Milanese churchmen—the bishop of Milan at the time, Ambrose, and his successor, Simplicianus—yet he appears to have coped solo with what Luigi Alici now calls the divine shock or spark (*étincelle*) that helped him make sense of his disenchantment—and ultimately prompted him to reconstruct religious subjectivity for Latin Christendom.[86] Augustine often repeated that complacency and concupiscence made all the more precarious the lives of Christians suspended between their love for God and their lust for things of this world. But his first pastors played only cameo roles in his awakening, and he was later heard to suggest that, without God's transformative presence *in corde*, pastors remained a rather powerless lot.[87] Unless God

84. Augustine, *Contra academicos* 3.20,43.

85. Augustine, *De natura et gratia* 48.56–51.59. Augustine's anti-Pelagian correspondence and treatises come to much the same conclusion, but the less polemical and most memorable statements about God's "residence" within the faithful (*in nobis . . . ut in Deo maneamus*) appear in his exposition of the Trinity—see, for example, Augustine, *De Trinitate* 15.19,37.

86. Alici, "*Interrogatio mea*," 379–81.

87. Augustine, *In epistolam Joannis ad Parthos* 3.12–13: *ubi illius inspiratio et unctio non est, forinsecus inaninter perstrepunt verba.*

moved Christians from within, sermons were ineffective—sounds without significance. Yet, once seeds were planted, Augustine explained, exploiting a familiar biblical metaphor, pastors worked on externals (*forinsecus*). The orchard's seeds required God's sowing. Otherwise, they could never take root. Pastors labored to ensure that the saplings became sturdier and that the harvest was bountiful. Only if God supplied seed (*si autem det*) could pastors be productive (*valet aliquid quod plantamus et rigamus, et non est inanis labor noster*).[88] Alexander Faivre may be correct to say that early clerical Christianity was a social reality seeking "a coherent, systematic theological justification," but Augustine appears to have been rather successful articulating a pastoral justification or challenge (to go along with his many polemical challenges) that featured collaboration between God's work, *intrinsecus*, and pastors' strenuous efforts, *forinsecus*.[89]

Promises

In his controversy with the Donatists, Augustine alluded to God's planting or internal work as an invisible ministry. He was countering the secessionists' breathtaking claim that a pastor's sins could, in effect, block God's work imparting grace to the baptized. Augustine knew that much depended on pastors' diligence, but he was unwilling to concede that sacraments over which they presided were their work. God did the cleansing at baptism, requiring no impeccable pastor to be present.[90] Besides, as Augustine made abundantly clear against Pelagians, although pastors' probity was to be highly prized, impeccability in this wicked world was impossible. God's grace and the faith of the faithful spurred personal transformations from weakness to strength in struggles against temptations, not from imperfection to perfection.[91]

What the baptized received in their initiation, Augustine explained in his *City of God*, was a token (*pignus*), a promise of sorts that, as adopted sons of God, by grace and not nature, they would gradually change for the better by their participation in God's righteousness. They would become less self-confident, more readily detect heretical or sectarian preachers trying to lead them astray with promises of some earthly perfection, and

88. Augustine, sermon 152.1, commenting on 1 Cor 3:6–7.
89. Compare Faivre, *Chrétiens et Églises*, 271–72.
90. Augustine, *Contra litteras Petiliani* 3.49,59.
91. Tornau, *Zwischen Rhetorik und Philosophie*, 288; Couenhoven, *Stricken by Sin*, 54.

learn to rely on God's promises in the gospels. Meanwhile, their pastors persuaded them that they belonged to a celestial city on pilgrimage in time. They remained at risk, at war with themselves (*secum pugnat*). Their longing for peace was tested tediously by an irrepressible, inordinate desire for name and fame or wealth and position, Augustine's *City* tells us, echoing his sermons' suggestions that pastoral leadership succeeded to the extent that God's internal work—an inspiring fire in the *City* or a planting in his preaching—was fueled or fertilized, respectively, by parishioners' hopes for peace, their faith that it would come to pass, and their love for others as they waited.[92]

Pastors faced multiple challenges sustaining faith, hope, and love. Augustine appreciated how ecclesiological, doctrinal, and political crises could complicate those challenges and would thus constrict, if not confound, pastoral care. As noted, he probed the practical consequences of an unequivocal commitment to Christianity without sustained clerical counsel when he was in Milan. He discovered that the imperative to love God unstintingly entailed loving neighbors as well.[93] In his polemical work against the Manichees and Donatists, he probed the relationship between the summons to love even hostile sectarians, which prompted his yearning to have them embrace promises that enriched Catholic Christianity, and his temptations rhetorically to throttle them, to compel them to relinquish their opposition. Less controversially, he spelled out the responsibilities of the faithful and their pastors to refractory others whose resistance to what was in their best interests took none of his close colleagues by surprise. One of his sermons imagined two avid sports fans, a Christian and his ungodly comrade, intending to attend the games. The former stirred early and disturbed his friend's sleep; together, they rushed to the arena and got superb seats. The latter and lazier was grateful for his rude awakening. Their favorites may not have won the contest, Augustine added, but the gratitude of the ungodly would be undiminished, nonetheless, because both spectators were well positioned to view the contest. Augustine lodged his lesson at the anecdote's end. The faithful could not force God's grace or God's promises on others, but they might snatch the unfaithful (*rapis*), ideally, to bring them to witness what God accomplished and promised. Before closing, he stipulated, as he would have had all pastors do, that Christians' love for

---

92. Augustine, *De civitate Dei* 21.15.
93. Müller, *Willensschwäche*, 322–23; Kaufman, *Incorrectly Political*, 26–31.

God should not be called well grounded (*vera*) unless it encompassed love of neighbor.[94]

A few years later, in another sermon, Augustine returned to the amphitheaters, although, as we have come to expect, he expressed displeasure with the faithful's fondness for games. On this visit, however, the ungodly were not racing for seats. Augustine's sermon had them leaving their shows and pitying the Christians who had been dissuaded by their pastors from joining their party. Their pity was perverse, Augustine said, yet the pagans were kind to have wished their fun on the faithful. That the Christians had not been equally considerate was regrettable, he went on, instructing them to coax unbelievers to share their enjoyment, not in coliseums, of course, but in churches where they could hear pastors preach about God's promises. And that good news might lead to conversions. Still, Augustine reiterated, nothing would result, unless God's grace moved within those whom the faithful had moved to come.[95]

Emphasis on interiority might have led to what Jean-Marie Salamito describes as the "privatization" of the Christian faith, which would hardly have been conducive to its churches' growth. One suspects Augustine increasingly enlisted the aid of the laity, in collaboration with their pastors, to draw the ungodly within range of sermons that proclaimed promises made to the faithful, in part, because his Pelagian critics and competition catered to the masses by presenting a Christianity that was meritocratic and, therefore, more comprehensible. It gave greater weight—or to be precise, its God seemed to give greater weight—to the laity's striving for improvements deemed to deserve salvation. Matching effort to reward and optimistically looking ahead to the conquest of concupiscence, as Pelagians purportedly did, probably appealed to ordinary people more than preaching uncertainty. Discussing that appeal, Salamito refers to Pelagianism as "a massification" of Christianity.[96] Moreover, the Pelagian deity—suspending judgment, awaiting then rewarding moral behavior, and punishing malfeasance—must have seemed more attractive as well as more intelligible than a god, who, according to Augustine, condemned unbaptized infants who had died before recording their first sin. The Pelagians capitalized on Augustine's insistence on infant baptism to portray his God as tyrannical. God's severity figured in Christianity's sacred texts, Augustine responded;

---

94. Augustine, *sermones nuper reperti*, Dolbeau 11.11–13.
95. Augustine, *Enarrationes in Psalmos* 147.8. Also see Augustine, epistle 140.71.
96. Salamito, "Ambivalence de la christianisation," 72–73.

prophets as well as patriarchs experienced divine wrath. The Apostle Paul's letter to the Romans had God abandoning the ungodly to their wickedness. Augustine's prolific Pelagian nemesis countered that Paul could only have been exaggerating.[97]

One could infer from his polemical treatises that Pelagians' rejoinders nearly drove Augustine to distraction during the second and third decades of the fifth century. They did not drive him from his refuge in God's promises. God's severity was a prelude for the fortunate to whom grace and salvation were promised. Pastors reminded the faithful that their sins had been forgiven yet their growth in grace required struggle.[98] Their ordeals were less onerous, in part, because God's grace, the faith and love it deposited in the faithful, and pastoral guidance made inordinate desires less intense. Concupiscence, Timo Nisula proposes, became "more a sparring partner than a dangerous enemy."[99] Nothing changed the fact that the faithful had been displaced from Eden and saddled with mortality. But recovery could begin with baptism, and the mothers hastening to have their newborn baptized must have seemed to vindicate Augustine's sense that a flinty deity could retain the veneration of Christians who counted on their God, not simply to punish wickedness but also to keep generous promises. Those mothers believed what Julian and other Pelagians did not, that to deny their youngsters the remission of the sin of their first parents—the sin that made them sinful and mortal—on the grounds that ostensibly innocent infants had not yet sinned was heartless.[100]

The Pelagians' repudiation and occasional ridicule of infant baptism only stiffened Augustine's resolve to defend it. His was no desperate sortie into troubled waters; given his premise about the ineradicable stain of sin and pervasive imperfection, he formulated a well-reasoned argument for forgiving those who seemed in no need of forgiveness. The Donatists' insistence that the effectiveness of the sacrament depended on the virtue of pastors presiding over that sacrament as priests required Augustine to tread carefully, for, as Adam Ployd says, Africa's "traditional ecclesiological culture" emphasized, as did Donatists, the importance of clerical character. Augustine, at this point, was the renegade. He contended that the virtues

---

97. Augustine, *Contra Julianum opus imperfectum* 6.23; Augustine, *Contra Julianum haeresis Pelagianae defensorem* 5.3,10, discussing Rom 1:28–32.

98. Augustine, sermon 158.4.

99. Nisula, *Functions of Concupiscence*, 351.

100. Augustine, sermon 293.10–11.

or vices of pastors officiating had no bearing on the effectiveness of the baptisms of infants and adults. Baptisms need not be repeated, even if presiding clerics were extortionists, adulterers, blasphemers, or murderers.[101] Because baptism signaled rebirth and, ideally, would be the beginning of a Christian's good run at redemption, it was not left to the presiding pastor to transfer grace or virtue from what some dissidents imagined to be his stock. Christ baptized, Augustine asserted; pastors as priests at the sacraments could neither transmit (by having an unobjectionable record of selfless service) nor block (by having misbehaved) the grace God chose to bestow. Pastors as priests at baptism were conduits.[102]

Donatists, in effect, disqualified pastors affiliated with Catholic Christianity. Christians they had baptized would have to be rebaptized, if they elected to join the secessionists' sects. In Augustine's judgment, rebaptism was unnecessary for reasons just revealed. Donatist baptisms were valid; God's grace had been bestowed on the baptized, but a lack of charity in dissident congregations, of which Donatists' resistance to reconciliation with Catholic Christians was symptomatic, Augustine said, meant that their baptized would be deprived of an atmosphere necessary for their growth in grace. A pastor's principal role, therefore, was not sacramental. Pastors were to maintain a climate in which—or, contemplating something less meteorological and more managerial, one could say a network through which—compassion conserved churches' unity.[103] Ernst Dassman depicts the pastor's role as parental, insofar as, promoting parishioners' mutual affection, pastors were also disciplinarians, preaching humility to those tempted by their baptisms to think God's work on and with them had been done to perfection.[104]

At the ready, pastors had tales of martyrs, whose fortitude and humility, to the point of self-sacrifice, ought to have convinced Christians to stop their boasting of baptisms and of God's apparent favor. Pastors' sermons could draw on the church's memory bank for the inspiring tales of heroism under fire, as it were. Yet with martyrs came miracles, either performed by them or at their tombs or shrines, where their powers as well as God's were

---

101. Augustine, *In Evangelium Joannis tractatus* 5.9; Ployd, "Power of Baptism," 519–21.

102. Augustine, *Contra Cresconium* 2.25,30; Augustine, *De natura et gratia* 4.4; Burns, "Baptism as Dying and Rising," 428–29, 434–35; Crespin, *Ministère et sainteté*, 247.

103. Augustine, *De baptismo* 3.13,18: *in unitatis vincula caritate operante*.

104. Dassman, *Eine Kirche in vielen Bildern*, 39–40.

reputedly still at work. The sick and crippled were healed. Anne Fraïsse suggests that such wonders were seen to be "the word of God in action."[105] Before he had gained experience as a pastor, Augustine wrote a treatise to his longtime friend Romanianus agreeing that it had been necessary to tell miracle stories to satisfy demands for visible proofs during Christianity's early years but arguing that the practice outlived its purposes.[106] Soon after, however, the objectives of narratively, strategically deploying martyrs and miracles seemed more agreeable. Stories lodged in sermons or circulated less formally confirmed the faith of the faithful generations removed from the sacrifices inspired during previous persecutions (and centuries removed from the sacrifices reported in their sacred literature) and sustained the solidarity pastors were able to create in their churches.[107]

Early in his career, Augustine complained about Socrates, Plato, Porphyry, and Plotinus, who, to his mind, had been insufficiently critical of the miracle stories circulating in their times, despite their opinion that the fuss made over idols was laughable. The philosophers' opposition to superstition seemed to him tepid, at best.[108] But he does not appear to have reconsidered his indictment after he turned martyrs and their miracles loose in his treatises and sermons. Late in his career, finishing his *City of God*, he assembled a number of sensational stories in a lengthy chapter of its last book, a treasure trove for pastors interested in recycling stories for purposes Augustine approved. He supplied details of many miracles that, he maintained, confirmed the truth of Christianity's supreme miracle, which—as the pastors reading would know—vouchsafed the salvation of their parishioners (*multa miracula . . . grandi salubrique miraculo*). He retailed stories of miracles that had occurred decades before and were widely reported. Others had only recently happened. *Etiam nunc*, even now, Augustine claimed, miracles at martyrs' shrines, as well as those in the sacraments, proved that God's power was at work in the world. A Syrian Christian brought his sick daughter's cloak to a shrine near Hippo and prayed to the martyr honored there for her recovery. Returning home he draped the cloak over her lifeless body, which immediately came alive. Also current, a woman anointed with a pastor's tears was dispossessed of a demon. Augustine's *City* rehearsed such stories with gusto. Philosophers' skepticism, which he once thought

---

105. Fraïsse, "La théologie du miracle," 134–39.
106. Augustine, *De vera religione* 25.47.
107. Augustine, *De utilitate credenda* 16.34.
108. Erler reviews the complaints in "Die helfende Hand Gottes," 90–91.

toothless, may have been a distant memory by the time suspension of disbelief became second nature to him.[109]

He anticipated that pastors might have had one reservation about deploying miracle stories. They could well be asked how Christianity could boast of the strength of its faith and simultaneously rely on fabulous tales to fortify it. Why would a robust faith need the proof provided by miracle stories? The question would have sounded strange to the faithful in the fifth century, inasmuch as they believed their sacred texts were truthful—literature that featured stories of miracles and martyrs. Yet pastors—and Augustine—were wary of learned pagans' ridicule. And some were likely to join the less learned demanding, as proof of Jesus' divinity, wonders beyond those rehearsed for and by the faithful (Jesus' creation of a parallel world, say). Christianity's critics taunted pastors, claiming that most miracles in their Bible and all those inventoried in Augustine's *City* were too slight or superficial to substantiate the sanctification of those who performed them.[110] Predictably, Augustine thought otherwise. Nonetheless, he was concerned more with the effectiveness of miracles among Christians. It would be no exaggeration to say that he believed miracles had made the faith's first pastors. The apostles had wavered (*nutabat infirmitas*) when they heard Jesus; miracles were necessary to overcome their doubts.[111] Those miracles, retold in pastors' sermons, became parts of the faith. The martyrs' deaths and miracles during the centuries that followed the resurrection reinforced or, Joost van Neer avers, "built up" the faith. And, as Augustine explained, miracles of restoration and healing foreshadowed a final restoration, the resurrection of the faithful, of which Jesus' resurrection was the promise.[112]

Pastors were left to put that promise in perspective, specifically, to deploy the church's sacraments, martyrs, and miracles in their sermons so parishioners' morale might be sustained while their expectations for a modicum of peace on earth were increasingly and excruciatingly disappointed. Their world was coming apart. Augustine trusted that the rise and fall of empires was divinely choreographed. He was encouraged because, despite political fragmentation, the powerful were coming to Christianity. The religion spread and sprawled across a world that remained more wicked than good, although the faith's success gave its pastors opportunities to

---

109. Augustine, *De civitate Dei* 22.8.
110. Augustine, epistle 147.14; Tornau, *Zwischen Rhetorik und Philosophie*, 220–21.
111. Augustine, sermon 88.2–3.
112. Ibid., 8–9; Augustine, *De civitate Dei* 22.9; Neer, "Bouwen aan het geloof," 356.

influence the influential. Nonetheless, Christianity's growth also brought the wickedness of the world into the church. But before we discuss that development, we must attend to Augustine's resolve—which pastors would have noticed and, plausibly, taken as a model—specifically his resolve to prepare parishioners to embrace the promise of resurrection and long for celestial rewards, that is, to have them lift their spirits above the corruption around them. To clarify, a sermon he preached before the sack of Rome in 410—but after the disintegration of the western empire could no longer be disregarded—used topographical imagery borrowed from the prophet Isaiah to offer the church as a mountain and a refuge from all the disappointments and chaos in the late fourth and early fifth centuries. Yet Augustine did not dwell on the safety in the institutional church but quickly shifted focus. He introduced the eternal church, the celestial city, intimating that pastors preparing parishioners to reach that safer refuge should persuade them to admit their defilement—*surrexit libido, iam coinquinatus est spiritus*—and curse their surging lusts and desecrated spirits. For to become heirs to the promise of resurrection parishioners in this—Augustine's—politically disintegrating, morally compromised world must labor to purify themselves.[113]

Augustine believed disintegration told against pagans who made felicity one of their gods. The old Roman cults were crowded with deities, yet, he pointed out, not one of them was willing or able to preserve Romans' control over the western portions of their empire. Moreover, those Romans considered such control—the expanse of empire, which was so closely associated with glory—along with prosperity the preconditions for felicity. Augustine countered that lasting felicity arrived with grace and faith, as a gift from the Christians' God. It was possessed as hope for happiness in the hereafter and not as contentment or pleasure here and now, possessed *in spe* rather than *in re*.[114] Catholic Christians who trusted that advantages here and now would remain secure were disappointed. Many were euphoric when Emperor Constantine committed to their faith. The Caecilianists, whose descendants we now know as Catholic Christians, were glad to have him endorse the European church councils' decisions against proto-Donatist bishops. Yet the endorsement was not followed by enforcement. Constantine had to attend to a commotion in the East. Neither he nor his successors creatively and conclusively settled African Christianity's

---

113. Augustine, sermon 45.6–8, citing Isa 57:13.
114. Augustine, *De civitate Dei* 4.21.

quarrels. The hostility between Donatist secessionists and Catholic Christians was ongoing. The prospects for temporal felicity or security seemed remote when Augustine returned from Italy in the late 380s. During the first decade of the next century, as we learned, he reported progress in his diocese where dissidents were evacuating rural Donatist congregations, turning or returning to Catholic Christianity.[115] Yet the schism persisted, even after the Council of Carthage in 411 proscribed Donatism—after Emperor Honorius and his African deputies discountenanced the secessionists. Too many pagans held their ground; Pelagians remained combative; Vandals invaded Africa from Spain. Embattled Augustine cherished a promise, *in spe*, a promise that pious pilgrims in time would find places in the celestial city. Their pastors would see to it that pilgrims' faith, hope, and love would be portals through which a felicity, vastly different from what was promised pagans, would make itself known.[116]

Distress and Discipline

Augustine was keenly aware of the world's wickedness, which created problems for faithful pilgrims and their pastors. For the latter, none was more important than the need to devise discipline and find ways to restrict the influence of those parishioners who were more forward than others in the congregations yet less able to resist doubt and temptation. Churches were *permixta*. The weak among the strong and especially reprobates among the faithful could be a stifling presence or, when assertive, would lead others to take their pleasures in time rather than in their expectations of salvation. *Ecclesia . . . sola spe gaudens, quando sanum gaudet*; a sound church rejoices only in hope, so the faithful must learn to live differently from the thorns and tares among them (*discretae vivite*), but not to live separately as many dissidents directed.[117] For it was not unthinkable that the love of faithful congregants and a pastor's discipline would work wonders on the surliest Christians admitted into fellowship.[118]

Evidence for Augustine's position on rehabilitation is clearly presented in a sermon delivered in the summer of 401. Faustinus, an influential

---

115. Augustine, *sermones nuper reperti*, Dolbeau 27.2.

116. Kaufman, "Augustine's Dystopia," 69–74.

117. Augustine, *De civitate Dei* 15.26 and 18.49; Dassman, *Eine Kirche in vielen Bildern*, 116–17.

118. Augustine, *Enarrationes in Psalmos* 47.11.

pagan who had made enemies among the faithful, asked to be admitted to their church in Carthage. They doubted his sincerity, and he apparently retained some doubts about what they believed. Augustine acknowledged that doubt weakened Faustinus' faith yet urged Christians to be compassionate, confident that compassion would overcome whatever remained of Faustinus' (*amore vestro amovete de corde infirmi dubitationem*). His request to join the church, after all, had alienated his former friends, so new friends, Augustine reasoned, would be welcome indeed and would become part of Jesus' ministry to outcasts. Carthage's pastors responded favorably to Faustinus' overtures; they had considered parishioners' opposition. They concluded that his previous prejudices did not disqualify him. Augustine's sermon seconded their decision. Pastors and parishioners must live with those whose repentance they suspected of being disingenuous—and whose faith might seem flawed—Augustine explained, if only to allow God and the churches' warm reception to complete the regeneration of ostensibly irresolute Christians.[119]

To be sure, there were some who entered or stayed in the churches for the wrong reasons. Plausibly some assumed that listening to sermons or attending the sacraments would compensate for their foul behavior, their fondness for sorcery, or their addiction to spectacles and pageantry. Augustine thought they were deluded, as were parishioners who presumed that their minimal, intermittent, even fraudulent contrition sufficed to save them. They seemed carefree (*securi*), unashamed that they were adding to their pastors' burdens.[120]

To this collection of nominally or minimally Christian souls, whom the most persistent pastors would have had difficulty disciplining and reorienting, Augustine added those who began with or developed a sincere faith but who lacked fortitude. Perseverance was a gift from God, not given to everyone in church. A few of the faithful might have appeared to their pastors and fellow parishioners to be making progress, although, indiscernibly, they had stalled. Others returned to superstitious practices and deplorable behavior more conspicuously. Augustine speculated that such backsliders could have been dropped into their congregations as an antidote to arrogance, alerting the faithful that only God knew who would remain steadfast, that no one in the church should be sure of staying power,

---

119. Augustine, sermon 279.11–12.
120. Augustine, *De civitate Dei* 21.20–25.

either of others' or of their own. Augustine believed this was yet another argument for humility.[121]

Starting his ministry in 391, Augustine condensed what the faithful ought to be taught about God's purposes and power, emphasizing then (as he often would later) that God meant to make good use of the wicked. That was why the stalled, unsteady, arrogant, carefree, and outright malevolent had been set alongside the good in the churches. Persecutors' enmity, the devil's devices, and Judas' greed were regrettable; nonetheless, the results—Jesus' atonement and the examples of the martyrs' forbearance and courage—redeemed and enlightened the faithful. Augustine's rich farrago of exegesis and exhortation drew ethical inferences, counting on God to forge advantageous results from the setbacks that Christians encountered.[122] That reliance was a premise informing everything he wrote about pastoral leadership and extending into his ecclesiology. One could argue that it had to, given what historian Claude Lepelley calls Augustine's "pessimism," which was prompted by a congregation that included incompletely converted Christians. Slips and obvious backsliding gave pastors good reason to distress and discipline parishioners. Obligations of that sort were unenviable but necessary, occasioned by what Lepelley characterizes as the "inevitable compromises" that Christianity had made when the faith became respectable and extensive—and when its churches became inclusive.[123]

Pastors' rebukes were intrusive, but Augustine thought them necessary. He assumed that the intractably unrepentant could not be reached, but one could not be sure in advance how hard or impenetrable their hearts would be.[124] Besides, reprimands were absolutely critical if pastors were to police their parishes and care for parishioners, notwithstanding delinquents' preferences to be forgiven without a fuss. Augustine held that pastors who combined either private or public rebuke with preaching grace—aiming to cure rather than simply to accuse—did great service to the faith. The more puritanical among their parishioners may have considered pastors too subtle, for Augustine appeared to be defending pastoral discretion when he argued that censures should be tailored to fit situations

121. Augustine, *De dono perseverentiae* 8.19.

122. Augustine, sermon 214.3: *novit quemadmodum malis Deus bene utatur*. For the good coming from Rome's humiliation in 410, see Augustine, *De excidio urbis Romae* 8–9.

123. Lepelley, "Augustin face à la christianisation," 272–73.

124. Augustine, sermon 71.21.

of which most members of congregations were best left unaware. He urged parishioners to trust pastors to train sinners' consciences without publicly embarrassing them.[125] His message for the reprimanded, particularly those who hated being confronted with their sins, was that their displeasure was incontestable evidence that they needed the pinch and sting of censure (*correptionis aculem*) that jarred them to repent.[126] Augustine disclosed that pagan pundits objected to his line of argument. They protested that a powerful God could put miscreants on a path to righteousness without pastors' scolding. Augustine understood why a pagan would have thought that pastors' were expendable. Why would pastoral discipline be a critical part of an omnicompetent God's *modus operandi*? But pagans were outside the faith looking in; Christianity required faith that God's plan was wise as well as secret and sublime (*abdito altoque consilio*), faith that rebukes were justifiable ways to move people to pray for grace that, according to plan, they were destined to receive.[127]

Pastors, as disciplinarians, were at a disadvantage. After infractions, they could usefully direct their efforts, but the idols in the hearts of parishioners were harder to locate than those in temples; residual paganism among the faithful, that is, was difficult to detect. Not all Christians who were fond of excess openly displayed their predilections, and the lack of fortitude was hard to predict. Early in his career, Augustine packed a sermon with both threats and consolations yet confided in a letter to Alypius that its effectiveness should be attributed to its conclusion wherein he commiserated with sinners he berated. Empathy got their attention; he wept as they wept, and, he explained to Alypius, he was supremely confident that commiseration was responsible for his auditors' regeneration.[128] He trusted as well that compassion not only reinforced congregants' resolve but also made congregations more appealing to outsiders, inviting secessionists and other strays (as well as pagans) into Catholic Christian churches. Historian Mickaël Ribreau notes that Augustine fundamentally disagreed with influential colleagues in Rome and Jerusalem: whereas some of them looked to exclude or eradicate dissidents, he wanted to incorporate them.[129]

---

125. Augustine, sermon 82.11.
126. Augustine, *De correptione et gratia* 5.7.
127. Augustine, *Contra Julianum* 4.28.
128. Augustine, epistle 27.7: *plenissima spe correctionis*.
129. Ribreau, "Quelle est la place de l'heretique," 272–73.

To the extent that discipline as well as compassion shaped an attractive community, ideally, it encouraged growth. What made discipline delicate was that it could also discourage parishioners and lead the disconcerted to defect. Arguably, Augustine intended to be a whetstone for his colleagues when he wrote his *Confessions*, illustrating the anxieties that afflicted ordinary Christians. And he seems to have had the same intent when he circulated his counsel in sermons and correspondence. Foregoing, for the most part, philological analysis and extensive contextual or historical commentary, he underscored practical, pastoral applications of his interpretations of biblical passages. He prized those that documented Jesus' and the apostles' humility, knowing the empathy he extolled would be sabotaged by pastors' and bishops' self-importance, if their arrogance was unchecked. He obviously worried that temptations to create a clerical aristocracy would overtake his colleagues and undermine their pastoral care along with their congregations' solidarity. The vulnerabilities they shared with all Christians, which were occasioned by their first parents' sin, ought to be mentioned often, Augustine stressed, to remind bishops and pastors that, notwithstanding their leadership and their commission to feed their flocks, they were bit players in the big picture.[130]

In that big picture, God determined the retention (or the disaffection) of disciplined parishioners, the rehabilitation of rebuked sinners, and the reclamation of entire congregations. God determined the setbacks experienced in the European portions of Rome's empire and was therefore responsible for the sadness that must have seemed irrepressible since Emperor Valens' defeat at Adrianople in 378. For most of Augustine's pontificate, however, Hippo was, in Peter Brown's terms, "an oasis of Roman order," which suited its bishop, whom Brown described as "conscientious and mild. But the diocese stretched many miles into the countryside, presenting the pastors Augustine appointed with formidable challenges. Donatists had dominated there for decades. They remained active even after the Council of Carthage outlawed them. "In that rough-and-ready land" (Brown again) the power rested with the owners of the vast estates on or near which Catholic Christian churches were built.[131] Pastors came to rely on their provision and protection. Augustine seems seldom to have visited either the clerics or the rural despots on whom they came to depend, yet

---

130. Augustine, sermon 340A.3: *nos debemus conferre portiunculas nostras*.
131. Brown, *Augustine*, 186–87.

tried to ensure that pastors fluent in the local dialects were sent with the truths of their faith to the laity in the countryside.[132]

Augustine did not personally travel far from the African coast often, yet his sermons and correspondence did. In both he made it clear that their parishioners' solidarity was in the top tier of pastors' resources. "To the ear of faith," if one may borrow William Wordsworth's poetry to present possibilities with which Augustine tried to inspire the clergy and animate the Christian ministry, pastors would impart

> Authentic tidings of invisible things;
> Of ebb and flow, and ever-during power;
> And central peace, subsisting at the heart
> Of endless agitation.[133]

Agitation or distress came with the territory, so to speak, if only because concupiscence never ceased to tempt and trouble the faithful who experienced, as did their pagan neighbors, political insecurity, even in Augustine's "oasis of order." He never abandoned his concentration on what scholars depict as interiority. He turned his insides out in his *Confessions* and instructed pastors to monitor parishioners' receptivity to God's grace working within them. His instructions could have been taken as obstacles to achieving discipline and solidarity, had his exegesis not covered social outcomes as well as incoming grace.[134] The latter was what confirmed God's promises of imperishable rewards for cultivating gifts divinely bestowed—peace or contentment in terrestrial cities that extended into the celestial city of God. It was left to pastors to help their parishioners patiently endure the stresses or distress of this world and to present an affecting and compelling vision of what they were entitled (or elected) to expect. Augustine preached as much with the imperative that the faithful endure the former, as Jesus did, and hope for the latter: redemption, resurrection, and eternal life.[135]

Augustine suggested that endurance and hope were more easily sustained in community, almost certainly sensing that church solidarity would always be a work in progress, a work that required pastors persuading parishioners to interrogate the unprincipled pursuit of what the world so highly prized: gain and glory. Cultivating Christian compassion, which was

132. Augustine, epistle 84.1-2; Brown, *Augustine*, 186–87.
133. Wordsworth, *The Excursion*, book 4, lines 1144–47.
134. See Piccolo, *Processi di apprendimento*, 234–37.
135. Augustine, sermon 279.8: *patere quod suscepit, spera quod ostendit*.

the foundation for the church's solidarity, could only follow a far-reaching restructuring of parishioners' desires. As historian Frank Vander Valk suggests, Augustine was particularly effective in promoting emotions clearly distinct from the bonds of friendship or patronage to which orators appealed to inspire civic responsibility in late antiquity and to shore up the *polis* in times of crisis.[136] And what Augustine promoted in theory, pastors put into practice. He would have had them exhort the faithful, intent on having their God at hand, to care for each other, for the unity of their congregations, and for the unity of the African church. God gave grace to the faithful so they might love unity and dread separation. Nothing ought to terrorize parishioners more than the latter. Relaying just that to the laity, disciplining Christians and dispossessing them of improper and unbecoming desires, pastoral leadership translated much of what Augustine tried to express polemically into pastoral care.[137]

---

136. Vander Valk, "Friendship," 140–42.

137. Augustine, *In Evangelium Joannis tractatus* 27.6: *ut amemus unitatem et timeamus separationem. Nihil enim sic debet formidare Christianus quam separari a corpore Christi.*

4

Augustine's Statesmen

The Business of Babylon[1]

AUGUSTINE WAS IN MILAN in 386, when the Court requested, then demanded, that Bishop Ambrose surrender one of the city's churches for the use of anti-Nicene Christians. He refused, and the young emperor's soldiers surrounded the basilica he and his rather overbearing mother, Justina, wanted. Ambrose stayed and prayed in another church with a cohort of partisans, which included Augustine's mother. Some parishioners staged a sit-in at the church under siege. The standoff could have ended with Ambrose's incarceration—or worse—yet the Court capitulated, the siege was lifted, and the bishop's success, for centuries, inspired church authorities who dared to resist government interference.[2]

Had he made himself indispensable, as he seems to have intended, Augustine could well have been among the courtiers advising the regime that had tried diplomacy and intimidation to outmaneuver Ambrose, to no avail. For, prior to the government's confrontation with the bishop of Milan, Augustine had come from Rome with a letter from Symmachus, the influential prefect of the old capital, and was looking to make his mark. He delivered orations, and collected clients. His mother came from Africa to arrange a marriage that would further advance his career. Yet, as we know,

---

1. Augustine, *Enarrationes in Psalmos* 51.6: *Babyloniae negotia*.
2. Augustine, *Confessiones* 9.7,15; McLynn, *Ambrose*, 187–96; Colish, "Why the Portiana?," 361–72. For the bishop's deployment in the sixteenth century, see Collinson, "If Constantine, then also Theodosius," 205–29.

Augustine changed his mind; he became disenchanted. Clients paid him to flatter them and advance their careers by exaggerating their virtues. A coup or two in public relations should have landed him a place among the statesmen he served—conceivably, a place at the Court that challenged Ambrose's authority. Like several others who started their careers as he did, he might even have been appointed a provincial governor. Yet telling lies about the highly placed to their colleagues, who no doubt recognized them as lies, demoralized him. A decade later, he confided that he had renounced secular ambition (*contempta spe saeculi*) by the time Ambrose defied the Court. And, by then, Augustine had also taken to the bishop's—and his mother's—faith, returning from Italy as a *servus Dei*, a contemplative heading with several colleagues for his family estate in Thagaste. He did not return, as he probably had planned, as a magistrate sent to Cirta to serve with the governor of Numidia or to Carthage to assist the proconsul, one of Rome's highest-ranking provincial governors. He did not become a public official responsible for construction and maintenance of public works, the collection of revenues, the administration of justice, and the enforcement of edicts from the Court. He would occasionally correspond with and try to counsel—but would not serve among—the empire's officials strategically positioned in Africa to carry on the business of Babylon.[3]

On the whole, the larger cities in Numidia and Proconsular Africa, the provinces in which Augustine spent nearly all his time after he returned to Africa, accommodated Roman rule. Rome was resented for generations after its conquest of the Carthaginian Empire, but Hippo Regius, the venerable Punic port settlement, where Augustine served as priest and bishop, had commissioned statues to honor Emperor Claudius and his deputy Soranus—a signal that citizens were resigned to their fate by the first century CE.[4] African insurgencies in the countryside attest that resistance continued, but Marcel Bénabou suggests that the belligerence and "turbulence" were used to the occupiers' advantage and that pacification was not a high priority. Rome's representatives were more interested in maintaining and managing local factions and feuds that kept Africans from uniting against the empire's garrisons and provincial governments.[5]

---

3. Augustine, *Confessiones* 5.13,23 (Symmachus' recommendation); 6.6,9 (orators' lies); 8.7,18 (*spe saeculi*).

4. Osgood, *Claudius Caesar*, 82–83.

5. Bénabou, *La résistance africaine*, 176–80, 248–50, and 425. Lepelley accounts for several regional variations in resistance ("La période romaine," 65–66).

Augustine saw Rome's political practice in Africa differently. He appreciated officials' willingness to collaborate with his Catholic Christian colleagues to proscribe pagans' worship and to dismantle Donatism, the one Christian faction that worried him from the time he assumed pastoral responsibilities in the early 390s well into the fifth century. Government censures at the time were emphatic, but enforcement was uneven. Augustine prized the decrees from the Courts of Theodosius and Honorius, yet he seemed more concerned with statesmen's piety than with their policies. He noticed that Christians among provincial and metropolitan authorities worked within a narrow imaginative range; they craved celebrity, much as their pagan peers did. They often acted as if they were less interested in the eternal celestial rewards promised in their gospels than in statutes and statues subject to perpetual perishing.[6]

We now know that Augustine thought Emperor Theodosius the exception, a statesman whose humility was remarkable—and rare. But emperors could do little in the provinces without provincial governors and civic leaders or *curiales* to represent their interests and implement the imperial chancery's projects. Once back in Africa, Augustine acknowledged that local deputies were seldom selfless. He became convinced that virtuous candidates for regional and municipal offices were difficult to find.[7] To his mind, Theodosius must have appeared to complicate the problem by delegating power to pagans. Christianity's pastors and bishops had been gratified to see idols removed from temples, which were either left in disrepair or turned to other uses, but it was another thing altogether for officials to legislate and lure pagans into churches. In a letter to authorities in Madaura, where he had been sent for school before going to Carthage, Augustine expressed his dissatisfaction. His correspondents had not hesitated to address him respectfully, because they wrote to ask a favor, yet they hesitated to go to church. He complained that they acted as if they would have to climb a rock wall to enter.[8] The imperial government had not prevailed on them to convert to Christianity, which was in the ascendant, to be sure, but which was far from having colonized the African bureaucracy. There was no discernible drift toward Christian theocracy during the tenure of Emperor

---

6. Augustine, epistle 155.2. Dodaro finds Augustine acknowledging occasionally that officials' civic pride could be devoid of self-interest, yet never consistently enough to pass as paradigmatic ("Augustine and the Possibility of Political Conscience," 236).

7. Augustine, epistle 138.16.

8. Augustine, epistle 232.1–2: *rupium praerupta*.

Theodosius, who, as Marianne Kah confirmed, had opened rather than foreclosed the debate between Christianity and paganism. And advances during the reign of his son, Honorius, had not terribly impressed Augustine.[9] The consensus among historians is that political life in the African provinces during Honorius' tenure exhibited signs of considerable vitality, but Christianity's pastors and bishops were left with the challenge of ensuring that the statesmen responsible behaved less as masters of their region's destiny (and of their own) and more as tenants—or, Augustine preferred, as pilgrims—that they displayed signs of Christian as well as civic piety.[10]

There were also signs of economic vitality. African provinces, especially Proconsular Africa and Numidia, experienced what Serge Lancel characterizes as "the Indian summer" of empire in the late fourth and early fifth centuries. Excavations lead archeologists to conclude that Carthage then reached its greatest extent while "extensive and profitable" rural settlement put resident landed gentry in positions to compete with municipal powerbrokers for influence with governors and their legates.[11] *Curiales* participated in the larger towns' councils (*curiae*); they were members of their cities' socioeconomic elites responsible for their municipalities' basic services. They adjudicated civil and criminal cases and collected revenues for their provincial and central governments. Tensions between the *curiales* and the landed gentry probably derived from the former's demands on what Bryan Ward-Perkins calls "the taxable countryside."[12] The Court was constantly in need of subsidies for its various war efforts and, therefore, intensely interested in recruiting effective members of the *curiae* and in keeping them on task so that "Indian summer" would not turn frosty. If revenues collected seemed inadequate, the *curiales* would have to compensate for shortfalls. That obligation predictably dampened the enthusiasm for public service. Both the Court across the Mediterranean and provincial officials, therefore, were troubled by what Peter Brown describes as a "discreet and persistent withdrawal of collaboration of the local notables." The governors, however, could do little more than worry. Nearly all were sent from Rome and remained in Africa for little more than eighteen months, at

9. Kah, *"Die Welt der Römer"*, 127–28.

10. For the efflorescence, see, for example, Lepelley, "L'Afrique à la veille de la conquête vandal," 65–67.

11. Lancel, "L'Antiquité tardive," 236–38; Eck, "Der Episkopat," 275–76. Hippo Regius was in Proconsular Africa, although Augustine's diocese stretched into the province of Numidia.

12. Ward-Perkins, "Cities," 375–76, 404–8.

most. Brown thinks that provincial governors were simply listening posts.[13] The duties related to monitoring municipal elites fell to the provincial bureaucracy staffed by Africans who were charged with maintaining efficiency, while the proconsuls' legates were empowered to umpire disputes related to finance and public works, although final determinations were reserved for their superiors.[14]

Positions in government were for sale. Augustine seems to have witnessed a transition from bureaucracies that were wholly dependent on patronage networks to administrations that relied as well on informal networks, which allowed statesmen to serve if they were prepared to purchase the privilege. The traditional routes to promotions were not closed, but avenues were opened by financial exchanges.[15] Corruption, prevalent when favors were granted, became epidemic when coin advanced careers. When the costs were considerable, they were passed along to ordinary subjects, victimizing the powerless. So said Salvian of Marseilles, whose outrage, years after Augustine's death, made the latter's reactions to corrupt practices seem subdued and, to historian Ramsay MacMullen, diffident. MacMullen believes that Augustine winked at corruption, rather scornfully citing his remarks about court registrars who charged litigants for expediting the resolution of their cases. MacMullen called it bribery, although it could be construed as something less sinister. Minor officials (*personae inferioris loci*) hardly extorted large sums; they simply solicited or accepted fees or tips. The custom was regrettable, Augustine admitted, yet less damaging than the perjury, malicious prosecutions, and racketeering he explicitly condemned, as he did the behavior of advocates who justified deceit and scandalous court tactics as the vigorous pursuit or defense of their clients' legitimate interests. To Augustine, the fees and tips were disconcerting features of advocacy and arbitration in late antiquity. But he chose not to antagonize those giving and getting; instead, he exhorted the recipients of gratuities to be charitable and dedicate a part of their perks to relieve the plight of the poor.[16] Meaningful change, however, was unlikely, Augustine conceded; justices, lawyers, litigants, and the courts' clerks or

---

13. Brown, *Power and Persuasion*, 23–25, 32–33.
14. Hugoniot, "Les légats du proconsul d'Afrique," 2085–86.
15. Kelly, *Ruling the Later Roman Empire*, 103–4; 170–71.
16. Augustine, epistle 153.24–26. MacMullen (*Changes in the Roman Empire*, 153) compares Augustine to Salvian, citing the latter's *De gubernatione Dei* 4.4–7. Also see Kaufman, "Augustine and Corruption," 50–51.

registrars were schooled to chase the almighty drachma. The courts simply reflected conventional priorities. People were content if public roads were repaired in a timely fashion, entertainments supplied at others' expense, and the good fortune of the wicked did not diminish their own returns. People ranked material sufficiency and gain above moral improvements. Yet Augustine believed that was a problem to be tackled pastorally; only minimal structural change could be expected.[17]

Still, the structures were oppressive; competition for gain, Kevin Uhalde surmises, left overwrought prelatical and secular magistrates "neck deep in the treachery of human society."[18] To manage conflict and, ideally, resolve complaints before they clogged the courts, ombudsmen (*patroni* or *defensores plebis*) were appointed in some cities. Their commission appears to have been to protect the relatively powerless from powerful and sometimes scurrilous neighbors, but François Jacques alleges that ombudsmen became ciphers by the early fifth century. He thinks that Augustine knew as much, yet, to spare himself the necessity of confronting local officials with commoners' grievances, he asked that a *defensor* be appointed to umpire cases and keep him from turning on—and trying to turn out of office—corrupt or ineffective officials.[19] He did not relish that prospect. He was ill at ease in their company. In a sermon preached at the start of the fifth century he told parishioners of one harrowing and humiliating experience he had trying to intercede for parishioners cheated by corrupt customs officials. He was startled by how little influence he was able to exert.[20] He later acknowledged that churches could not force-feed the local authorities remedies for extortion and fraud. To do more than sigh for the unfortunate was to risk reprisal. Moreover, public declarations against magistrates amounted to a daft marketing strategy for a faith still looking to win over pagans who suspected that the Christians' churches harbored excessive political ambitions. Calling for ombudsmen with determination, ingenuity (*sollertia*), rank, and respect seemed the best way to assist corrupt officials' casualties.[21]

But because most statesmen valued their reputations, church authorities did have one arrow in their quivers capable of taking down and

17. Augustine, epistle 138.14.

18. Uhalde, *Expectations of Justice*, 66–67, 135–37.

19. Compare Jacques, "La défenseur de cité," 58–60, 71–73 with Lepelley, *Aspects de l'Afrique romaine*, 365–66.

20. Augustine, sermon 302.17.

21. Augustine, epistle 22*.3–4.

keeping down corruption. Augustine knew that retaliation usually followed denunciation but that the threat of the latter might serve as well as, or better than, an uttered accusation or censure to discipline those who desperately wanted to remain irreproachable in the eyes of their public. In his *City of God*, he rehearsed Sallust's vivid descriptions of older noble Romans eager for acclaim and terrified of shame. Honor mattered; it was *finis virtutis*, the culmination or consummation of all virtues.[22] The worst persons (*pessimi*) would do nearly anything to avoid ruining their reputations, to keep their fame safe (*fama salva*). Statesmen especially feared disgrace. Whereas ombudsmen might protect ordinary citizens from nefarious officials, to a point, the dread of pastors' and bishops' antipathy, which would lead to public exposure of their misdeeds, might keep officials—if not in line—at least from monstrously wicked behavior. Augustine let it be known that the church would see to it that authorities who wantonly harmed others heard that they were also harming themselves.[23]

Yet would they listen? Augustine calculated that censures likely had only limited effects as long as lust for power and domination irrepressibly drove statesmen from post to post, up their career ladders. Ambition might be leavened for a time—officials may be contented, provisionally—but Roman statesmen generally considered ambition critical to the wellbeing of their terrestrial cities.[24] In a perfect world, the political cultures of, and political practices in, such cities would have been reconstituted according to lessons drawn from Christianity's sacred texts. But it was not a perfect world and never would be. Augustine was an imperfectionist, resigned to the presence of the wicked and mischievous in public office.[25] A year or two after admitting as much in the first few books of his *City of God*, he sent them to Macedonius, who was then vicar of Africa (413), and—echoing the psalmist—Augustine elaborated: God's gift was the deliverance of those still in this world (*in hoc saeculo maligno*) from this wicked world where there could be no genuine justice, where people judged material convenience worthy of their best efforts, filling their cellars, expanding their flocks, and giving no thought to their rescue or rebirth (in the faith). They became lovers of this world (*dilectores hujus mundi*) and grew certain that their exertions merited material reward. Augustine explained they were cursed

22. Augustine, *De civitate Dei* 5.12.
23. Augustine, epistle 151.10: *sibi igitur ille nocuit, quidquid nocuit.*
24. Augustine, *De civitate Dei* 1.31.
25. Ibid., 2.19.

with that certainty. He said that their inability to transcend the vanity and insanity of investing all their hope in this world would cost them the world to come.²⁶ Vicar Macedonius might apply his skills to creating an order to please the misguided, to keep them safe or unmolested and prosperous, but they would not turn their peace or prosperity to eternal advantage, Augustine argued, while they were insensitive to Catholic Christianity's summons to faith, hope, and love. The truth was that Macedonius' craft, which earned him citizens' gratitude, was unimportant *sub specie aeternitatis*.²⁷

And, despite Macedonius' magnanimity and policy as well as other statesmen's initiatives, the terrestrial cities continued to be dangerous places filled with misery and care, Augustine alleged in his *City of God*—dangerous and wretched not only for their leadership but also for ordinary residents. Affairs in this world were characterized by mistrust, envy, injuries, and enmity (*injuriae, suspiciones, inimicitiae*); friendly gestures concealed malice, even within homes (and families), which seemed to supply no refuge from the evils of the city. Forums were filled with nonsense and—always—with rancorous citizens. Courts were crowded with venomous litigants.²⁸

Perhaps, if the righteous indignation that surfaces in parts of Augustine's *City* describing inescapable evils had been expressed more emphatically and more frequently in his sermons and correspondence, he might have inspired a war on corruption. He might have stirred the faithful to oppose business as usual, that "business of Babylon," more energetically. Yet, as we shall see, he advised statesmen deferentially—delicately. On occasion he exhibited frustration and foreboding; he voiced his misgivings about what good could be expected from political practice. He would never, however, be taken as an insurgent. As John Parrish proposes, "Given the risk of moral corruption, Augustine [thought Christians] should prefer even to endure the rule of an unjust government rather than hazard [their] own moral purity unnecessarily."²⁹ Besides, the celestial city was on pilgrimage, and the elect were in diaspora. Their expectations and affections—what Augustine called their "loves"—were different from those who made this world troubled and treacherous.³⁰

---

26. Augustine, epistle 155.6–8.
27. Ibid., 10: *nihil tibi prodest ad vitam vere beatam tantus labor.*
28. Augustine, *De civitate Dei* 19.5.
29. Parrish, *Paradoxes of Political Ethics*, 95.
30. Augustine, *De civitate Dei* 18.54.

Could those different, celestial expectations and affections make this world better in ways that Augustine would approve? To some extent, surely; scholars differ, however, when they posit to what extent. What one could call an optimistic view—because it casts Augustine as a political optimist and as a resource for theorists interested in relating Christianity to political liberalism—has him presuming that significant political changes in the early fifth century could develop from statesmen's and citizens' personal conversions. Historian Robert Dodaro, one of the most erudite proponents of this position, correctly reminds us that Augustine was far from counseling others to abandon terrestrial cities, as we conceded in this study's introduction, yet Dodaro also claims Augustine had ambitious plans for terrestrial reform. Dodaro, that is, has him proposing that the virtues of humility and forbearance need not keep Christian statesmen from "shaping society and political forms according to Christian ethics." There is no denying Augustine's judgment that the "ultimate objectives framed" by celestial expectations and affections were beyond a magistrate's abilities to realize. Dodaro argues that Augustine proposed nonetheless that Christian statesmen could and, of course, should fashion an alternative order without resorting to the sordid political practices that prevailed. They need not return from their pastors' lessons to their civic duties empty-headed. Dodaro's reconstitution of Augustine's confidence, which has influenced the optimism of some prolific political ethicists, suggests that the bishop believed it possible to reconstitute or rehabilitate the terrestrial city.[31]

Some basis for this upbeat reading of Augustine can be found in his response to Tribune Marcellinus, about whom we shall hear more shortly. The tribune had relayed several questions from Proconsul Volusianus, who declined to be baptized but remained curious about dilemmas that, he imagined, Christian statesmen were forced by their faith to face. Although their pastors told them to be peaceable, defending their empire sometimes required them to be savage. Would they warehouse religious precepts when they encountered intruders on the frontiers or prosecuted criminals in the cities? How ready were they to cope with conditions that called for brawny, even brutal responses—situations in which submissive responses would

31. Dodaro, *Christ and the Just Society*, 203–5, and Dodaro, "*Ecclesia* and *Res Publica*," 242, 248–50, 256. For "expanding Augustinian liberalism" into a "robust civic humanism," see Gregory, *Politics and the Order of Love*, 47–56, 107–25. And, for summaries of Dodaro's and Gregory's impressions of Augustine's thinking on piety and politics, see Bruno, *Political Augustinianism*, 197–203, 219–23, and Kaufman, "Christian Realism," 703–13.

be tantamount to subversion of the government? After he confronted the problems head-on (answering that Christianity opposed unnecessary violence and directed that wars be waged benevolently), Augustine mused that if the Christian faith ever informed political practice, the commonwealth would be invigorated, enriched, and consecrated (*constitueret, consecraret, firmaret, augeretque*).[32] By referring to consecration, Augustine seemed to formulate a manifesto of sorts, a statement that seems to substantiate the notion that he meant to reform and rededicate political culture. Yet his letter concedes that its counsel was intended more for the cultivation of personal virtue than for an overhaul of public policy.[33] And, as the letter's replies to the proconsul's inquiry conclude, he confided his hope that the faith of Christian statesmen might encourage apolitical expectations and affections that their faith might keep them from participating in the deceit so common in back-room bargaining, which was often fueled by politicians' lust for domination.[34]

Those apolitical expectations and affections were normative for Augustine—central to the interior lives of the faithful. But Robert Dodaro is more bouyant than Augustine was; he believes Augustine expected the expectations and affections of the faithful would issue in their purposeful and politically unconventional piety with a potential to evangelize the public realm.[35] Augustine explained to Vicar Macedonius that the celebrity associated with public office could be perilous. Statesmen were as defective as the ordinary citizens they governed. Good qualities were God's gifts to human nature, but that nature, Augustine continued (along the lines drawn more sharply in his anti-Pelagian treatises) was stained indelibly by the sin of humanity's parents, Adam and Eve. So when Augustine praised Macedonius, he was anticipating that the vicar would know well enough to attribute all his virtues to God. Statesmen acquired celebrity and a reputation for righteousness—but not righteousness itself—by leaving behind viaducts, theaters, and other civic upgrades. Yet, notwithstanding their judicious management of affairs, kindnesses, and legacies in marble, they must never claim to be unsoiled. They were good, Augustine maintained, when their

---

32. Augustine, epistle 138.10.

33. Ibid., 13: *magis ad praeparationem cordis quae intus est quam ad opus quod in aperto*.

34. Ibid., 17: *ne mala suadentium, vel in mala impellentium*.

35. See Dodaro, "Augustine's Secular City," 231–59, responding to the discussion of Augustine's supposedly authoritarian political theology in Connolly, *The Augustinian Imperative*. Also see Dodaro, "Augustine on the Statesman," 388–92.

admirable qualities outweighed their character flaws, when they owned and confessed the latter, and when they gave God credit for the former. To say that diligent statesmen performed irreproachably was not pretentiously to claim that they were sinless but only to say they sinned insignificantly (*peccat minimum*). To think otherwise was to reinforce reluctance to take refuge in God's grace (*gratiam confugiendum*).[36]

Dodaro thinks Augustine's endorsements of Christian statesmen's worthiness presumed a transformation of civic virtues—prudence, conscientiousness, temperance, and impartiality—by the virtues associated with Christianity: faith, hope, humility, and charity. The transformation was an enhancement central to what Dodaro calls Augustine's "theory of Christian political conscience." Yet the coherence of that theory may be in the eye of the beholder rather than in that of Dodaro's subject. For it is far from incontrovertible that Augustine would have extended his "theory" and awaited a reorientation of government, which would have profoundly affected what James K. A. Smith describes as the "mutually exclusive *teloi* of practices which give [Christianity and politics] their identity-forming capacities."[37]

Smith updates, referring to the antithesis between Christian discipleship and liberal democracy in his discussions of various adaptations of Augustine by advocates of the latter, although his remarks apply equally well, if not better, to the exclusive *teloi* or objectives of Roman rule and personal righteousness. The conflict between them is splendidly illustrated by the agonizing consequences for Christian statesmen of the conflict between their commitments when their faith dictated compassion and their duties required torture. The custom was to extort truths from witnesses as well as from the accused by subjecting them to pain. The practice was valued in the terrestrial city; Augustine argued for limits. Christian magistrates, he suggested to Marcellinus, should resort to beating, much as parents, teachers, and (infrequently) even bishops did at that time. But magistrates ought to forego branding the flesh and distending limbs. Milder forms of corporal punishment avoided undesirable, occasionally lethal outcomes.[38] Augustine

---

36. Augustine, epistles 104.10–11 (answering epistle 103.2) and 153.12: *sed eum dicimus bonum, cujus praevalent bona, eumque optimum qui peccat minimum*.

37. Compare Dodaro, "Augustine and the Possibility of Political Conscience," 229–33, with Smith, "Politics of Desire," 217–19.

38. Augustine, epistle 133.2. In this connection, see Lepelley, *Aspects de l'Afrique romaine*, 371–72.

preferred to have magistrates retain their humanity than to see what passed as justice—restitutions, for example—that resulted from torture.[39]

But torture was commonly thought to prevent perjury. Christian magistrates, therefore, were expected to rack those charged and their accusers. Augustine advised them to do their duty, to despise it, and to decathect. They ought to conform to citizens' expectations, but disassociate and pray for deliverance from that "necessity."[40] Augustine would have Christians serve when called to do so, despite what one might now call moral compromises. His was a measured version of what Charles Mathewes terms "a theology of engagement." It neither "finally rest[ed]" nor measured its success "in sheer accomplishment."[41]

Statesmen's engagements, just as ordinary citizens' engagements with the government, rendered unto Caesars what was due. To disarm suspicions that faith was necessarily betrayed when political authorities were obeyed—or political practices followed—Augustine recycled the gospels' reminder that Caesars' images were on the coins *curiales* collected. Taxes belonged to the government, but Augustine also reminded his parishioners that the image engraved on their souls was that of God who, as creator and redeemer, had every intention of taking and retaining what could be called a monopolistic position. Christians belonged to their God, so—on moral and spiritual matters—they were bound to defer to what was revealed in their scripture, honoring their pastors' interpretations and applications when sacred literature's meanings seemed obscure.[42]

In a sermon preached in Carthage perhaps as early as 399, Augustine made much the same point, adapting a bit of political wisdom that Christian statesmen and pagan colleagues would have readily appreciated: beware of offending higher-ups. For the faithful, God was the highest up, so to speak; hence, Christian statesmen's political engagements must never present them with a lastingly vexing conflict of loyalties.[43] Yet, if Robert Dodaro is correct and faithful statesmen, from Augustine's perspective, were to promote "an alternative social order," political conflicts would sure-

---

39. Augustine, epistle 153.20.

40. Augustine, *De civitate Dei* 19.6, quoting Psalm 25: *in ista necessitate miseriam eamque odit in se et, si pie sapit, clamat ad Deum: "De necessitatibus meis erue me."*

41. Mathewes, *Theology of Public Life*, 31–33.

42. Augustine, *Enarrationes in Psalmos* 94.2.

43. Augustine, sermon 62.8, discussed by Horn, "Augustinus über politische Ethik," 61–62.

ly follow. And one passage in his *City of God* suggests he was preparing for that conflict. If celestial goods are neglected, he prophesied, temporal goods that worldly persons consider superior would preoccupy the governed and government alike. Misery must follow, and present misery would become more galling, he added, nearly turning his warning into a call for a reinvention of public administration. Yet Augustine characteristically imagined that chasing after temporal goods was unstoppable. The best one could expect in society (although he hoped for a better result within individuals) would be damage control, not an end to misery in this wicked world but something of a prophylactic—something to limit the scope or reach of misery, which was inevitable this side of the grave. Conceivably, then, the surges of misery could be capped—made less chafing. Misery kept humanity company, however, because concupiscence afflicted human will as the punishment for humanity's original sin of disobedience. That is the theme of the first four—and, arguably, of several more—books of Augustine's *City of God*, which preface its warning ("if celestial goods are neglected") in the fifteenth. A quick thumb-through of the *City's* prophetic remarks would have persuaded readers that, for Augustine, the political was not just an extension but also an amplification of everyone's personal predicament.[44]

The world seemed to him to be traveling away from God, putting a premium on gain and, more dramatic still, shamelessly encouraging ambition and greed. Those unable—or unwilling—to peer beyond their terrestrial horizons were adept at the business of Babylon but could only grope awkwardly after anything greater than their immediate temporal interests. But the faithful were pilgrims in this world and were headed in a different direction. They were still sinners, we have heard Augustine repeatedly say; they had discreditable desires yet usually refrained from acting on them.[45] The problem for the Christian magistrate was how to serve this world without being carried away in its direction. As Miles Hollingworth says, Augustine understood that statesmen among the faithful were "just as much afflicted by the itchy sore of *libido dominandi*," lust for power, but were "enjoined not to scratch it."[46] Augustine would have them become martyrs at heart in their terrestrial cities where the premium put on temporal advantage in the business of Babylon was unquestioned. Faithful statesmen had to face

---

44. Augustine, *De civitate Dei* 15.4: *si negelctis melioribus, quae ad supernam pertinent civitatem . . . necesse est miseria et quae inerat augeatur.*
45. Augustine, *De spiritu et littera* 36.65.
46. Hollingworth, *Pilgrim City*, 69–70.

temptations with a near ascetic self-discipline; above all, they must avoid the trap of mistaking politics for piety. The glory hounds around them sought rewards and celebrity by expanding their regime's reach, conquering their neighbors' territories, and touting civic virtues, which, Augustine thought, only the unschooled and irreverent mistook for true virtue.[47] Plausibly, he arrived at that conclusion after he became acquainted with *curiales* in Hippo or Carthage. Provincial officials, as Neil McLynn infers from Augustine's correspondence, were generally beyond his range. He seems to have had very little contact with proconsuls. Persons of senatorial rank fled to Africa after 410, yet Augustine was either indifferent or relatively unwelcoming. He would have seen many of them, one suspects, clutching what was left of their possessions and so, in his estimation, still traveling—with the world—in the wrong direction.[48]

So, although Augustine allowed that Christians should participate in public service, he kept his distance, encouraging Christian statesmen, as pilgrims, to keep their emotional distance. Hence, historians who describe his conduct, character, and counsel as "politically remote" are not far off the mark, although he figured that statesmen's devotion to Rome was only problematic if it overwhelmed their religious devotion, that is, if they forgot that their affections, expectations, and the rewards they would receive for preserving both were celestial, and if they forgot that the secular, wicked world they served was, despite their best efforts at damage control, headed away from God.[49] His *City of God* underscores that last point, stipulating that earth's cities had been founded by Cain after he had murdered Abel. The faithful, as pilgrims, lived among, but would never be at home with, Cain's kind.[50]

As Timo Weissenberg explains, Augustine increasingly considered that bloodshed was emblematic of the terrestrial city. He came to think that the rulers of this world generally were unprincipled as well as unruly. The best intentions of the few who nurtured them would prove powerless to counter the thrusts of the passions for power that motivated most. Would

---

47. Augustine, *Contra Academicos* 3.17,27 and Augustine, *Contra Julianum haeresis Pelagianae* 4.3,26.

48. For the refugees, see Augustine, *Gesta collationis Carthaginiensis* 1.149. McLynn argues compellingly that Augustine was "politically marginal" ("Augustine's Roman Empire," 36–40).

49. See Fortin, "Justice as the Foundation," 133–38, and Horn, "Augustinus über politische Ethik," 59–60.

50. Augustine, *De civitate Dei* 15.1.

Augustine have agreed that politics was war by other means? The savagery was in evidence; the devastation less conspicuous, although quite corrosive. Belligerence fueled by ambition took many forms, all of which raged on the wrong side of the threshold that marked off Christianity's noble affections from the *amor sui* that inspired Cain and his heirs brooding over the business of Babylon in the terrestrial city.[51]

In 409, a year before Rome was sacked, Augustine declared to a troubled colleague that belligerence was inescapable.[52] History might appear to be a series of alternating successes and failures, but, as Charles Mathewes points out, for Augustine, the *distensio* of worldly existence became "one long lesson" in patience. Statesmen's civic virtues—which, to his mind, were only ostensible or supposed rather than authentic virtues—and statesmen's services aside, Christians would be naïve to look for or to plump for a final resolution to the war of all against all among Cain's kind.[53]

Augustine's accounts of pervasive war fever, inflamed by the lust to dominate that was present in the powerless as well as among the highly placed, occasionally cited the arrangements made to secure a modicum of peace. They were advantageous for the church, Augustine allowed; peace made parishioners feel safe. Peace comforted pilgrims. Peace on earth, of course, could not compare with peace in the celestial city, a peace pilgrims possessed within as a foreshadowing of a flawlessly formed, harmonious fellowship with God—and with each other (*ordinatissima . . . et concordissima societas fruendi Deo et invicem in Deo*). Yet that possession, along with pilgrims' otherworldly expectations and the ardent affections that distinguished them from the less selfless, suffused them with a conviction that they were divinely ordained beneficiaries of the armistices governments negotiated. Peace on earth, furthermore, enabled Catholic Christianity to withstand its critics and assailants more expeditiously, and—just as significant for Augustine—peace on earth would have made it possible to circulate the gospels' good news widely and to colonize from all tribes (*ex omnibus gentis*)—in effect, universalizing the church.[54] Statesmen's severity, soldiers' weapons, and executioners' apparatus inspired fear, permitting the

---

51. Weissenberg, *Die Friedenslehre des Augustinus*, 111–12.

52. Augustine, epistle 111.1: *totus quippe mundus tantis affligitur cladibus.*

53. Mathewes, *Republic of Grace*, 234–35.

54. Augustine, *De civitate Dei* 19.17: *ex omnibus gentibus . . . peregrinam colligit societatem . . . servans ac sequens quod licet diversum in diversis nationibus, ad unum tamen eumdemque finem terrenae pacis intenditur.*

good to live unmolested by the wicked. Force and fear deterred the latter, Augustine suggested, and might also undermine their resistance to pastoral counseling.[55]

Marcellinus

We have already learned how important the government's agents were to the church's leadership, to bishops and pastors in their efforts to protect the churches from violent factions among Donatist secessionists. We need now to revisit the Donatists' persistence to appreciate statesmen's efforts, as Augustine did, efforts to reconcile the dissidents and to resolve crises related to the schism, specifically, efforts that culminated with the intervention of Marcellinus, the military commander and official in the imperial chancery sent from Italy to Africa early in the second decade of the fifth century. Donatism preoccupied Augustine from the start of his pontificate in the late 390s—when he prodded Eusebius, an official in Hippo, to influence the city's Donatist bishop, Proculianus—and into the fifth century, during and after his apparent triumph, over which Marcellinus presided at the Council of Carthage in 411.

The tone of Augustine's letter to Eusebius suggests the latter's reluctance to intervene. He might have been a pagan whose hesitation to stage a debate between the two Christian factions in Hippo simply reflected his desire to be impartial. Or he might have been a Donatist who did not want to see his bishop embarrassed by a cosmopolitan Catholic Christian.[56] Augustine referred to himself as a raw recruit (*tiro*) but was far from it. True, he was new to the episcopacy, and he importuned Eusebius because Proculianus had refused to confer with him about the character of Christians whom the Donatists welcomed into their church. One abominably treated his mother, a widow, for whose safety Augustine was concerned. Another recent convert from the Catholic Christian camp had seduced several nuns who, along with their seducer, were welcomed by the Donatists. Augustine may have believed that informing Eusebius would tilt him against his own clerics' recklessness (*coerceat insaniam clericorum suorum*). And he may have deliberately left unspecified the nature of that *insania*, because what he most wanted was the chance to talk with Proculianus about their differ-

---

55. Augustine, epistle 153.16.
56. Lepelley considers both options without favoring one (*Aspects de l'Afrique romaine*, 350–51).

ences. No referee was necessary, Augustine assured Eusebius, who probably dreaded the prospect of assuming such a role. Augustine was pleased to let bystanders judge the merits of the two competing versions of Christianity.[57]

By the early fifth century, after Catholic Christians in Africa had again gotten favorable attention from the imperial government, its provincial and municipal deputies presumably were more inclined to acquiesce to Augustine's overtures than Eusebius had been. Emperor Honorius' principal military commander, Stilicho, unequivocally supported Catholic Christianity.[58] Edicts directed local authorities to close secessionists' churches. Government intimidation drew many Donatists from their sects, but Augustine preferred colloquies to coercion. He was unable to get Proculianus or Eusebius to oblige, as we just discovered, so—after other attempts—he grudgingly concurred with colleagues who wanted to put the dissidents under duress. Yet when magistrates ordered death penalties Augustine seems well-meaningly to have taken extra pains to have the condemned spared. He advised magistrates to exhaust alternatives before ordering executions. And, writing to Marcellinus' brother Apringius, proconsul in Africa in 411, he proposed that outspoken dissidents be released if statesmen could not come up with a more compassionate, sensible (*providentiorem*) sentence than death.[59] Augustine believed that the resistance of his most incorrigible rivals could be tested—to good ends—by clemency, whereas cruelty would only stiffen their resolve. He asked statesmen commissioned to enforce government edicts to correct rather than kill offenders.[60]

Enforcement was critical. When personnel changes at Court appeared likely to limit the government's initiatives—soon after Stilicho had been killed—Augustine was quick to prevail on political authorities to sustain their anti-Donatist campaign. His motive and that of his Catholic Christian colleagues was not revenge, he assured one official, and his assurance signals that a complaint about their churches' vengeful, venomous efforts had been registered and had to be answered. Yet Augustine was most concerned with explaining why Roman officials in Africa and their African legates should couple their proper work—upholding laws and order—with their special work, which could be undertaken in concert with the amicable,

---

57. Augustine, epistles 34.6 and 35.5.

58. Di Berardino, "Rileggere il 410," 12: "*molto più deciso contro il paganesimo e i cristiani dissidenti.*"

59. Augustine, epistle 134.4.

60. Augustine, epistle 101.1: *corrigi eos cupimus, nec necari.*

charitable efforts of the Catholic Christian leadership. That special work reconciled dissidents and procured peace by recovering souls beguiled by heretics and lost in schism.[61]

Such were the Donatists' souls. Their secession divided the church, so, although they claimed that Caecilian had done so a century earlier, technically, the Donatists were in schism. The government had ruled in 314 that they left the church, and Augustine ruled that persistence in schism was heresy. Donatists, he went on, thought their rivals were flawed, inferior Christians. His rejoinder targeted the Donatists' sense of superiority, which, he said, was not only pretentious and an embarrassment to all other Christians who identified humility as the faith's cardinal virtue but was also a source of behavior to which statesmen could not be indifferent because it unsettled just what they were devoted to upholding; he and his colleagues, Augustine reported, had learned by trying to appease the Donatists that they despised peace.[62]

Such unsubtle statements served Augustine's polemical purposes. As we have seen, he commended clemency yet had to harp on his rivals' treacheries to retain government interest in their suppression. Historians Carles Buenacasa Pérez and Raúl Villegas seem especially astute when they suggest Augustine crafted his categorical characterizations of Donatists' *furor* and *insania* both to warn authorities in Africa that the confessional civil war was a grave threat to public order and to ensure them that Catholic Christian interest in stability spurred the faithful in communion with Augustine stridently to censure dissident neighbors. He appealed for clemency, as we now know, but he insisted that he, his clerical colleagues, and the Catholic Christian laity had a duty to discipline and correct errant others. Should they be less than dutiful on that score, although their dereliction might pass unnoticed by most, Augustine was certain the negligent would regret their inattention if, to perpetuate goodwill, they declined to be disagreeable and scold friends who sinned.[63]

In the context of the anti-Donatist campaign, to be disagreeable was to insist that regime officials enforce prohibitions against secessionists. After

---

61. Augustine, epistle 86.1. For Augustine's supposed "consent" to the partnership between church and government that developed in the "post-Constantinian" period, compare Lienemann, "Eschatologik als Antipolitik," 423–25, with Kaufman, *Redeeming Politics*, 143–45.

62. Augustine, *Enarrationes in Psalmos* 119.9: *his qui oderunt pacem sumus pacifici.*

63. Augustine, *De civitate Dei* 1.9; Buenacasa-Pérez and Villegas, "Agustín, autor intelectual," 633–36.

the emperors restricted the jurisdiction of the churches' courts, bishops and their deputies relied on the government to combat heresy.[64] Statesmen were responsible for returning to Catholic Christian clergy the churches unlawfully taken over by Donatists, Augustine said (*illicite usurpantur*), because even the most moderate among their bishops, he believed, were likely to become associated with the sect's lunatic fringe eventually, which attacked Catholic Christians whom the statesmen should be protecting.[65]

It bears repeating that the coalition was not one that Augustine discussed in person with highly placed statesmen. He established some connections through correspondence yet nothing surfaces in the letters that would lead him to count on consistently favorable responses when he asked for favors. He was less adept at courtship than was Bishop Ambrose. As an orator, Augustine deployed hyperbole expertly, but an artistry or dexterity of a different sort was required in delicate political deliberations. And he seems to have had few occasions to practice diplomacy, save for conversations during church councils. There is no evidence he had contact with proconsular legates who likely set up headquarters near his basilicas in Hippo. In sum, he cannot be said to have had easy access to Roman dignitaries or to their African deputies.[66] Yet he regularly preached in Hippo—and frequently in Carthage—within earshot of the influential. The effects of his sermons on statesmen who heard them or heard about them or heard paraphrases in lessons preached by his colleagues are incalculable. Yet the subject that would have attracted the magistrates to Augustine's anti-Donatist rhetoric was the universality of Catholic Christianity. A statesman, he mused, might have thought secession was defensible, had the dissidents done the impossible and altogether avoided sedition and sin. But they did not, for they could not, from Augustine's perspective; everywhere, *per totum mundum*, wheat and weeds were mixed. Yet what must have startled him was that Donatists seemed not to have had the foggiest idea why officials anxious about the empire's territorial integrity and preoccupied with the security of Africa, which supplied staples to Italy, favored Catholic Christianity's claim that the faith's sacred texts, the literature it shared with Donatism, invited all peoples into communion.[67]

---

64. See, for example, Dossey, "Judicial Violence," 99–100.
65. Augustine, *Contra litteras Petiliani Donatistae* 2.19,43; Augustine, epistle 185.14.
66. McLynn, "Augustine's Roman Empire," 34–35.
67. See, for example, Augustine, sermon 47.18, and Tholen, *Die Donatisten*, 339.

Nonetheless, it did seem to surprise the secessionists that their reading of the sacred texts' invitation was unpopular with a government that reached well beyond Africa and that the tribune sent from Rome to convene a conference between Donatists and Catholic Christians would favor terms conducive to the unity of Christian churches everywhere the empire was trying to defend. Marcellinus summoned prelates to a council in Carthage in 411. He suspended the enforcement of edicts against the Donatists, pending the council's determinations. Augustine could have met informally with him before the first of the council's three sessions opened. Both the bishop and the tribune were in Carthage a few months before the clergy from both sides gathered. To infer that Augustine rehearsed or readied Marcellinus, however, seems overreaching. Whatever had passed between them, the tribune would have been inclined by the rivalry's history and by his government's interests to treat Donatists as plaintiffs.[68] Constantine and two European church councils regarded the sect's founders similarly nearly one hundred years before. And plaintiffs' complaints were similarly dismissed in 411. At the council's third session, Marcellinus argued that he could hardly enter into evidence unproven accusations against either Bishop Caecilians' supporters in the early fourth century or against Augustine and Catholic Christians in the early fifth.[69]

The Donatists were accustomed to disappointment. Edicts working to their disadvantage since 403, which Marcellinus had agreed to suspend for a time, probably were responses to their refusal to confer with Catholic Christians and their constant complaints about them. To be sure, those complaints echoed their predecessors' protests against early fourth-century prelates, who retained bishops whose credibility had been compromised because, allegedly, they had betrayed the faith during the previous persecution. The Donatist secessionists got no satisfaction from the government in the fourth century, save for the eighteen months when Emperor Julian ruled. Still, as we learned, they outnumbered their rivals in Africa when Augustine returned. If the surviving Catholic Christians' correspondence can be trusted, however, Donatists became panicky as their rivals took a more active role in helping authorities and promoting the defections of Donatist priests.[70]

---

68. But see Moreau, *Le dossier Marcellinus*, 110–11.
69. *Gesta Conlationes Carthaginiensis* 3.140: *quod necdum est adprobatum.*
70. Augustine, epistles 88.6–9 and 105.3.

Such developments probably prompted the Donatists to risk the Council of Carthage in 411. And they might have been more inclined to accept Marcellinus' invitation to confront Catholic Christians when they heard that Augustine had abandoned his objections to the use of force and fear. For his part, Augustine continued to stress the theme that catered to the government's interests, locating arguments for the universality of the church in the Bible, which, on his reading, promised that the faith must spread, as the empire once seemed to, over the known world. The psalmist, Pentateuch, prophets, gospels, and Pauline epistles composed a resounding rejoinder to African secessionists. Compare them to strays, Augustine counseled, and compare Catholic Christians to the stars in the heavens and the sand on a vast seashore.[71]

But in Africa, as we now know, the Donatists were numerically superior, and that, too, might have influenced their decision to come to Carthage for the council. In Byzacena, south of Proconsular Africa and east of Numidia where Donatists predominated in the rural parishes, the two factions were roughly equal. Marcellinus, however, must have known the importance of the other two provinces. The Donatists demanded a roll call at the first session so he would see *their* many bishops and, perhaps, dismiss Augustine's rhetorical flourishes about sand and stars. Yet, at this distance, intentions are difficult to discern; for whatever reason, when the tribune agreed to suspend enforcement of the edicts against them, Donatists came. They scored well at the first session but not as decisively as they must have hoped. Numbers from Numidia gave them an edge, but there were more Catholic Christian bishops than Donatist prelates from Proconsular Africa at the council. Marcellinus, however, seems to have disliked the numbers game. So he simply pronounced excuses for absences plausible, and the council count reflected bishops on the ground, as it were, and not just at the conference. He then probed to see whether reconciliation or more mutual recrimination would follow from his efforts to arbitrate.[72]

After the presence and absences of bishops had been registered, Marcellinus required the parties to delegate representatives so the discussion would be orderly. The ruling was unpopular among the Donatists. Reliance on delegations negated their numerical advantage. Augustine may

71. Augustine, epistle 93.28–30, citing Gen 22:17. On this letter, in which Augustine somewhat tentatively justified yielding to Catholic Christian colleagues who had determined that fear and force would be useful (in Augustine's terms, not unuseful [*non videtur inutile*]; epistle 93.1), see Cazier, "La *compelle intrare* d'Augustin," 29–31.

72. *Actes de la conférence* 1.144–45.

have expected secessionists to nominate moderate delegates. He was likely in earnest, expressing his desire that the conversations be more collegial than adversarial.[73] But Marcellinus forced the Donatists' hand, and the Catholic Christians who were appointed to participate could not have been displeased. Their critics were compelled to recycle the suit against Caecilian and his partisans, because the Donatists' claim that communion with Catholic Christians contaminated Christianity rested on the guilt of the early fourth-century prelates. Marcellinus, therefore, would have to listen to plaintiffs argue against statesmen who had heard their predecessors' allegations and who had vindicated the accused. Charges that Caecilianists were spineless—*traditores* or the friends of such traitors—would be heard again, and dismissed.

Augustine almost certainly expected the tribune to have a predilection for consistency that could only have told against the Donatists' case. Moreover, if the Donatists were persuasive and prevailed, their sense that every sacrament performed by their opposition was invalid would have made for utter confusion in the Christian empire. If Catholic Christianity's ordinations and consecrations were charades, Africa was filled with ineffective priests and bogus bishops. And Marcellinus would have collaborated in flooding the provinces with doubts about the clergy as well as about the quality or validity of the church's sacraments. Augustine's position, articulated against Donatists and—later—Pelagians, must have seemed to be more reasonable. Turning one of the former's favorite analogies against them, he agreed that the world was in a terrible condition and that the church was a refuge. But no sanctuary or ark could seal off imperfection. As Noah's ark accommodated both crows and doves, the churches contained laity and clergy whose virtues, when sifted at the final judgment, would be deemed exceptional or found wanting, if they were found at all.[74] Augustine reiterated his case along those lines during the council yet reinforced the tribune's procedural decision by throwing down the gauntlet; dissidents must either present new evidence that previous verdicts that favored Caecilian's party were mistaken or Marcellinus must consign the entire affair, *de re tota*, to history and ratify the acquittals.[75] Augustine, during deliberations, repeated his charges that the Donatists were unwise and uncharitable,

---

73. Ibid., 3.20: *conlatores magis quam litigatores*.

74. Augustine, *In Evangelium Joannis tractatus* 6.2: *quia necesse est ut in isto diluvio saeculi utrumque genus contineat Ecclesia, et corvum, et columbam*.

75. *Actes de la conférence* 3.110.

but he made no effort to relieve them of the plaintiffs' obligation and turn them into defendants. For it was incumbent on the plaintiffs to present new, compelling evidence that Catholic Christianity's existence in fifth-century Africa derived from a false start—or to yield.[76]

Before proceedings opened Catholic Christian prelates wanted to impress Marcellinus with their benevolence. Although they likely assumed his gavel would work to their advantage, they formulated and sent him concessions that would have appealed to the government's interest in unity. They offered Marcellinus and the dissident bishops a plan according to which the latter would be allowed to retain their sees while uniting with Catholic Christian colleagues (*nobiscum teneant unitatem*).[77] If Marcellinus found in favor of Donatists, the concession would have been moot. Catholic Christian prelates promised to resign. Better to restore unity than to cling to their positions, they declared, presumably after having cleared their tactics with Augustine, who may have scripted their proposal. Its argument was fashioned to appeal to statesmen who appreciated the values of unity and continuity. The Catholic Christians made that appeal explicit by recalling that the first verdicts against their rivals were delivered just as Christianity had gotten a toehold at Court, a few years after Emperor Constantine had converted. Since then, Catholic Christianity fortified its hold over the imaginations and allegiances of inhabitants in a large part of the world and seemed to some to be on the threshold of completing its conquest of the rest. If Marcellinus revisited the Donatists' original complaints and found them cogent, the authors of the letter confided that they and the other Catholic Christian bishops in Africa were ready not only to resign their sees—as noted—but also to resign themselves to the finding that the sole authentic fragment of the faith belonged to fourth-century critics of Caecilian and their Donatist heirs, whose practices and pretensions were quite distinct from those of the immensely successful, universal church. Could Marcellinus have failed to realize that, on this count, his Catholic Christian correspondents were disingenuous? Possibly, for they were cleverly so and had annexed to their contingency plans—to word of their readiness for defeat and retreat—a fairly detailed scheme that merged the ministries of the rival factions when Marcellinus found in their favor. One suspects that the purpose was to discourage the tribune from proposing a two-church solution by substituting a two-bishop resolution. According to that plan,

76. Ibid., 3.115–16.
77. Augustine, epistle 128.2.

when Marcellinus found in favor of Catholic Christianity, Donatist and Catholic bishops would preside in their respective basilicas in the presence of their former rivals and welcome them as colleagues. Seating as well as some liturgical arrangements would signal the preeminence of incumbent bishops, who, if formerly Donatists, would demonstrate that they accepted Marcellinus' and thus the council's condemnation of their previous convictions by the affection they showed their new colleagues.[78]

The council adjourned in June 411. Donatist bishops, having refused to consider the two-bishops-one-church solution, returned to their sees. Early in 412, Marcellinus circulated an edict making it a crime to remain a Donatist and assessing fines against sectarian clergy and laity who did not comply and conform. The tribune was commissioned to stay in Africa and granted near proconsular powers, in part, one infers, to oversee the edict's enforcement.[79] Petilian, the Donatist bishop of Cirta in Numidia, one of his faction's outspoken prelates at the council, had anticipated its outcome and fell back on the dissidents' refrain, decrying their rivals' ostensible alliance with statesmen. Petilian thought it lunacy to hitch African Christianity's fate to "the state." Catholic Christianity not only had done so, Petilian said, but also had encouraged the government representatives with lethal rhetoric (*lingua carnifice*), to lethal effect. Naturally, Augustine saw developments differently. The regimes in Rome and Africa were Babylon, he conceded, yet they could be served by emissaries from Jerusalem. The conflicts between terrestrial and celestial cities, in time, never ceased, but even when the former persecuted the latter, citizens of the pilgrim celestial city should allow themselves to be pressed into service. The precedent had been set by Shadrach, Meshach, and Abednego, whom Nebuchadnezzar had promoted to positions of authority. Augustine admitted it was more common in the Bible and in the first few centuries of the church's history to have the unsavory (*cives malae civitatis*) govern Jerusalem, but times had changed; increasingly, Christians carried on the business of Babylon as judges, magistrates, and military commanders—not to mention, as emperors. Marcellinus was in good company. The faith was well served by faithful statesmen.[80]

---

78. Ibid., 2–3.

79. Moreau, *Le dossier Marcellinus*, 114–15.

80. Compare Augustine, *Enarrationes in Psalmos* 61.8, citing Dan 3:30 with Augustine, *Contra litteras Petiliani Donatistae* 2.93,202.

The result in this case, as in others—notably, in Emperor Theodosius'—however, fell well shy of a comprehensive remedy for humanity's servitude to envy and ambition. Concluding his *City of God*, Augustine stipulated that despite God's grace, which afforded only a foretaste of celestial blessings, there was no liberation from the hell on earth created by ineradicable sinful instincts.[81] There were consolations (*solacia*) this side of the grave. Humans were creative and procreative. Their networks of arteries and veins attested the creator's craftsmanship. Humanity was inventive; wit occasionally was put to odd uses, defending fanciful ideas, but it powered the arts and sciences. Improvements in health care and navigation as well as culinary advances made humanity seem convalescent and not fatally ill and ill-tempered. Conspicuously absent from the *City*'s list of consolations or advances, however, was meaningful political melioration.[82]

Had Marcellinus not fallen victim to what has been described as a political "witch-hunt" soon after the Council of Carthage adjourned, Augustine's *City of God* might have conveyed a rosier picture of political culture. But he was profoundly disturbed by the tribune's misfortune. We know too little about the charges against Marcellinus to separate fact from fantasy, but we know that the Roman senate became frightened in 413, soon after Heraclian had been appointed consul and had sailed from Africa to Ostia with a large fleet. The possibility that the new consul intended to replace Emperor Honorius alarmed the Court. Troops commanded by Count Marinus were sent to intercept Heraclian, who was defeated, pursued to Africa, and executed. The senate or emperor directed Marinus to mop up what was left of the suspected rebellion, and enemies of both Marcellinus and his brother, Proconsul Apringius, seized their chance to accuse the two and be rid of them.[83] After their execution Augustine posted a brief account of what he considered a tragedy to the man who advised Marinus during the purge and who succeeded Marcellinus as special envoy. Although the letter exonerated Marcellinus and his brother, Augustine prudently was stingy with details. Still, it is impossible to miss the sense of dread, which corresponds with his and his *City*'s general sentiments about this world's wickedness and the unsavory business of Babylon, because Augustine closed the letter

---

81. Augustine, *De civitate Dei* 22.22: *ab hujus tam miserae quasi quibusquam inferis vitae non liberat nisi gratia.*

82. Ibid., 22.24.

83. Oost, "Revolt of Heraclian," 239–41.

with the lament that the malice of a single informant (*uno teste*) had been allowed to put the innocent in jeopardy.[84]

Marcellinus and Apringius were officially, posthumously vindicated. The regime had refused to circulate pardons, Augustine explained, because their issue would have implied that the two had been Heraclian's accomplices. The letter to Marcellinus' successor was unsparing; the deceased tribune's courage, piety, and—of course—innocence were trumpeted, and Marinus' insensitivity and ignobility were underscored. He had currishly deceived and demoralized the church, Augustine said; he had promised to delay Marcellinus' and Apringius' executions to accommodate bishops who were formulating an appeal, only to hasten their deaths on hearing that an African prelate was en route to the emperor in Ravenna.[85] The loss of those two valued allies in the African provinces, in effect, disarmed Catholic Christianity. Augustine and his colleagues had counted on Marcellinus to enforce edicts against the Donatists. For nothing discredited the faith as effectively as schisms. The secessionists were plagued by secessions, which delighted Christianity's pagan critics (but on which Augustine's polemics capitalized).[86] The saber-rattling that accompanied every controversy proved to its enemies that Christianity was incapable of achieving consensus. Augustine knew that among Christians and pagans alike, fissures in the history of any cult, especially those that led to enduring divisions, were the devil's work.[87] Marcellinus' death struck him as a blow that made more remote the possibilities for the reunification of African Christianity. Political intrigue, to his mind, had exacted a terrible price.

Claude Lepelley agrees that Marcellinus' fate confirmed Augustine's pessimism about political culture.[88] He may have been recalling Marinus' purge and drawing on his own reserves of resentment when he echoed Terence's pronouncement in his *City of God*, claiming that enmity and treachery so filled the world that every peace was impermanent. Statesmen's honor seemed to govern policy, but the ulterior motives of those who professed to favor peace and to negotiate suitable settlements to preserve it usually dictated changes of course destabilizing whatever peace was in

---

84. Augustine, epistle 151.4.
85. Ibid., 10–11: *atrociter contristavit Ecclesiam*.
86. See, for example, Augustine, sermon 71.4.
87. Sieben, "Augustins Auseinandersetzung," 195–96, 248.
88. Lepelley, "Augustine face à la christianisation," 277–78.

place.[89] Christoph Hugoniot correctly concludes that the crisis in 413 reinforced Augustine's ambivalence about government service, an ambivalence that Hugoniot traces to Augustine's work as orator and politicians' publicist in Milan. Augustine admitted that he was unhappy with his character and career path. He wearied of dragging—or of having been dragged by—his ambition from Rome (*trahens infelicitatis meae sarcinam*), and, we learned, he despised the immodesty of his clients even as—and presumably because—his advancement then depended on his stocking his speeches about their virtues with lies.[90] Yet, later, when he returned to Africa and became a bishop, he had to avoid letting his resentments ripen into rejections of the authorities. Their assistance was critical if Catholic Christianity's critics were to be answered effectively and perhaps silenced. Moreover, as pastor, Augustine could hardly have excluded municipal elites and other officials from his flock without betraying his vocation and without seeming to be more perfectionist than his Donatist and Pelagian adversaries.

Yet Augustine was known to have protested the immunities statesmen enjoyed. They were a breed apart. They scoffed at excommunications. They counted on their status to protect them from confinement or from corporal punishment, to which others who offended as they did were subject. During the 420s, Augustine sent a memorandum to Alypius, his friend and by then his fellow bishop, deploring the exemptions that enabled political elites to sin with impunity. He cited the example of a municipal official who dared to appeal to the bishop of Rome against the local cleric in Africa who had flogged him for seducing a nun. The seducer, it seems, had every expectation that the man who punished him would be punished for trampling on a privilege enjoyed by men of standing. Augustine was thunderstruck; he predicted to Alypius that the highly placed would soon be dancing in churches. There was no telling what an atrociously indiscreet yet influential person might yet do, if traditional immunities went unchallenged.[91]

The Marcellinus who seems to have lived on in Augustine's memory and who surfaces in his correspondence was unimpeachable. Conceivably, Augustine counted on him to alter African officials' sensibilities and, as imperial commissioner, to trim those time-honored immunities that subverted discipline. He likely would have enforced the prohibitions he composed

89. Augustine, *De civitate Dei* 19.5.

90. Augustine, *Confessiones* 6.6,9 and 8.7,17 (*tanto exsecrabilius me . . . oderam*) and Hugoniot, "Les légats du proconsul d'Afrique," 2067.

91. Augustine, epistle 9*.2; Lepelley, *Aspects de l'Afrique romaine*, 363–64; Brown, *Power and Persuasion*, 52–53.

and circulated to reunify the African church. Historian Émilienne Demougeot imagines Augustine regretting that local and provincial authorities were relatively uninterested in preventing the Donatists' resurgence in the wake of Marcellinus' execution. Had he lived, local magistrates might have guarded more zealously the ground Catholic Christian prelates thought they gained from their sectarian rivals at the Council of Carthage.[92]

Marcellinus was also missed because he had served as something of a stand-in for the governing elites. He was a perfect interlocutor, a pragmatic statesman who challenged Augustine to make sense of Catholic Christianity's more controversial doctrines and, therefore, to anticipate and undermine the Pelagians' appeal to highly placed officials. The tribune arrived in Africa at about the same time as did the pamphlets and partisans bearing Pelagius' ideas. Marcellinus had not shied from asking hard questions. At his instigation, Augustine drafted his most energetic and emphatic rebuttal to Pelagians, whom he called the enemies of God's grace. Marcellinus required explanations. His inquiries prompted Augustine to educate statesmen, whose linear, logical thinking prepared them to direct policy but also inclined them to Pelagians' expositions of Christianity's mysteries, expositions that were simple, straightforward, and—Augustine said—inaccurate. In matters of faith, simple or logical explanations were sometimes untenable. It took nerve and nuance, even with influential backing, to disclose how God's direction of history did not rob humans of their freedoms.[93]

The expectations just attributed to Augustine as well as the questions Marcellinus raised for (or relayed to) him can lead scholars to exaggerate their intimacy. Madelaine Moreau thinks that they were "constant companions." Neil McLynn supposes Augustine hoped he might "gain purchase on the governing elite of the empire" in Marcellinus' company. But McLynn's footing seems more secure when he suggests that, after the tribune had been exonerated and Augustine had dedicated his *City of God* to him, he was gratified to have a magistrate-cum-martyr on the title page of his tome, which recommended that statesmen cultivate martyrs' sentiments.[94]

---

92. Demougeot, *De l'unité à la division*, 555.

93. Augustine, *Retractionum libri duo* 2.37,64; Augustine, *De spiritu et littera* 30.52.

94. Moreau, *Le dossier Marcellinus*, 171–73; McLynn, "Augustine's Roman Empire," 42–43; Augustine, *De civitate Dei* 5.14–16.

Counseling Statesmen

That recommendation resurfaced often in Augustine's pastoral counsel. The martyrs' mentality was urged on ordinary as well as politically influential parishioners. But counseling the latter, Augustine may have more conspicuously registered his mistrust of moral clarity, as Charles Mathewes suggests, because statesmen usually placed inordinately high priorities on material gain and glory as they formulated and implemented policy. But Mathewes's claim that Augustine's mistrust of even ostensibly high-minded motives made choices in this wicked world "always morally ambiguous" does not appear to withstand close scrutiny.[95] Martyrs' sentiments and virtues were unambiguous, as were Augustine's commendations of them, which, to an extent, applied the ethos of the celestial city to circumstances statesmen encountered in terrestrial cities, provinces, and imperial chanceries. So Augustine answers to Christoph Horn's descripion of "an eschatological moralist."[96] As Otfried Höffe maintains, the place that Augustine reserved in his thinking for eschatological or celestial perspectives may have privatized or personalized virtue, yet it incontestably relativized the state. No form of government was normative.[97] The contours of political culture that preoccupied statesmen and political theorists were irrelevant; Augustine announced in his *City* that it should not matter to Christians who was ruling or how they ruled as long as their rule did not impose on their subjects an obligation to be impious.[98]

A few years before he set aside the form or structure of government operations as if they did not matter, Augustine wrote to colleagues about the difficulties that church statesmen faced. His assessment could just as easily have been about problems facing secular magistrates. Causes affecting their neighbors' interests came before both sets of justices. So the decisions of both sets ordinarily angered plaintiffs or defendants aversely affected by them. Statesmen were thought by some to be not only mistaken but mean-spirited. Uncertainties plagued the process. To serve the interests of some against those of others, Augustine admitted, left magistrates exposed, because they had to proceed with what must necessarily be only partial knowledge of choices that petitioners or plaintiffs made and with

---

95. Mathewes, *Republic of Grace*, 214–15.
96. Horn, "Augustinus über politische Ethik," 65.
97. Höffe, "Positivismus plus Moralismus," 287.
98. Augustine, *De civitate Dei* 5.17.

no sense of their hidden deficiencies and infirmities (*occultissimas*; *infirmitates*). Angry litigants might well misjudge justices' meanness, but it proved impossible to guard against mistakes. The best course, Augustine said, was to serve interests that corresponded with the hopes and compassion associated with the celestial city. Statesmen, at their best, in his opinion, served pilgrims forced—for a time, in time—into the business of Babylon rather than the interests of any terrestrial state.[99]

Augustine set the dichotomies between pilgrims' (or Jerusalem's) expectations and Babylon's outlook in fascinating fashion, yet they may have had less connection with or bearing on statesmen and parishioners than he would have wanted. Historian Eric Rebillard's contention rings true: "Bishops . . . forced the distinction between religious and secular on their [indifferent] congregations." Rebillard files a brief for "the intermittency of Christianness" in late antiquity. He proposes that the on-again, off-again character of religious commitment was "structurally consistent [with] the everyday life of Christians" and that the categories highly placed prelates used to shape their challenges and pastoral counseling did not match views from the pews. Rebillard's proposition, however, does not tell against the value of those categories for understanding Augustine's look at leadership.[100]

The categories and contrast come out clearly in one of the most notorious passages in Augustine's *City of God*, which compares politics to piracy. He borrowed a well-traveled story about Alexander the Great's conversation with a pirate he had apprehended and asked why his ship sank other vessels after making off with their cargoes. The pirate replied that he had done just what Alexander did. It was called a crime when a single ship wreaked havoc but was called empire when fleets were afloat. Augustine put the pirate's punchline at the back end of his story, which followed an inquiry. Could it be that, *remota justitia*, justice removed, rule was larceny on a grand scale?[101] The anecdote was Augustine's answer; the buccaneer, his seer. So the question turned out to be a rather astounding accusation that put politics in its place, in no uncertain terms.

Statesmen who served their emperors were accomplices—hence, necessarily, scoundrels. The conclusion seems wholly inconsistent with Augustine's counsel that they think as martyrs while acting as magistrates,

---

99. Augustine, epistle 95.4–5; Clair, *Discerning the Good*, 99–102.

100. Rebillard, *Christians and Their Many Identities*, 96–97.

101. Augustine, *De civitate Dei* 4.4: *remota itaque justitia quid sunt regna nisi magna latrocinia?*

which is anything but transparent, but which sets the bar far too high, unless we translate his ablative absolute (*remota justitia*) as conditional. If or when no genuine justice survived in this wicked world, statesmen became pirates' apprentices. But the causal—not the conditional—reading (because there is no justice in this wicked world) is more consistent with Augustine's previous descriptions of the pervasiveness of the lust for domination. He explained earlier in the *City* that nearly every imperial, provincial, and municipal leader was so infected by lust and by self-love that genuine justice was unattainable in time. Alongside that explanation, the causal rather than the conditional reading becomes more compelling, if far less charitable, and, consequently, Augustine's *City of God* ought to be read as one symptom of his disenchantment with civic pieties. Certainly the pirate's passage—and, arguably, the *City* itself—considered statecraft per se not just morally objectionable but without moral foundation.[102]

The passions and ambitions of the powerful were not solely to blame for having turned government into a den of thieves. Although Augustine frequently criticized officials' unbridled pursuit of possessions and reputations, he understood that ordinary people as well as statesmen missed signals in sacred literature that humanity was created to be compassionate. Unfortunately, they formed entanglements that led them into the "temptations" against which Matthew's Gospel warned (6:13). Compassion should have overruled temptation, yet few knew as much. The Bible, after all, chronicled the creation of but one at the start. But Augustine elaborated, instructing that Adam's solo did not tell against the importance of compassion. His appearance alone was meant to alert humanity to the importance of unity. Genesis generally spoke of couples and, he went on, ought to inspire creatures to be companionable, not reclusive or contentious. Nonetheless, rancor ruled. People became envious, malicious, and gratingly discordant.[103] Augustine encountered many litigious parishioners in his court, and, as we learned discussing bishops' leadership, he detested that part of his job. But truculence was a constant feature of social interaction that, therefore, required and justified the existence of governments, notwithstanding their piracy. Magistrates were needed to adjudicate disputes and keep antagonism from spiraling out of control. Church officials, according to Augustine, were to assist with counsel. Macedonius, whom we

---

102. Augustine, *De civitate Dei* 2.21, for *vera justitia*. Also see Höffe, "Positivismus plus Moralismus," 265–66, and Kaufman, *Incorrectly Political*, 116–17.

103. Augustine, *De civitate Dei* 12.28.

already met in this chapter, was curious about the relative roles of statesmen and clerics. He was not unresponsive when Augustine asked him to pardon offenders. He wrote back, supposing that he and fellow magistrates were able, unaided, to ascertain whether anyone convicted in his court was beyond redemption—*nulla spes est*, when there was no hope for amendment. He suggested that clerical interference was inappropriate.[104]

Augustine did not think his intervention or counsel constituted interference. He assured Macedonius that he was not challenging the vicar's prerogatives or jurisdiction. Augustine had no desire to grandstand or assert the church's authority. He accepted the legitimacy of punitive measures Macedonius prescribed. He conceded that statesmen were needed to protect societies from their most unruly members and that fear of punishment tended to deter the sinister from assailing their virtuous neighbors. Asking Macedonius for clemency or amnesties, Augustine granted that recidivism could not be ruled out, that pardoned offenders might resist reintegration, and that unforeseeable and undesirable consequences might follow if the vicar agreed (*sequuntur aliquando quae nolumus*). But Augustine asked him to think of good results that ought to follow when pastors counseled magistrates on the prospects for rehabilitating convicted offenders and then counseled the offenders who had been given time to repent and reform.[105]

Generally, repentance and reformation followed because God was patient and merciful. When Julian of Eclanum crafted an answer to his insistence on infant baptism, Augustine let the premise stand: only a tyrant would punish promiscuously, and God was no tyrant. Clemency was part of God's plan, which reclaimed sinners.[106] Augustine anticipated Julian's maxim and related God's mercy to the principle he closely associated with Christianity's (especially with martyrs') morality: one should not conquer evil with evil and return injury for injury. Writing to Proconsul Apringius, he submitted that the stories of martyrs' fortitude were somehow stained when, in the name of justice, statesmen demanded their persecutors' blood.[107]

The letter to Apringius anticipated themes that Augustine replayed for Macedonius years later. But, in Madelaine Moreau's opinion, he was less

---

104. Augustine, epistle 152.2–3.

105. Augustine, epistle 153.18.

106. Augustine, *Contra Julianum opus imperfectum* 5.64,1: *liberalitas ergo in peccatores exercita abducit a malis*.

107. Augustine, epistle 134.3.

self-assured writing to the proconsul than he had been, or would be, corresponding with other magistrates. Yet Augustine could be excused, for he faced a formidable challenge. He was asking Apringius to spare some Donatist extremists who had confessed to mutilation and murder. Unprovoked, they attacked two Catholic Christian priests. Apprehended, they showed no remorse. The proconsul considered their lives forfeit, but Augustine reminded him that a reluctance to return wound for wound had been fundamental in his faith's response to wickedness from the first. Moreau's assessment of that reminder's tone—that it was tentative, yet solemn—seems to catch the first part of the letter's critical line but not the last: he asked as a Christian that a milder (*lenior*) punishment apply and, only then, warned as a bishop. If no milder measure were practicable, if execution was the only option, Augustine told Apringius that he would prefer to see the murderers set free, for vengeance would dishonor their victims.[108] To Apringius and, later, to Macedonius, he allowed that punishments protected society from scoundrels. Moreover, he held that they could also be therapeutic. Cruelty in some circumstances was a kindness; fathers struck their children whose delinquencies, if overlooked, developed into self-destructive as well as socially disruptive behavior.[109] Augustine was no categorical critic of draconian measures, he clarified; despite the biblical directives to return good for evil, some crimes and some characters called for grim discipline. Statesmen would benefit, nonetheless, if they let prelates sift circumstances and characters and advise on the appropriate responses.[110]

Augustine had no interest in supplanting secular magistrates. He was terribly unhappy umpiring disputes in his church's court, a chore he relinquished to a lieutenant late in his career. He was emphatic: rather than unseating or superseding statesmen, prelates ought to support and advise them. His sermon on the psalmist's lectures "to all who judge the earth" was an exercise in deflation. He reminded statesmen of their fallibility. They were no more than earth judging earth (*terra judicans terram*), or, as we might say today, statesmen with feet of clay, and they would be wise to confer with prelates. Without clerical counsel, Christian statesmen probably would forget that their faith dictated punishment of sins not sinners, in large part because the distinction was all but incomprehensible. Hence,

---

108. Ibid., epistle 134.2–4: *christianus judicem rogo, et christianum episcopus moneo*; Moreau, *Le dossier Marcellinus*, 39–40.

109. Augustine, sermon 13.9: *pater . . . quando ferit, amat*.

110. Augustine, epistle 153.19.

prelates' insights should be useful as magistrates determined how to punish piously and where they might find the extra patience when sinners were incorrigible and incessantly scuffled with authorities.[111]

Pondering Augustine's letters about punishments and pardons, Robert Dodaro aptly refers to Augustine's purpose as "broaden[ing]" all statesmen's "ethical horizons."[112] To parse that objective and to reinforce the distinction between counseling statesmen to develop personal dispositions and counseling them to develop social programs, we should look again at one letter to Marcellinus that vividly presents patience as a preeminent virtue. It begins with an admission that slowing statesmen's and victims' rush to revenge would always be a problem. The church's task was to explain that retribution risked more than the suspension of one virtue. Lose patience, and the temporal crowds out the celestial, jeopardizing peace of mind and peace on earth.[113] Augustine was relaying answers through Marcellinus to Proconsul Volusianus, who had posed questions about Christianity's compatibility with civic duty, specifically concentrating on the possibility that the directives to return good for evil would undermine local law enforcement and civil defense. Might Christianity's "turn the other cheek" leave unprotected those whom statesmen had been commissioned to protect? The unruly would rule, undeterred by the prospect of some reckoning. Augustine clarified: the other-cheek directive did not preclude self-defense. He added a predictable caveat, however: severity increased the likelihood of reprisals and stoked an all but uncontrollable fury that would probably prevent statesmen from promoting reconciliation effectively. Also in this letter to Volusianus, through Marcellinus, Augustine labored the limit he placed on counseling officials to get the word out: pastors aimed to prepare or sway statesmen's hearts. Social policy might change, if the ministry was successful in countenancing patience, pardons, repentance, and compassion. But, for Augustine, the changes were incidental—not central—to the pastors' and the faith's mission.[114]

111. Augustine, sermon 13.4–8. Augustine's distinction between punishments that help and those that harm surfaced often in his anti-Donatist treatises, sermons, and correspondence, because dissidents insisted that the punishments assessed against them amounted to persecution. For his typical responses, see Augustine, *Contra litteras Petiliani Donatistae* 2.89, 194–95; Augustine, epistle 93.8; and Lamirande, "Aux origines du dialogue," 217.

112. Dodaro, "*Ecclesia*," 246. Also see Clair, *Discerning the Good*, 148–52.

113. Augustine, epistle 138.12.

114. Ibid., 138.13: *denique ista praeceptae magis ad praeparationem cordis quae intus est, pertinere, quam ad opus quod in aperto fit.*

He supposed that statesmen who heeded the counselors Christianity supplied would undoubtedly give greater weight to constituents' long-term interests than to their preferences.[115] In 408, a few years before he wrote as much in a letter to Marcellinus, he scolded Nectarius of Calama for doing just the reverse. Nectarius appealed for Augustine's help, identifying himself with his clients' sense that poverty was a fate worse than death. Possidius, Calama's bishop, had left for Court to prevail upon the chancery to collect hefty fines from pagan offenders. Nectarius anxiously pressed Augustine to intervene, trusting that he could influence his colleague to drop the suit. Nectarius claimed he was interested in the prospects for peaceful coexistence between pagans and Christians, which would assuredly be undermined, he said, if the former were forced to forfeit considerable sums. If pagans were impoverished, he continued, tensions between them and the Calama Christians would be exacerbated. Hard feelings, he added, were no foundation for toleration.[116] We have already introduced the episode, discussed Nectarius' advocacy, and mentioned the ambiguities that plague efforts to establish his confessional commitments, but it will be useful to take a last look at his statesmanship and Augustine's response to contextualize the latter's views on political conduct and political culture.

Nectarius need not have been a Christian to have known Augustine urged the faithful to be compassionate. As Calama's advocate, therefore, he probably expected his appeal would get a favorable hearing in Hippo. Moreover, as either a member of Calama's *curia*—or as a friend of its members—he must have been aware that municipal elites in Africa were losing ground to bishops, notwithstanding assorted squabbles perpetuated by Catholic Christianity's rivalry with Donatists. Indeed, if Peter Brown is right, the rivalry may even have contributed to "the assertiveness of the churches in local society."[117] Yet, if Nectarius had assumed that Augustine would be supportive, he was sorely disappointed. He believed his argument had seized the moral high ground. Surely, restoring tolerance served the long-term interests of Calama's Christians and pagans alike. But Augustine defined "long-term" differently. Even if the pagans were permitted to retain their possessions and came grudgingly to abide the presence (or

---

115. Ibid., 14.

116. Augustine, epistle 103.3-4.

117. Brown, *Power and Persuasion*, 89. Imperial law did not explicitly require bishops' participation in municipal affairs until 409, the year after Nectarius approached Augustine; see Rapp, *Holy Bishops in Late Antiquity*, 288.

predominance) of Christians in Calama, their longest-term interests would be ill-served. Their poverty was likelier than prosperity to prompt them to repent; the threat of destitution generated feigned, insincere remorse. Augustine would have had Nectarius become a more discerning statesman, one prepared to free his Calama clients from their love of money, which Augustine elsewhere identified as a colossal obstacle to developing love for God and trust that celestial rewards awaited those who longed for them. The responsible statesman looked after constituents' longest-term interests and looked to create that longing.[118]

No Angels

Augustine left behind no master plan for deploying squadrons of statesmen as politically powerful evangelists, although, corresponding with Nectarius, he seems to have been trying to nag or scold one into existence. For his part, Nectarius was glad to read Augustine's description of celestial rewards (*libenter audivi*), he said, yet he proposed that fulfilling civic duties was one way to acquire them.[119] We have no evidence that Nectarius abandoned the notion and indulged Augustine. No statesman would have had an easy time indulging or gratifying Augustine, whose sermons against the spectacles prominent civic leaders were expected to sponsor, entertainments that reminded him of the old Roman cults, would have been difficult for them to abide. So local statesmen who may have wanted to oblige the bishop were, on one important matter, compelled to disoblige him as long as proconsular legates encouraged them to subsidize and preside over pageants in their cities' amphitheaters to build civic solidarity and remind Africa of Rome.[120] Most municipal officials in Africa, moreover, had to cope with a robust paganism, with which some were in sympathy. So it is hardly a mystery why the *curiales* in Calama were slow to respond to Christians' complaints about pagans' pageants, despite imperial edicts prohibiting them.[121] And the odds were against other statesmen clearing Augustine's bar by prying clients or constituents from their obsessions with possessions. Menus of

118. Augustine, epistle 104.9; Augustine, *In Evangelium Joannis tractatus* 40.10: *non amat multum nummum, qui amat Deum*.

119. Augustine, epistle 103.2.

120. Hugoniot, "Les légats du proconsul d'Afrique," 2069–72; Brown, *Through the Eye of the Needle*, 353–54.

121. See Augustine, epistle 91.8, and Shaw, *Sacred Violence*, 257.

what civil servants were expected to serve up would not have included the responsibilities Augustine urged on Nectarius. Officials in Africa probably would have agreed with the latter who exhibited an uncomplicated notion of what churches preaching mercy should and likely would do: bishops would forgive, inasmuch as forgiveness and redemption appeared to be central to their faith. How could they preach about pardons yet dispossess their neighbors for having insulted or injured them? Augustine's answers could only have appeased exceptional statesmen ready to acknowledge their other-than-secular responsibilities to relieve the sinners they served or ruled of the resources that enabled them to practice vices that kept them from the celestial city.[122]

Might either Emperor Theodosius or Marcellinus have complied? Augustine lavished time lecturing Nectarius, but did he expect him to convince his clients to repent as instructed? Statesmen ordinarily achieved mastery and reputations as advocates, magistrates, or rulers by having excelled at channeling their lust for domination to great effect—although only God knew to what ends—and promotions depended on their abilities to articulate and defend the prevailing preferences of their clients rather than on formulating a contrary, more abstract and theological interest. They were no angels. They had not been commissioned as apostles. The faithful were told by their sacred literature to obey those statesmen and to trust that their God's distribution of authority in political cultures was for the best, Augustine reminded them, adding that the faithful were pilgrims in an unfair world, in which the obedient would often be better persons than those whom they obeyed.[123]

They were not better because they were beyond ambition. Inordinate desires for fame, fortune, and power infected everyone. Numbers of the faithful were better than most statesmen because, finding themselves captives to lust, they refused to consent. Much like the Apostle Paul, they acknowledged their imperfection and declared war on concupiscence.[124] Augustine realized that pilgrims' subjection to self-absorbed statesmen was unjust, so it is no wonder he abandoned Cicero's definition of political culture, which was based on its pursuit of justice. The cornerstone of political

---

122. Augustine, epistles 91.10 and 104.11 and 16. Also see Weissenberg, *Friedenslehre des Augustinus*, 172–73.

123. Augustine, *Enarrationes in Psalmos* 124.7.

124. Augustine, sermon 154.3: *homo . . . vitium agnovit, bellum indixit, captivitatem invenit.*

practice in terrestrial cities, according to Augustine, was self-love. Having given rein to their ambition, successful statesmen were worse than their acquiescent subjects. The powerful created structures that committed them and their constituents to pursuits inferior to those the faithful knew to be ennobling. If the substance and tone of Augustine's remarks are any measure, they mistrusted authority, but Christianity sanctioned disobedience only when authorities demanded something contrary to the faith. And when the faithful were pressed into service, Augustine advised that their compliance be conditioned by their detachment.[125] For they should count on the sordid system they served winning over all who chased power and promotion. The bishop might well have concurred with Otfried Höffe, whose analysis of late antique leadership supposed that the politically prominent put in place secondary, "subsidiary forms of justice" for damage control. But, insofar as self-love had become the very foundation of political culture, in Augustine's view, that damage, dated to humanity's exile from the garden, could only be controlled and never undone or significantly repaired. Hence, whereas just outcomes occasionally came out, statesmen, who ought unfailingly to have reconciled factions, too frequently incited rivalries to divide and conquer. And statesmen whose powers extended to depriving subjects of property, standing, and life itself could exercise those powers—and too often would do so—with impunity.[126]

Augustine allowed for exceptions. He celebrated statesmen who drafted edicts against secessionists that echoed his sermons' justifications for an invasive policy. Vicar Macedonius, for one, explicitly condoned coercive measures by citing the long-term interests of the coerced and of the African church. Macedonius, Augustine said, had a magistrate's pen or—figuratively—sword in hand as he decreed punishments, but his mind was on the celestial city.[127] Presumably, Augustine hoped that his correspondence and sermons would curb the ruthlessness spawned by political ambition. In at least one instance a proconsul seemed to abet his confessional initiatives. Having agreed to restore a statue of Hercules at the request of pagans in Carthage, the proconsul shaved off its beard. Decapitation would have led to protests and made the proconsul's job more difficult. But a beard-

---

125. See, for example, Augustine, *De civitate Dei* 19.6, and Ruokanen, *Theology of Social Life*, 28, 69–76.

126. Höffe, "Positivismus plus Moralismus," 277.

127. Augustine, epistle 155.17: *ut te appareat in terreni judicis cingulo, non parva ex parte coelestem rempublicam cogitare.*

less Hercules alerted pagans to the government's waning support and let Christians know that their preachers' opposition to idolatry was having an effect. Augustine admired the tactic, delighted that the statue had become a symbol of idols' impotence.[128]

Augustine preached about the beardless Hercules, but there is no evidence he ever wrote to the proconsul or met with him. He was often in Carthage, but a proconsul's tenure ordinarily was brief—a matter of months rather than years—and, as we learned, Augustine had very limited access to the politically powerful. His friendship with Marcellinus was exceptional. He wrote a short, hopeful note to Darius, another statesman who had been sent from Rome to negotiate with insurgents in 428. Augustine knew him only by reputation, which was sufficiently impressive to have inspired him to imagine the emissary slaying war with words (*ipsa bella verbo occidere*).[129] The bishop advocated peace but realistically doubted that Christianity (or Christian statesmen) could achieve lasting peace.[130] Nothing that sublime could be expected from political culture in this wicked world, which, James Wetzel appreciates, was, for Augustine, mired "in materiality." Even at the courts or conferences, over which the likes of Darius, Macedonius, or Marcellinus presided, their "ragingly imperfect," often overwrought colleagues would be prowling for personal advantage, even if horrible consequences for the commonwealth attended their pursuits.[131]

Augustine scattered extended comments about this wicked world in his *City of God*, completed not long before Darius arrived in Africa and then the Arian Christian Vandals, who made Augustine's clutch of claims about evil days seem prophetic.[132] Early in his monumental work he conceded that the late Roman republic and early empire had achieved wonders, in part, because statesmen and soldiers sacrificed private interests for public profit. They accumulated tribute and territory. Their laws were reasonable, and Rome's prominent citizens valued honor and glory as well as wealth and power. Statesmen who built so well, Augustine said, ought to have had no cause to complain. They had received their reward (*perceperunt mer-*

---

128. For Hercules, see Augustine, sermon 24.6, and Oliveira, "*Ut maiores pagani non sint!*," 253–55. More generally, see Weissenberg, *Friedenslehre des Augustinus*, 228–30, and Dodaro, "Political and Theological Virtues," 442–43.

129. Augustine, epistle 229.2.

130. Curbelié, *La justice dans "La Cité de Dieu"*, 466–68. For one of Augustine's very rare spurts of optimism, see his epistle 138.10.

131. Wetzel, "Tangle of Two Cities," 7–12.

132. Augustine, *De civitate Dei* 18.49: *in hoc . . . saeculo maligno, in his diebus malis*.

cedem suam). Yet this line about the sufficiency of their reward obliquely refers to the lines in the Gospel of Matthew that refer to the good name or fame that hypocrites had earned by having given alms, although they gave grudgingly.[133] So, at precisely this point, the knowledgeable reader would have caught Augustine lathering his commendations with contempt. For he seems to have put Rome's glory—along with its statesmen's strategies and sacrifices—in comparative perspective, and the comparison plainly worked to the disadvantage of statesmen who labored long before—and in—his time for merely human glory (*propter hominum gloriam*).[134] Wolfgang Lienemann assumes that Augustine received numerous requests to formulate and circulate that perspective while some western parts of the empire were overrun.[135] Be that as it may, the bishop stressed that the faithful were pilgrims in this world but citizens of an imperishable, celestial city, the glory of which made Rome's terrestrial successes seem trifling.

Recall, then, as we near the conclusion of our chapter on Augustine's statesmen, that surviving correspondence suggests that he only infrequently wrote provincial governors and their legates, although their services in Numidia and Proconsular Africa brought them within his range. He "had no privileged access to the machinery of government," as Neil McLynn says; he "was groping through a fog in the hope of grasping and manipulating the dimly perceived [and] barely accessible levers of power." But "groping" may not be the right word. For McLynn's mention of manipulation suggests that Augustine wanted greater "pull" or influence than he had. A contrary case can be made, inasmuch as those "levers" were parts of the complicated political games he seems to have been uninterested in playing. Perhaps, then, he was not widely, warmly received by either local or provincial officials in Africa because—save for several sermons and a small pouch of his letters—his efforts to advise, lobby or just encourage statesmen were few. He volunteered no comprehensive social program and deposited candid, critical assessments of the "levers of power" into his *City of God*.[136]

There, at the end of the fifth book, we found his expressions of gratitude for the two fourth-century emperors who had dramatically improved the standing of Catholic Christianity. Augustine honored Constantine for his conversion, Theodosius for his character, and both for having undermined

133. Augustine, *De civitate Dei* 5.15, suggesting Matt 6:2.
134. Ibid., 5.16.
135. Lienemann, "Eschatologik als Antipolitik?," 415.
136. Compare McLynn, "Augustine's Roman Empire," 40.

the prestige and abridged the prerogatives of Rome's old cults.[137] When support from the Court across the Mediterranean became more routine and occasionally less reliable—certainly less spectacular—Augustine went on attributing Christianity's successes to statesmen who served both the empire and what he took to be God's purposes. His colleagues generally agreed. But Bishop Hesychius of Salona surveyed the history of his faith's progress, presuming that it had crested and that the end of history was near. Until persecutions ceased, Hesychius wrote to Augustine, Christianity's influence increased only slowly. Governments' support accelerated the religion's growth. Bishops and pastors spread the gospel everywhere, swiftly (*ubique in parvo tempore*). Yet the good times had gone, and, Hesychius said, doubts about the future of the brittle western empire after Valens' defeat in 378 and Alaric's sack of Rome in 410—and even their religion's apparent ubiquity—signaled the end of time.[138] Augustine believed that his correspondent had mistaken the signs of the time. The chaos and tribulation to which Hesychius referred bore no resemblance to what their scripture revealed about history's end. No, something more devastating was in store.[139]

Besides, Christianity had not finished growing, Augustine prophesied, and the fate of Christianity was not inextricably bound with that of the empire. Hesychius' diocese of Salona was on the Dalmatian Coast. From that vantage, the sudden changes precipitated by the Goths' crossing the Danube and their movement through Thrace and to the West might have appeared apocalyptic. Augustine suspected that Hesychius knew little about the extent of Christianity in Africa, where work remained for missionaries. Proconsuls and their legates replaced many tribal leaders in coastal provinces, and Christianity replaced indigenous cults. But, *interiores*, far from the Mediterranean, there were tribes that as yet knew nothing of the gospel. Augustine assured Hesychius that their faith eventually would reach them, because the psalmist, channeling God, promised that their church would extend to the ends of the earth. And going global, Augustine asserted, did not depend on Rome's survival as an empire.[140]

Equally to the point, the psalmist had not pledged that statesmen would continually assist bishops. Nor should Christians look to the

---

137. Augustine, *De civitate Dei* 5.25–26.
138. Augustine, epistle 198.5–6.
139. Augustine, epistle 199.37.
140. Ibid., 46–47, referring to Psalms 72:8 and 86:9.

psalmist or to other canonical authors for explanations of how the church could expand while what had become a defective empire contracted. Nothing would come of compiling a roster of possible ways and means; much of God's commerce with this wicked world would forever remain mysterious, according to Augustine, who advised trust rather than further investigation. God would fulfill what the psalmist promised. To be sure, the troubling times made it hard to maintain trust, yet Rome's setbacks were lessons. Not even the goodwill of emperors and other statesmen could give Christianity untroubled ascendancy. For, when the strains or troubles seemed less severe, then temptations arose, and pastors needed to preach patience, restraint, and compassion.[141]

Troubles and temptations did not cause Augustine to swerve from the theme his sermons and correspondence featured prominently. He stayed on message developing his justification for Catholic Christianity's alternative to what he perceived and detested as Donatists' and Pelagians' conceits. The message was unmistakable: churches should encourage the laity and clergy alike to confess and repent their sins. As Robert Dodaro registered, in exchanges with powerful figures in government and in the churches, Augustine forged "the link he want[ed] to establish between the humble acknowledgement of sinfulness and virtuous leaders."[142] Perhaps his sermons converted members of Hippo's *curia* and some *curiales* elsewhere. Might one say that he drew Marcellinus into his orbit? We know that his few brushes with highly placed statesmen did nothing to qualify his statements about pervasive, destructive ambition. His criticisms settle strangely alongside his censures of arrogant others who tended to think the worst of their associates, yet he persisted to berate figures who failed to live up to his high expectations. And a few bad apples, he preached, naturally caused one to dispraise the whole bushel. Remedies were at hand, of course; one need only to live humbly as one would want others to live.[143] By the time he wrote the last books of his *City*, if not before, he had lowered his expectations. He hoped statesmen would be moved to preserve what was left of the *pax Romana* and to protect the faithful who passed as pilgrims, as undistracted and undeterred as possible by troubles plaguing terrestrial cities.[144]

---

141. Augustine, sermon 335M.1: *Refrigium enim in hoc saeculo, cui, unde plena sunt omnia tribulationibus, et quando tribulationes parcunt, plena sunt temptationibus.*

142. Dodaro, *Christ and the Just Society*, 201–2.

143. Augustine, *Enarrationes in Psalmos* 30(3).7.

144. Augustine, *De civitate Dei* 19.7.

For their part, pilgrims would pray for their magistrates and peacekeepers, unbelievers as well as Christians pressed into secular service. To illustrate and inspire just that, Augustine recalled what the prophet Jeremiah told Israel in exile: Israel ought to pray for its captors—the faithful for their statesmen—for temporal peace maintained by the Babylonians and by Roman authorities in Africa engaged in "the business of Babylon" benefited the highly placed and the displaced alike.[145]

Augustine might have lowered his expectations yet never relented or significantly mellowed, after he had learned that statesmen neither were nor ever would be angels. He continued to pray that they might repent and preached to disquiet them, to arouse those who judge others ("the earth") to judge themselves.[146] His emphasis on introspection characterized his appeals, as it indelibly marks his general approach to religious development. But Otfried Höffe is likely right to conclude that a concentration on personal piety and on eschatological consolations for the demoralization occasioned by the apparent disintegration of the western empire came to eclipse Augustine's interests in statecraft. He often pivoted from thinking about magistrates to remembering martyrs.[147]

---

145. Ibid., 19.26, citing Jer 29:7.
146. Augustine *In Evangelium Joannis tractatus* 33.5: *se non perspicieabant*.
147. Höffe, "Positivismus plus Moralismus," 281.

Conclusion

DEVELOPMENTS DURING THE FIRST decades of the fifth century did not inspire faith in Roman statecraft. The empire's enemies continued crossing the Rhine frontier. Rome was sacked in 410 after negotiations with the Goths miscarried. Emperor Honorius fumbled often, and on his death in 423, the political climate in the old capital was stormy and remained so several years after his half-sister's six-year-old son was recognized as Emperor Valentinian III in 425. Textbooks generally associate his mother's reign as regent—and his own, which ended in 455—with the dismantling of the Western Empire. New lows seemed to follow, one after another.

During the late 420s Rome's panicky attention turned to Africa where Boniface, who commanded the regime's regiments there, was thought to be too powerful. Factions in the old capital feared he would cut off the grain supply to their city and further complicate its already disturbed state. Boniface feared that the Court would have his head. Either taking advantage of his predicament or at his invitation, Gaiseric led an army composed of Vandals and some Goths across the Strait of Gibraltar into Africa. He had his way, even before Boniface was recalled to Rome. Too little assistance from Constantinople came too late to make a difference. Augustine died shortly before—or just as—Gaiseric reached Hippo, which was besieged for more than a year and then taken (430–31). The Vandals occupied Carthage by 439.[1]

They were Arian Christians. During his career, Augustine had tried to undermine the force of the Arians' opposition to the christological settlement reached at the Council of Nicaea in 325. He acknowledged that the formula sanctioned there contained extrabiblical terminology but argued the propriety of the bishops having done so. Correspondence making that

---

1. Berndt, *Konflikt und Anpassung*, 133–34; Shaw, *Sacred Violence*, 772–73.

point could be dated to the late 420s.² Yet there is no sign that Augustine had anticipated the Vandals' invasion or the brutality with which they ousted pro-Nicene clergy. Later in the fifth century, Victor of Vita chronicled Gaiseric's savagery, suggesting wholesale slaughter.³ Perhaps the Vandals were as ruthless in the early stages of their campaign, as Victor reported, but they soon settled alongside their new neighbors. Native Africans who had resented Roman control possibly welcomed them. But Augustine's colleagues, refusing to disavow Nicene Christology, seemed to find their situation suffocating (*in medio Wandalorum nostri nullatenus respirant*).⁴ Still, the scholarly consensus is that "the decline of Roman Africa was . . . less pronounced than that of the rest of the Western Empire." Commerce with Europe and with the East was pretty much uninterrupted. Municipal administration ran smoothly.⁵

But significant changes in municipal government preceded the Vandals' conquests. Decisions during the late fourth century increasingly were made at Court, which eroded the cities' autonomy. At roughly the same time, economic burdens dissuaded elites from public service, as did what Bryan Ward-Perkins calls "the collapse of security." As we noted in the chapter on Augustine's statesmen, bishops often informally assumed greater responsibilities; Peter Brown refers to them as "the new urban leadership."⁶ It is hard to imagine Augustine becoming enthusiastic about such developments. Grin-and-bear may have characterized his compliance until he surrendered his daily duties to his successor in 426.⁷ We have already discussed his repudiation of political ambitions; the officials who inspired him to do so found prominent places in his *Confessions*, where the selflessness of the ascetic Saint Anthony made several statesmen (and later Augustine) thoroughly ashamed (*repletus pudore*) of their grasping for

---

2. Augustine, epistle 238.4–5. For dating, see Heil, "Antiarianisches in den neutestamentlichen Predigten," 379.

3. Victor of Vita, *Historia persecutionis* 1.5: *praeclari pontifices et nobiles sacerdotes, diversis poenarum generibus extincti sunt.*

4. Ibid., 1.22. Shaw (*Sacred Violence*, 802–3) reminds us that Donatist bishops as well as Catholic Christian prelates were "blindsided by forces that were beyond their . . . comprehension . . . or control."

5. Berndt, *Konflikt und Anpassung*, 186; Mattingly and Hitchner, "Roman Africa," 210–11.

6. Brown, *Power and Persuasion*, 77; Ward-Perkins, "Cities," 409. Also see Rapp, *Holy Bishops in Late Antiquity*, 286.

7. Augustine, epistle 213.6.

Conclusion

glory.[8] Augustine learned from the fate of Marcellinus, if not before, how precarious both patronage and position had become in the empire's African provinces. Presumably, he became resigned to the inevitability that highly placed prelates would assume civic responsibilities as secular elites backed away from them. Parishioners and, perhaps, other locals turned to their cities' bishops in times of political crisis, in Africa, as others did in Gaul. With the Vandals, North Africans, particularly Nicene clergy, faced crisis and, as just noted, jeopardy.

At least one Numidian bishop turned to Augustine to resolve a dilemma posed both by the Vandals' progress and by what seemed to be conflicting counsel offered by sacred literature. Jesus explicitly told his disciples to flee persecutors yet also seemed to warn against abandoning their posts. Augustine explained that the disciples' ministry was mission. Their assignment kept them on the road. Unlike most fifth-century bishops and pastors, they were itinerants. They had no settled congregations, which, in times of crisis, especially needed to have their pastors close; Honoratus and his colleagues could hardly be dutiful and simultaneously oblivious to the laity's fears as the Vandals approached. Yet the latter, at their worst, Augustine continued, would only threaten the corporeal wellbeing of the faithful. Parishioners' spiritual welfare would only be in danger if clerical leaders left their sheep.[9] Augustine anticipated some questions raised during and after previous persecutions. Was discretion the better part of valor? Or was Bishop Cyprian wrong to have fled Carthage in the third century during the Decian persecution so that the church's enemies could not claim its leadership among their victims? Had he been imprudent years later, remaining to face persecutors and lose his life? Might one argue that escape was the only responsible option, insofar as it enabled the ministry to revive when refugee bishops returned? Incumbents' deaths, noble as they were, invited squabbles over succession once persecutions concluded. Augustine discussed several options to immediate evacuation. Clerics might leave with their parishioners, he said, if they all agreed to go. And, should swarms of hostiles attack, mass exodus might be the only viable option for congregations. Yet, if some stayed and were likely to survive, Honoratus ought to trust resourceful laity to conceal their bishops and other pastors, Augustine

---

8. Augustine, *Confessiones* 8.6,15.
9. Augustine, epistle 228.2–6, discussing Matt 10:23 and John 10:12–13.

said, adding that the remnant, in distress and *in situ*, would have need for clerical leaders—for consolation and inspiration to keep the faith.[10]

The letter to Honoratus nowhere mentions magistrates and suggests Augustine's abiding respect for martyrs. The Vandals, in effect, became an occasion to repeat the theme he had been featuring forthrightly since Marcellinus' murder and, arguably, from the time he abandoned his political ambitions in Milan: leaders who emulated martyrs' humility, compassion, and courage were what the church wanted at all times and needed in trying times. They were what Pierre-Marie Hombert, presuming to channel Augustine, calls "living examples of grace."[11] Their presence among the faithful (and in memory) reminded Christians of their predicament, one that the Vandals' invasion, the empire's setbacks in Europe, and even the dissidents' and delinquents' assaults on Catholic Christianity dramatized: history was not reliably, consistently on the side of the pious, so to speak. Augustine told them to prepare for periodic harassment. Citizens of the celestial city on pilgrimage in time were different from many of their neighbors whose intolerance of that difference surfaced in relatively harmless disrespectful remarks but could also erupt in violence that required a strong faith to endure. There was no escaping the predicament: Christians were pilgrims in a persecuting world (*mundus persequens*).[12]

Augustine preached about the near-permanent persecution or harassment for at least ten years before he finished composing his *City of God* and, responding to the Pelagians, decided to put pilgrims' proper response to their predicament—stamina or grit—in theological perspective. Pelagius and his colleagues were persuading Christians to take credit for their determination to persevere—for their grit. But Augustine saw their initiative as a threat to divine sovereignty. He figured that Pelagians and those they persuaded looked for reasons to forget their frailties. The truth, he went on, was that the trespass of their first parents made their progeny—all humanity—weak-willed.[13] They were too coarse to be constant. Their perseverance, therefore, was a gift from God, as was faith. The latter was given so

---

10. Ibid., 11–13.

11. Hombert, "Augustin, prédicateur de la grâce," 241. Also see Zocca, "La figura del santo vescovo," 90–91.

12. Augustine, *De civitate Dei* 14.28 and 15.2; Augustine, sermon 96.7–8.

13. Augustine, *De dono perseverentiae* 5.8. Wetzel suggests Augustine considered the forgetful to be "fifth column Pelagians" (*Augustine and the Limits of Virtue*, 161).

Conclusion

that Christians could draw close to God (*ut accedamus*); and the former, so they would not withdraw from God (*ne discedamus*).[14]

The faithful prayed for fortitude in a persecuting world, and Pelagians—ignorant of how powerless creatures were—interpreted prayer as worthy of reward. Augustine deplored that turn; prayers, he knew, were far from superfluous, but Pelagians' interpretations only displayed their stepped-up self-reliance. For Augustine, prayers were of paramount importance because they reminded the prayerful of their unworthiness, of the gratuity of the faith they received, and of God's responsibility for the fortitude or perseverance they practiced.[15] So their perseverance, one could say, was theirs and not theirs. God predestined their ordeals, from murderous assaults to petty insults, but God also provided pilgrims with the resolve and resilience to bear them—and with a foretaste of the celestial city. Not all the faithful received such gifts in equal and sufficient measure, and those who ceased to profess their faith under duress tempted the persistent to claim too much credit for their persistence. Augustine advised that they should rather rejoice in God's choice, trusting that it had favored them (and not others) without respect to merits.[16] He knew why the faithful and favored found their good fortune hard to accept humbly. Their hardships tested them, as did the mysteries of their election and their endurance. But pilgrims could not rely on pastors to offer reasons for God's decisions. That some rather than all received the gift (or grace) of perseverance was and would remain as unknowable (*inscrutabilia*) as the reasons God led the Vandals to Africa and the Goths to Rome.[17]

In a sermon preached at about the time news of Alaric's descent into Italy had reached Africa, Augustine suggested that his contemporaries were doomed to improvise stuttering efforts to survive among the ruins of an empire built by Romans' lusts. Debris was their inheritance, yet Christians lived in hope of a new inheritance (*novam hereditatem speras*). They were still subject to the devastation and aftershocks but had divested or decathected and therefore had been able to keep relatively calm.[18] Another of Augustine's sermons held that the coherence and endurance of congregations depended as much on parishioners' courage as on the leadership of

14. Augustine, *De dono perseverentiae* 7.14.
15. Ibid., 7.15.
16. Ibid., 13.33.
17. Ibid., 8.18.
18. Augustine, sermon 25.2.

bishops or pastors, although the clergy, as we learned, would have to see to it that the laity was inspired to sow good works to keep their communities viable.[19] Predictably, alms were important, but the bishop defined the seeds to be sown more broadly. Often, he noted, the poor would be sturdier than the well-off, whose pampering ill prepared them for crises. Is it altogether improbable that he had future crises in mind as he tried to create conditions in which a sensitivity to the various needs of others pervaded congregations? During normal times, sensitivity of that sort would be hard to sustain. Temptations to look after oneself or one's family must have overcome impulses to be more comprehensively generous. Also, as Augustine said, the lusts to possess or dominate obliterated desires to cooperate. But to signal that he was not preaching in or about normal times, he referred to a conscientious farmer, undeterred by sudden squalls (*imber*) or icy winds (*frigidus ventus*) from sowing his seeds. Nor did all the gloom Augustine packed into his sermon daunt or deter his farmer. Sowing compassion was too important, for it united Christian communities when heavy weather in this "persecuting world" came upon them.[20]

Robert Markus concludes that Augustine, during his first years as bishop, was pleased with "the sudden acceleration" of what had been "the gradual Christianization" of the empire after Constantine's conversion.[21] In 391, Emperor Theodosius seemed to have kick-started a brisk campaign against idolatry and heresy. From that time, edicts from the imperial chancery endorsed Catholic Christian orthodoxy. But Augustine, as we discovered, stopped well short of endorsing or extolling political culture, perhaps because enforcement of government edicts was uneven. Markus, however, sees things differently. He claims that Augustine initially participated in the "euphoria" that attended and followed Theodosius' prohibition of public pagan worship as well as the Court's other restrictive measures in the early 390s. That participation diminished, he allows, noting that Augustine's *City of God* would later deflate Christianity's political optimism, wreck its theological premises, and profess "radical agnosticism about God's purposes in human history."[22] Markus's observations of subsequent developments seem sound. But what appears to have been Augustine's political disenchantment—and, arguably, his cynicism—originated in Milan during the

---

19. Augustine, *Enarrationes in Psalmos* 125.11.
20. Ibid., 13: *compingitur et adunantur in caritate*.
21. Markus, "*Tempora Christiana* Revisited," 202–3.
22. Ibid., 206–7.

Conclusion

mid-380s, if we may trust his *Confessions*. Marcellinus' fate almost certainly shored up his discontent with political maneuvering, as—conceivably—did church politics, which locked African prelates in several struggles with Roman pontiffs and their legates.[23]

Yet church politics in Africa stirred Augustine and his Catholic Christian colleagues to maneuver government authorities into place to suppress Donatist dissidents. Sometimes all that was required was rhetoric, the deployment of terms that triggered provincial officals' concerns about confessional conflict leading to political disobedience and civil war.[24] Preaching against the Circumcellions, for example, Augustine took care to deny the self-styled martyrs the dignity they claimed for themselves, claims that their self-sacrifices replicated those of early Christians. To Augustine, the comparison (or supposed continuity) was absurd. Donatist extremists, he said, had been frenzied and dangerous rebels, from the start of their secession into the fifth century.[25] He was grateful for the government's commitments to prosecute them, although nothing he had experienced dealing with local or provincial officials—save, perhaps, his association with tribune Marcellinus—tempted him to reverse his earlier judgment about pervasive political deceit and hypocrisy. He berated prelatical as well as secular statesmen who failed to appreciate that the prestige and power of office paled before the experience of finding within oneself the gifts of God. Bishops' leadership as well as that of municipal and provincial authorities preserved the peace of churches where those discoveries were most often made, where pastoral leadership shaped the laity's inward searches for a set of dispositions worthy of pilgrims—for the love of God, love for the good, and compassion for others.[26] Those inward discoveries or sentiments raised seemingly endless questions that pastors could help frame but not satisfactorily answer. Nonetheless, Augustine would have had bishops and pastors preserve parishioners from the profusion of appalling errors that the Manichees, Donatists, and Pelagians promoted about incorruptibility or sanctity. Yet the truth about God's gratuitous redemption of imperfection resided within the faithful as faith and as God's love, along with the human compassion

---

23. Marschall (*Karthago und Rom*, 67–71, 184–203) characterizes the struggles as a battle for African autonomy (*autonomiebestrebungen*), but also consult Pietri, *Roma Christiana* 2:1271–75, and Merdinger, *Rome and the African Church*, 183–99.

24. Buenacasa Pérez and Villegas, "Agustín, autor intelectual," 643–44.

25. Augustine, sermons 62.17 and 313(E).7.

26. Augustine, *De civitate Dei* 11.28.

that God's compassion inspired; find those, Augustine preached, and the faithful would have no cause to celebrate leaders and make them celebrities—surely not Arius or Donatus—not even Augustine.[27]

---

27. Augustine, *Enarrationes in Psalmos* 149.4: *si . . . caritas ibi habitat, Deus ibi habitat. . . . laetetur non in Ario . . . non in Augustino.*

Bibliography

Primary Sources Cited

References to Augustine's treatises are given by title and the customary section divisions. References to his epistles and sermons are given by number and section. During the composition of this study I have consulted the two online editions, http://www.augustinus.it/latino/index.htm, which reproduces the edition in J. P. Migne's Patrologia, series Latina, and a subsequent edition of many of Augustine's treatises and correspondence in the Corpus Scriptorum Ecclesiasticorum Latinorum, http://www.earlymedievalmonasticism.org/Corpus-Scriptorum-Ecclesiasticorum-Latinorum.html. *Sermones nuper reperti* refers to the relatively recently discovered sermons edited by François Dolbeau, first published in 1996 but now available online with the Migne Patrologia.

Actes de la conférence de Carthage en 411. Edited by Serge Lancel. Paris: Cerf, 1972–91.
Ambrose. *Epistulae et acta*. Edited by Otto Faller. Vol. 1. Corpus Scriptorum Ecclesiasticorum Latinorum 82. Vienna, 1968.
———. *Expositio Evangelii secundam Lucam*. Edited by Carolus Shenkel. Corpus Scriptorum Ecclesiasticorum Latinorum 32. 1907.
———. *De fide*. Edited by Otto Faller. Corpus Scriptorum Ecclesiasticorum Latinorum 78. Vienna, Hoelder-Pichler-Tempsky, 1962.
———. *De obitu Theodosii*. Edited by Otto Faller. Corpus Scriptorum Ecclesiasticorum Latinorum 73. Vienna, 1955.
Hegemonius. *Acta Archelai (The Acts of Archelaus)*. Translated by Mark Vermes. Turnhout: Brepols, 2001.
Imperatoris Theodosii Codex. http://ancientrome.ru/ius/library/codex/theod/liber16.htm.
Possidius. *Sancti Augustini vita*. Edited by Herbert Weiskotten. Princeton: Princeton University Press, 1919.
Prudentius. *Contra Symmachum*. Edited by Hermann Tränkle. Turhout: Brepols, 2008.

Bibliography

Sozomenus. *Church History*. Revised by Chester D. Hartranft. In vol. 2 of *Nicene and Post-Nicene Fathers*, Series 2, 237–427. Reprint, Peabody, MA: Hendrickson, 1995.

Synesius. *De regno*. In vol. 2 of *Synesii Cyrenensis hymni et opuscula*, edited by Nicola Terzaghi. Rome: Typis Regiae Officinae Polygraphicae, 1944.

Themistius. *Orationes*. Edited by G. Downey and A. F. Norman. 3 vols. Leipzig: Teubner, 1965–74.

Victor of Vita. *Historia persecutionis africanae provinciae*. Edited by Michael Petschenig. Corpus Scriptorum Ecclesiasticorum Lationorum 7. Vienna, 1881.

Zosimus. *Historia nova*. Edited by François Paschoud. Paris: Les Belles Lettres, 1971–86.

Secondary Literature Cited

Alici, Luigi. "*Interrogatio mea, intentio mea*: Le movement de la pensée augustinienne." In *Augustin: Philosophe et prédicateur*, edited by Isabelle Bochet, 371–87. Paris: Institut d'études Augustiniennes, 2012.

Barnes, Timothy D. *Constantine and Eusebius*. Cambridge: Harvard University Press, 1981.

Barreteau-Revel, Cécile. "Faire l'unité dans l'Église d'Afrique du Nord: La réintegration des donatistes à la transition des IVe et Ve siècles." In *Les Pères de l'Église et les dissidents: Dissidence, exclusion, et réintégration dans les communautés chrétiennes des six premiers siècles*, edited by Pascal-Grégoire Delage, 223–59. Royan: CaritasPatrum, 2010.

BeDuhn, Jason David. *Augustine's Manichaean Dilemma*. 2 vols. Philadelphia: University of Pennsylvania Press, 2010–13.

Bénabou, Marcel. *La résistance africaine à la romanisation*. Paris: Maspero, 1976.

Berndt, Guido M. *Konflikt und Anpassung: Studien zu Migration und Ethnogenese der Vandalen*. Husum: Matthiesen, 2007.

Bowlin, John. "Augustine Counting Virtues." *Augustinian Studies* 41 (2010) 277–300.

Brandenburg, Hugo. "Die Eroberung Roms durch Alarich im Jahre 410 und ihre Folgen: Die Wohnbebauung, die öffentlichen Monumente der Stadt und der Kirchenbau des 5. Jahrhundert, einige Beobachtungen und Überlegungen." In *Roma e il sacco del 410: Realtà, interpretazione, mito*, edited by Angelo Di Berardino et al., 229–73. Rome: Institutum Patristicum Augustinianum, 2012.

Bretherton, Luke. *Resurrecting Democracy: Faith, Citizenship, and the Politics of Common Life*. Cambridge: Cambridge University Press, 2015.

Brown, Peter. *Augustine: A Biography*. Berkeley: University of California Press, 2000.

———. *The Cult of the Saints: Its Rise and Function in Latin Christianity*. Chicago: University of Chicago Press, 1981.

———. *Power and Persuasion in Late Antiquity: Towards a Christian Empire*. Madison: University of Wisconsin Press, 1992.

———. *Through the Eye of a Needle: Wealth, the Fall of Rome, and the Making of Christianity in the West*. Princeton: Princeton University Press, 2012.

Bruno, Michael J. S. *Political Augustinianism: Modern Interpretations of Augustine's Political Thought*. Minneapolis: Fortress, 2014.

Buenacasa Pérez, Carles, and Raúl Villegas. "Agustín, autor intelectual del texto del Edicto de Unión del 405." In *Lex et Religion*, edited by Vittorino Grossi, 617–45. Rome: Institutum Patristicum Augustinianum, 2013.

Bibliography

Burns, J. Patout. "Baptism as Dying and Rising with Christ in the Teaching of Augustine." *Journal of Early Christian Studies* 20 (2012) 407–38.
Byers, Sarah Catherine. *Perception, Sensibility, and Moral Motivation in Augustine: A Stoic-Platonic Synthesis*. Cambridge: Cambridge University Press, 2013.
Cameron, Alan. *The Last Pagans of Rome*. Oxford: Oxford University Press, 2011.
Capatano, Giovanni. "Leah and Rachel as Figures of the Active and Contemplative Life in Augustine's *Contra Faustum Manichaeum*." In *Theoria, Praxis, and the Contemplative Life*, edited by Thomas Bénatouïl and Mauro Bonazzi, 215–28. Leiden: Brill, 2012.
Cary, Phillip. *Inner Grace: Augustine and the Traditions of Plato and Paul*. Oxford: Oxford University Press, 2008.
Cazier, Pierre. "La *compelle intrare* d'Augustin, mise en perspective." In *Violence et religion*, edited by Pierre Cazier and Jean-Marie Delmaire, 15–39. Lille: Université Lille, 1998.
Cimma, Maria Rose. *L'episcopalis audientia nelle costituzioni imperiali da Costantino a Giustiniano*. Turin: Giappichelli, 1989.
Clair, Joseph. *Discerning the Good in the Letters and Sermons of Augustine*. Oxford: Oxford University Press, 2016.
Colish, Marcia. "Why the Portiana? Reflections on the Milanese Basilica Crisis of 386." *Journal of Early Christian Studies* 10 (2002) 361–72.
Collinson, Patrick. "If Constantine, then also Theodosius: St Ambrose and the Integrity of the Elizabethan *Ecclesia Anglicana*." *Journal of Ecclesiastical History* 30 (1979) 205–29.
Connolly, William E. *The Augustinian Imperative: A Reflection on the Politics of Morality*. Newbury Park, CA: Sage, 1993.
Corsaro, Francesco. "Il trono e l'altare de Constantino a Theodosio: *De Obitu Theodosii* di Ambrogio." In *Vescovi e pastori in epoca Teodosiana*, 2:601–11. Rome: Institutum Patristicum Augustinianum, 1997.
Couenhoven, Jesse. *Stricken by Sin, Cured by Christ: Agency, Necessity, and Culpability in Augustinian Theology*. Oxford: Oxford University Press, 2013.
Courcelle, Pierre. "Jugements de Rufin et des Augustin sur les empereurs du IVe siècle et la défaite suprême du paganisme." *Revue des Études anciennes* 71 (1969) 100–130.
Crespin, Rémi. *Ministère et sainteté: Pastorale du clergé et solution de la crise donatiste dans la vie et la doctrine de saint Augustin*. Paris: Études augustiniennes, 1965.
Cristofoli, Roberto. "Religione e strumentalizzazione politica: Costantino e la propaganda contro Licinio." In *Istituzioni, carismi, ed esercizio del potere (IV-VI secolo d.C.)*, edited by Giorgio Bonamente and Rita Lizzi Testa, 155–70. Bari: Edipuglia, 2010.
Curbelié, Philippe. *La justice dans "La cité de Dieu"*. Paris: Institut d'études Augustiniennes, 2004.
D'Agostino, Francesco. "L'antigiurdismo di S. Agostino." *Rivista internazionale di filosofia del diritto* 64 (1987) 30–51.
Dassman, Ernst. *Die Eine Kirche in vielen Bildern: Zur Ekklesiologie der Kirchenväter*. Stuttgart: Hiersmann, 2010.
Decret, François. *Aspects du manichéisme dans l'Afrique romaine*. Paris: Études augustiniennes, 1970.
Demougeot, Émilienne. *De l'unité à la division de l'empire romaine, 395–410*. Paris: Adrien-Maisonnueve, 1951.
De Salvo, Lietta. "Gli spazi del potere ecclesiastico nella Ippona di Agostino." *L'Africa romana* 19 (2010) 1035–52.

Bibliography

Di Berardino, Angelo. "Rileggere il 410 altraverso le fonti letterarie." In *Roma e il sacco del 410: Realtà, interpretazione, mito*, edited by Angelo Di Berardino et al., 1–40. Rome: Institutum Patristicum Augustinianum, 2012.

Dodaro, Robert. "Augustine and the Possibility of Political Conscience." In *Augustinus: Ethik und Politik*, edited by Cornelius Mayer, 223–41. Würzburg: Augustinus-Verlag, 2009.

———. "Augustine on the Statesman and the Two Cities." In *A Companion to Augustine*, edited by Mark Vessey, 386–97. Malden, MA: Wiley-Blackwell, 2012.

———. "Augustine's Revision of the Heroic Ideal." *Augustinian Studies* 36 (2005) 141–57.

———. "Augustine's Secular City." In *Augustine and His Critics*, edited by Robert Dodaro and George Lawless, 231–59. London: Routledge, 2000.

———. *Christ and the Just Society in the Thought of Augustine*. Cambridge: Cambridge University Press, 2004.

———. "*Ecclesia* and *Res Publica*: How Augustinian Are Neo-Augustinian Politics?" In *Augustine and Postmodern Thought: A New Alliance against Modernity?*, edited by Lieven Boeve et al., 237–71. Leuven: Peeters, 2009.

———. "Political and Theological Virtues in Augustine, Letter 155 to Macedonius." *Augustiniana* 54 (2004) 431–74.

Dossey, Leslie. "Judicial Violence and the Ecclesiastical Courts in Late Antique North Africa." In *Law, Society, and Authority in Late Antiquity*, edited by Ralph W. Mathisen, 98–114. Oxford: Oxford University Press, 2001.

———. *Peasant and Empire in Christian North Africa*. Berkeley: University of California Press, 2010.

Drake, H. A. *Constantine and the Bishops: The Politics of Intolerance*. Baltimore: Johns Hopkins University Press, 2000.

———. "Intolerance, Religious Violence, and Political Legitimacy in Late Antiquity." *Journal of the American Academy of Religion* 79 (2011) 193–235.

Drecoll, Volker Henning. "Die Bedeutung der Gnadenlehre Augustins für die Gegenwart." In *Augustinus: Ethik und Politik*, edited by Cornelius Mayer, 129–50. Würzburg: Augustinus-Verlag, 2009.

Dupont, Anthony. "The Prayer Theme in Augustine's Sermons *ad populum*." *Zeitschrift für antikes Christentum* 14 (2010) 379–408.

Dupont, Anthony, and Matthew Alan Gaumer. "*Gratia Dei, Gratia Sacramenti*: Grace in Augustine of Hippo's Anti-Donatist Writings." *Ephemerides Theologicae Lovaniensis* 86 (2010) 307–29.

Duval, Yves-Marie. "L'éloge de Théodose dans la *Cité de Dieu*: Sa place, son sens, et ses sources." *Recherches Augustiniennes* 4 (1966) 135–79.

Ebbeler, Jennifer V. *Disciplining Christians: Correction and Community in Augustine's Letters*. Oxford: Oxford University Press, 2012.

Eck, Werner. "Der Einfluß der konstantinischen Wende auf die Auswahl der Bischofe im 4. und 5. Jahrhundert." *Ariel* 8 (1975) 561–85.

———. "Der Episkopat im spätantiken Africa: Organisatorische Entwicklung, soziale Herkunft, und öffentliche Funktionen." *Historische Zeitschrift* 236 (1983) 265–95.

Elm, Eva. *Die Macht der Weisheit: Das Bild des Bischofs in der "Vita Augustini" des Possidius und anderen spätantiken und frühmittelalterlichen Bischofsviten*. Leiden: Brill, 2003.

Erler, Michael. "Die helfende Hand Gottes: Augustins Gnadenlehre im Kontext des kaiserzeitlichen Platonismus." In *Augustinus: Ethik und Politik*, edited by Cornelius Mayer, 87–108. Würzburg: Augustinus-Verlag, 2009.

Bibliography

Ernesti, Jörg. *Princeps Christianus und Kaiser aller Römer: Theodosius der Große im Lichte zeitgenössischer Quellen.* Paderborn: Schöningh, 1998.
Errington, R. Malcolm. "Christian Accounts of the Religious Legislation of Theodosius." *Klio: Beiträge zur alten Geschichte* 79 (1997) 398–443.
———. *Roman Imperial Policy from Julian to Theodosius.* Chapel Hill: University of North Carolina Press, 2006.
Evers, Alexander. *Church, Cities, and People: A Study of the Plebs in the Church and Cities of Roman Africa in Late Antiquity.* Leuven: Peeters, 2010.
Faivre, Alexander. *Chrétiens et Églises: Des identités en construction; Acteurs, structures, frontiéres du champ religieux chrétien.* Paris: Cerf, 2011.
Ferraro, Giuseppe. "Lo Spirito Sancto nella esegesi agostiniana della prima lettera di Giovanni." *Teresianum* 60 (2009) 49–84.
Février, Paul. "Discours d'Église et réalité historique dans les nouvelles lettres de Saint Augustin." In *Les lettres de saint Augustin découvertes par Johannes Divjak,* edited by Johannes Divjak, 101–15. Paris: Études Augustiniennes, 1983.
Fortin, Ernest L. "Justice as the Foundation of the Political Community: Augustine and the Pagan Models." In *Augustine and Modern Law,* edited by Richard O. Brooks and James Bernard Murphy, 117–38. Burlington, VT: Ashgate, 2011.
Fraïsse, Anne. "La théologie du miracle dans la *Cité de Dieu* et le témoignage du *De Miraculis Sancti Stephani.*" In *Saint Augustin, la Numidie et la société de son temps,* edited by Serge Lancel et al., 131–43. Paris: Boccard, 2005.
Frakes, Robert M. *"Contra Potentium Iniurias": The "Defensor Civitatis" and Late Roman Justice.* Munich: Beck, 2001.
Galvão-Sobrinho, Carlos R. *Doctrine and Power: Theological Controversy and Christian Leadership in the Later Roman Empire.* Berkeley: University of California Press, 2013.
García Mac Gaw, Carlos. *Le problème du baptême dans le schisme donatiste.* Bordeaux: Boccard, 2008.
Gaudemet, Jean. *L'Église dans l'empire romain, IVe-Ve siècles.* Paris: Sirey, 1958.
Gebbia, Clara. "Sant'Agostino e l'episcopalis audientia." *L'Africa romana* 6 (1988) 683–95.
Gregory, Eric. *Politics and the Order of Love: An Augustinian Ethics of Democratic Citizenship.* Chicago: University of Chicago Press, 2008.
Groß-Albenhausen, Kristen. *Imperator Christianissimus: Der christliche Kaiser bei Ambrosius und Johannes Chrysostomus.* Frankfurt am Main: Marthe Clauss, 1999.
Hahn, Johannes. *Gewalt und religiöser Konflikt: Studien zu den Auseinandersetzung zwischen Christen, Heiden, und Juden im Osten des römischen Reiches von Konstantin bis Theodosius II.* Berlin: Akademie Verlag, 2004.
Hanson, R. P. C. "The Reaction of the Church to the Collapse of the Western Roman Empire in the Fifth Century." *Vigiliae Christianae* 26 (1972) 272–87.
Harding, Brian. "The Use of Alexander the Great in Augustine's *City of God.*" *Augustinian Studies* 39 (2008) 113–28.
Heather, Peter. *The Fall of the Roman Empire: A New History of Rome and the Barbarians.* Oxford: Oxford University Press, 2006.
Heil, Uta. "Antiarianisches in den neutestamentlichen Predigten von Augustinus: Eine Problemanzeige." In *Tractatio Scripturarum: Philological, Exegetical, Rhetorical, and Theological Studies in Augustine's Sermons,* edited by Anthony Dupont et al., 373–403. Turnhout: Brepols, 2012.

Hermanowicz, Erika T. "Catholic Bishops and Appeals to the Imperial Court: A Legal Study of the Calama Riots in 408." *Journal of Early Christian Studies* 12 (2004) 481–521.

———. *Possidius of Calama: A Study of the North African Episcopate at the Time of Augustine*. Oxford: Oxford University Press, 2008.

Höffe, Otfried. "Positivismus plus Moralismus: Zu Augustinus' eschatologische Staatstheorie." In *Augustinus: "De civitate Dei"*, edited by Christoph Horn, 259–87. Berlin: Akademie Verlag, 1997.

Hollingworth, Miles. *The Pilgrim City: St. Augustine of Hippo and His Innovation in Political Thought*. London: T. & T. Clark, 2010.

Hombert, Pierre-Marie. "Augustin, prédicateur de la grâce au début de son épiscopat." In *Augustin prédicateur (395–411)*, edited by Goulven Madec, 217–45. Paris: Institut d'études Augustiniennes, 1998.

Horn, Christoph. "Augustinus über politische Ethik und legitime Staatsgewalt." In *Augustinus: Recht und Gewalt*, edited by Cornelius Mayer, 49–62. Würzburg: Echter, 2010.

———. "Politische Gerechtigkeit bei Cicero und Augustinus." *Etica & Politica* 9 (2007) 46–70.

Hugoniot, Christophe. "Les légats du proconsul d'Afrique à la fin du IVe siècle et au début du Ve siècle ap. J.-C à la lumière des sermons et lettres d'Augustin." *L'Africa romana* 14 (2002) 2067–87.

Hunt, David. "The Church as a Public Institution." In vol. 13 of *The Cambridge Ancient History*, edited by Averil Cameron and Peter Garnsey, 238–76. Cambridge: Cambridge University Press, 2014.

Inglebert, Hervé. "Universitalité chrétienne et monarchie impériale dans les nouveaux sermons d'Augustin découverts à Mayence." In *Augustin prédicateur (395–411)*, edited by Goulven Madec, 449–70. Paris: Institut d'études Augustiniennes, 1998.

Jacques, François. "La défenseur de cité d'après la Lettre 22* de saint Augustin." *Revue d'études augustiniennes* 32 (1986) 56–73.

Jones, A. H. M. *The Later Roman Empire, 284–602: A Social, Economic and Administrative Survey*. Vol. 1. Norman: University of Oklahoma Press, 1964.

Kah, Marianne. *"Die Welt der Römer mit der Seele suchend . . .". Die Religiosität des Prudentius im Spannungsfeld zwischen Pietas Christiana und Pietas Romana*. Bonn: Borengässer, 1989.

Karfíková, Lenka. *Grace and the Will according to Augustine*. Leiden: Brill, 2012.

Kaufman, Peter Iver. "Augustine and Corruption." *History of Political Thought* 30 (2009) 47–59.

———. "Augustine's Dystopia." In *Augustine's City of God: A Critical Guide*, edited by James Wetzel, 55–74. Cambridge: Cambridge University Press, 2012.

———. "Christian Realism and Augustinian (?) Liberalism." *Journal of Religious Ethics* 38 (2010) 698–724.

———. "*Deposito Diademate*: Augustine's Emperors." *Religions* 6 (2015) 317–27.

———. "Donatism Revisited: Moderates and Militants in Late Antique North Africa." *Journal of Late Antiquity* 2 (2009) 131–42.

———. *Incorrectly Political: Augustine and Thomas More*. Notre Dame: University of Notre Dame Press, 2007.

———. *Redeeming Politics*. Princeton: Princeton University Press, 1990.

BIBLIOGRAPHY

Kelly, Christopher. *Ruling the Later Roman Empire*. Cambridge: Harvard University Press, 2006.

Kriegbaum, Bernhard. *Kirche der Traditoren oder Kirche der Märtyrer? Die Vorgeschichte des Donatismus*. Innsbruck: Tyrolia, 1986.

Laferrière, Anik. "The Augustinian Heart: Late Medieval Images of Augustine as a Monastic Identity." *Journal of Ecclesiastical History* 66 (2015) 488–508.

Lakhlif, Mustapha. "Saint Augustin et l'incident de 411 à Hippone." *L'Africa romana* 19 (2012) 1099–1108.

Lam, Qui Cong Joseph. "Die Menschwerdung des Gottessohnes: Christliche Identitätsfindung sowie theologisch-gesellschaftlichen Konsequenzen nach Augustinus von Hippo." *Augustiniana* 59 (2009) 227–46.

Lamirande, Émilien. "Aux origines du dialogue interconfessionnel: Saint Augustin et les donatistes, vingt ans de tentatives infructueuses (391–411)." *Studia canonica* 32 (1998) 203–28.

Lamoreaux, John. "Episcopal Courts in Late Antiquity." *Journal of Early Christian Studies* 3 (1995) 143–67.

Lancel, Serge. "L'affaire d'Antoninus de Fussala: Pays, choses et gens de la Numidie d'Hippone saisis dans la durée d'une procedure d'enquête épiscopale." In *Les lettres de saint Augustin découvertes par Johannes Divjak*, edited by Johannes Divjak, 267–85. Paris: Études Augustiniennes, 1983.

———. "L'Antiquité tardive et le christianisme." In *Algérie antique*, edited by Claude Sintes and Ymouna Rebahi, 236–48. Arles: Éditions du Musée de l'Arles et de la Provence antiques, 2003.

———. *Saint Augustin*. Paris: Fayard, 1999.

Lemmens, Leon. *Foi chrétienne et agir moral selon Saint Augustin*. Rome: Institutum Patristicum Augustinianum, 2011.

Lenski, Noel E. "Evidence for the *Audientia Episcopalis* in the New Letters of Augustine." In *Law, Society, and Authority in Late Antiquity*, edited by Ralph W. Mathisen, 83–97. Oxford: Oxford University Press, 2001.

Lepelley, Claude. "L'Afrique à la veille de la conquête vandal: Quelques aspects de l'administration des provinces romaines d'Afrique avant la conquête vandal." *Antiquité tardive* 10 (2002) 61–72.

———. "L'aristocratie lettrée païenne: Une menace aux yeux d'Augustin." In *Augustin prédicateur (395–411)*, edited by Goulven Madec, 327–42. Paris: Institut d'études Augustiniennes, 1998.

———. *Aspects de l'Afrique romaine: Les cités, la vie rurale, le christianisme*. Bari: Edipuglia, 2001.

———. "Augustin face à la christianisation de l'Afrique romaine." In *Le problème de la christianisation du monde antique*, edited by Hervé Inglebert et al., 269–79. Paris: Picard, 2010.

———. *Les cités de l'Afrique romaine au Bas-Empire*. 2 vols. Paris: Études Augustiniennes, 1979–81.

———. "Liberté, colonat et esclavage d'aprés la lettre 24*: La juridiction épiscopale *de liberale causa*." In *Les lettres de saint Augustin découvertes par Johannes Divjak*, edited by Johannes Divjak, 329–42. Paris: Études Augustiniennes, 1983.

———. "Le patronat épiscopal aux IVe et Ve siècles continuités et ruptures avec le patronat classique." In *L'Évêque dans le cité du IVe au Ve siècle: Image et autorité*, edited by Éric Rebillard and Claire Sotinel, 17–33. Rome: École française, 1998.

Bibliography

———. "La période romaine: Pouvoir et institutions politiques." In *Algérie antique*, edited by Claude Sintes and Ymouna Rebahi, 58–68. Avignon: Éditions du Musée de l'Arles et de la Provence antiques, 2003.

Leppin, Hartmut. *Theodosius der Große: Auf dem Weg zum christlichen Imperium*. Darmstadt: Primus, 2003.

Lettieri, Gaetano. *Il senso della storia in Agostino: Il "saeculum" e la Gloria nel "De civitate Dei"*. Rome: Borla, 1988.

Lienemann, Wolfgang. "Eschatologik als Antipolitik? Politische Ethik zwischen weltlichen Staat und christlichen Friedenzeugnis: Überlegungen im Blick auf Augustinus, De civitate Dei XIX." In *Alles in Allem: Eschatologische Anstösse*, edited by Ruth Hess and Martin Leiner, 409–25. Neukirchen-Vluyn: Neukirchener Verlag, 2005.

Lim, Richard. "Augustine and Roman Public Spectacles." In *A Companion to Augustine*, edited by Mark Vessey, 138–50. Malden, MA: Wiley-Blackwell, 2012.

Lippold, Adolf. *Theodosius der Große und seine Zeit*. Munich: Beck, 1980.

Lizzi, Rita. "I vescovi e i potentes della terra: Definizione e limite del ruolo episcopale nelle due partes imperii fra IV e V secolo." In *L'Évêque dans le cité du IVe au Ve siècle: Image et autorité*, edited by Éric Rebillard and Claire Sotinel, 81–104. Rome: École française de Rome, 1998.

MacMullen, Ramsay. *Changes in the Roman Empire: Essays in the Ordinary*. Princeton: Princeton University Press, 1990.

Mandouze, André. *Avec et pour Augustin: Mélanges*. Edited by Luce Pietri and Christine Mandouze. Paris: Cerf, 2013.

Marcos, Mar. "Anti-Pelagian Legislation in Context." In *Lex et Religio*, edited by Vittorino Grossi, 317–44. Rome: Institutum Patristicum Augustinianum, 2013.

Markus, Robert. *The End of Ancient Christianity*. Cambridge: Cambridge University Press, 1990.

———. *Saeculum: History and Society in the Age of Saint Augustine*. Cambridge: Cambridge University Press, 1970.

———. "Tempora Christiana Revisited." In *Augustine and His Critics*, edited by Robert Dodaro and George Lawless, 201–13. London: Routledge, 2000.

Marschall, Werner. *Karthago und Rom: Die Stellung nordafrikanischen Kirche zum apostolischen Stuhl in Rom*. Stuttgart: Hiersemann, 1971.

Mathewes, Charles. "The Liberation of Questioning in Augustine's *Confessions*." *Journal of the American Academy of Religion* 70 (2002) 539–60.

———. *The Republic of Grace: Augustinian Thoughts for Dark Times*. Grand Rapids: Eerdmans, 2010.

———. *A Theology of Public Life*. Cambridge: Cambridge University Press, 2007.

Matthews, John. *Western Aristocracies and Imperial Court, A.D. 364–425*. Oxford: Clarendon, 1975.

Mattingly, David J., and R. Bruce Hitchner. "Roman Africa: An Archaeological Review." *Journal of Roman Studies* 85 (1995) 165–213.

McLynn, Neil B. "Administrator: Augustine in His Diocese." In *A Companion to Augustine*, edited by Mark Vessey, 310–22. Malden, MA: Wiley-Blackwell, 2012.

———. *Ambrose of Milan: Church and Court in a Christian Capital*. Berkeley: University of California Press, 1994.

———. "Augustine's Roman Empire." *Augustinian Studies* 30 (1999) 29–44.

Bibliography

———. "*Genere Hispanus*: Theodosius, Spain, and Nicene Orthodoxy." In *Hispania in Late Antiquity: Current Perspectives*, edited by Kim Bowes and Michael Kulikowski, 77–120. Leiden: Brill, 2005.

———. "The Transformation of Imperial Churchgoing in the Fourth Century." In *Approaching Late Antiquity: The Transformation from Early to Late Empire*, edited by Simon Swain and Mark Edwards, 235–70. Oxford: Oxford University Press, 2004.

Meer, Frederik van der. *Augustine the Bishop: The Life and Work of a Father of the Church*. Translated by Brian Battershaw and G. R. Lamb. London: Sheed and Ward, 1961.

Merdinger, Jane. *Rome and the African Church in the Time of Augustine*. New Haven: Yale University Press, 1997.

Moreau, Madelaine. *Le dossier Marcellinus dans la correspondence de saint Augustin*. Paris: Études Augustiniennes, 1973.

Müller, Jörn. *Willensschwäche in Antike und Mittelalter: Eine Problemgeschichte von Sokrates bis Johannes Duns Scotus*. Leuven: Leuven University Press, 2009.

Nauroy, Gérard. "Le fouet et le miel: l'combat d'Ambroise en 386 contre l'arianisme milanais." *Recherches augustiniennes* 23 (1988) 3–86.

Neer, Joost van. "Bouwen aan het geloof: De twee Modeltoespraken in *De cathechizandis rudibus*." *Lampas* 43 (2010) 351–62.

Nisula, Timo. *Augustine and the Functions of Concupiscence*. Leiden: Brill, 2012.

Noethlichs, Karl Leo. "Materialien zum Bischofsbild aus dem spätantiken Rechtsquellen." *Jahrbuch für Antike und Christentum* 16 (1973) 28–59.

Oliveira, Júlio César Magalhães de. "*Ut maiores pagani non sint!* Pouvoir, iconoclasme, et action populaire à Carthage au début du Ve siècle." *Antiquité tardive* 14 (2006) 245–62.

Oost, Stewart Irvin. "The Revolt of Heraclian." *Classical Philology* 61 (1966) 236–42.

Osgood, Josiah. *Claudius Caesar: Image and Power in the Early Roman Empire*. Cambridge: Cambridge University Press, 2011.

Parrish, John. *Paradoxes of Political Ethics*. Cambridge: Cambridge University Press, 2007.

Perreau-Saussine, Emile. "Heaven as a Political Theme in Augustine's *City of God*." In *Paradise in Antiquity: Jewish and Christian Views*, edited by Markus Bockmuehl and Guy G. Stroumsa, 179–91. Cambridge: Cambridge University Press, 2010.

Petit, Jean-François. "Sur le phénomène amical: L'expérience de l'amitie chex saint Augustin." *Transversailités: Revue de l'institut catholique de Paris* 113 (2010) 47–63.

Piccolo, Gaetano. *I processi di apprendimento in Agostino d'Ippona*. Rome: Aracne, 2009.

Pietri, Charles. *Roma Christiana: Recherches sur l'église de Rom, son organisation, sa politique, son idéologie de Miltiade à Sixte II (311–440)*. 2 vols. Rome: École française de Rome, 1976–.

Ployd, Adam. "The Power of Baptism: Augustine's Pro-Nicene Response to the Donatists." *Journal of Early Christian Studies* 22 (2014) 519–40.

Potter, David S. *The Roman Empire at Bay, AD 180–395*. London: Routledge, 2004.

Raikas, Kauko. "*Audientia Episcopalis*: Problematik zwischen Staat und Kirche bei Augustin." *Augustinianum* 37 (1997) 459–81.

Rapp, Claudia. *Holy Bishops in Late Antiquity: The Nature of Christian Leadership in an Age of Transition*. Berkeley: University of California Press, 2005.

Rebillard, Eric. "Augustin et le rituel épistolaire de l'élite sociale et culturelle de son temps: Éléments pour une analyse processuelle des relations de l'évêque et de cité dans l'antiquité tardive." In *L'Évêque dans le cité du IVe au Ve siècle: Image et autorité*, edited by Éric Rebillard and Claire Sotinel, 127–52. Rome: École française de Rome, 1998.

———. *Christians and Their Many Identities in Late Antiquity, North Africa, 200–450 CE*. Ithaca: Cornell University Press, 2013.

Rémy, Gérard. "La notion de *medietas* chez Saint Augustin." *Revue des sciences religieuses* 85 (2011) 211–29.

Ribreau, M. Mickaël. "Quelle est la place de l'heretique dans l'église? L'exemple du *Contra Julianum* de Saint Augustin." In *Le Pères et l'Église et les dissidents: Dissidence, exclusion, réintégration dans les communautés chrétiennes des six premiers siècles*, edited by Pascal-Grégoire Delage, 261–80. Royan: CaritasPatrum, 2010.

Ruokanen, Miikka. *Theology of Social Life in Augustine's "De civitate Dei"*. Göttingen: Vandenhoeck and Ruprecht, 1993.

Sabw Kanyang, Jean-Anatole. *Episcopus et plebs: L'évêque et la communauté ecclésiale dans les conciles africains (345–524)*. Bern: P. Lang, 2000.

Salamito, Jean-Marie. "Ambivalence de la christianisation, frontières de l'église, identité chrétienne." In *Le problème de la christianisation du monde antique*, edited by Hervé Inglebert et al., 63–75. Paris: Picard, 2010.

———. "Constantin vu par Augustin: Pour une relecture De Civ. 5.25." In *Costantino prima e dopo Costantino*, edited by Giorgio Bonamente et al., 549–62. Bari: Edipulgia, 2012.

———. *Les virtuoses et la multitude: Aspects sociaux de la controverse entre Augustin et les pélagiens*. Grenoble: Millon, 2005.

Salzman, Michele Renee. *The Making of a Christian Aristocracy: Social and Religious Change in the Western Roman Empire*. Cambridge: Harvard University Press, 2002.

Schindler, Alfred. "Vermitteln die neuentdeckten Augustin-Briefe auch neue Erkentnisse über den Donatismus." In *Les lettres de saint Augustin découvertes par Johannes Divjak*, edited by Johannes Divjak, 117–21. Paris Études Augustiniennes, 1983.

Shaw, Brent D. *Sacred Violence: African Christians and Sectarian Hatred in the Age of Augustine*. Cambridge: Cambridge University Press, 2011.

Sieben, Hermann Josef. "Augustins Auseinandersetzung mit dem Arianismus außerhalb seiner explizit antiarianischen Schriften." *Theologie und Philosophie* 81 (2006) 181–212.

Smith, James K. A. "The Politics of Desire: Augustine's Political Phenomenology." In *Augustine and Postmodern Thought: A New Alliance against Modernity?*, edited by Lieven Boeve et al., 211–35. Leuven: Peeters, 2009.

Szidat, Joachim. "Constantin bei Augustin." *Revue des études augustiniennes et patristiques* 36 (1990) 243–56.

———. "Zum Sklavenhandel in der Spätantike." *Historia* 34 (1985) 360–71.

Tholen, Ivonne. *Die Donatisten in den Predigten Augustins: Kommunikationslinien des Bischofs von Hippo mit seinen Predigthören*. Berlin: LIT Verlag, 2010.

Tornau, Christian. *Zwischen Rhetorik und Philosophie: Augustins Argumentationstechnik in "De civitate Dei" und ihr Bildungsgeschichtlicher Hintergrund*. Berlin: de Gruyter, 2006.

Tuliere, André. "La politique de Théodose le Grand et les évêques de la fin du IVe siècle." In vol. 1 of *Vescovi e pastori in epoca teodosiana*, 45–71. Rome: Institutum Patristicum Augustinianum, 1997.

Uhalde, Kevin. *Expectations of Justice in the Age of Augustine*. Philadelphia: University of Pennsylvania Press, 2007.

BIBLIOGRAPHY

Vander Valk, Frank. "Friendship, Politics, and Augustine's Consolidation of the Self." *Religious Studies* 45 (2009) 125–46.

Vismara, Giulio. "Ancora sulla *episcopalis audientia.*" *Studia et documenta historiae et juris* 53 (1987) 54–73.

———. *Episcopalis Audientia: L'attività giurusdizionale del vescovo per la resoluzione delle controversie private tra laici nel diritto romano e nella storia del diritto italiano fino al secolo nono*. Milan: Vita e Pensiero, 1937.

Ward-Perkins, Bryan. "The Cities." In vol. 13 of *The Cambridge Ancient History*, edited by Averil Cameron and Peter Garnsey, 337–425. Cambridge: Cambridge University Press, 1997.

Weissenberg, Timo J. *Die Friedenslehre des Augustinus: Theologische Grundlagen und ethische Entfaltung*. Stuttgart: Kohlhammer, 2005.

Wetzel, James. *Augustine and the Limits of Virtue*. Cambridge: Cambridge University Press, 1992.

———. "A Tangle of Two Cities." *Augustinian Studies* 43 (2012) 5–23.

Whitby, Michael L. "Emperors and Armies, AD 235–395." In *Approaching Late Antiquity: The Transformation from Early to Late Empire*, edited by Simon Swain and Mark Edwards, 156–86. Oxford: Oxford University Press, 2004.

Wordsworth, William. *The Excursion*. Edited by Sally Bushell et al. Ithaca: Cornell University Press, 2007.

Ziolkowski, Theodore. "*Tolle Lege*: Epiphanies of the Book." *The Modern Language Review* 109 (2014) 1–14.

Zocca, Elena. "La figura del santo vescovo in Africa da Ponzio a Possidio." In *Vescovi e pastori in epoca teodosiana*, 2:469–92. Rome: Institutum Patristicum Augustinianum, 1997.

———. "L'identità Cristiana nel dibattito fra cattolici e donatisti." *Annali di storia dell'esegesi* 21 (2004) 109–30.

Index

Acta Archelai, 49, 169
Adrianople, battle of, 11, 23, 114
Agamben, Giorgio, ix
Alaric, Goth commander, 9, 157, 165
Alexander, emperor, 9–10, 146
Alici, Luigi 101, 170
Alypius, bishop of Thagaste, 3, 64, 68–69, 73, 89, 92, 99, 113, 143
Ambrose, bishop of Milan, 2, 31–33, 38, 48, 101, 135–37, 169
   influence and conflicts at the imperial Court, 12, 23, 41, 70–71, 117–18
Antoninus, bishop of Fussala, 40, 60–63
Antony, Egyptian ascetic, 162
Apostolic succession, 48–49
Apringius, proconsul, 133, 141–42, 148–49
Arbogast, Frankish general, 24–27
Arcadius, emperor, 11–13, 25, 33, 64–65
Arendt, Hanna, ix
Arius and Arian Christians (anti-Nicene Christologies), 22–24, 43, 75, 96, 168
Arles, council of (314), 15, 20, 50
Athanasius, bishop of Alexandria, 22
Augustine, bishop of Hippo Regius
   on ambition, 8–11, 29–30, 34–35, 153–56, 158–59, 162–63
   Christians as pilgrims, 71–73, 129–30, 146–47, 164–66

   on church courts, 40, 63–70, 147–50
   on church discipline, 2–5, 15–16, 81–91, 102–4, 111–16, 135
   on compassion and charity, 50–51, 55, 80–88, 94–95, 103–106, 113–16
   early career of, 2–3, 12, 35–38, 46–48, 71, 75–76, 107–8, 117, 143, 166–67
   on Emperor Theodosius' penance, 30–33, 119
   on humility, 30–31, 35, 43, 89–95, 99–101, 111–12, 138, 143, 158, 162–63
   on infant baptism, 5, 104–6, 148
   on law enforcement, 29–30, 55–56, 124, 143–44, 147–48
   and local governments 40–42, 119–23, 129–31, 143–44, 147, 153–55, 167
   on martyrs and miracles, 106–9, 145, 164
   on pagans' pageants, 80–81, 104, 152
   against perfectionism, 19, 48–50, 84–87, 91–95, 102–11, 138, 143, 158, 167–68
   on repentance, 8, 45–46, 54–57, 77–81, 99–102, 109, 126–27
   on slavery, 67–70
   on wealth and poverty, 7–8, 40–41, 58–60, 151–53, 166
Aurelius, bishop of Carthage, 73

Index

Aurelius, bishop of Macomades, 61, 63

Beduhn, Jason, 46–47, 170
Bénabou, Marcel, 118, 170
Berndt, Guido, 162, 170
Bishops, misconduct of, 59–63
Boniface, Roman commander, 161
Brandenburg, Hugo, 38, 170
Brown, Peter, 32, 93, 114, 120–21, 162, 170
Bruno, Michael, ix, 1, 125, 170
Buencasa-Pérez, Carles, 134, 170

Caecilian, bishop of Carthage, 15, 51, 83, 134
Carthage, council of (411), 39, 49–51, 60, 76, 82, 89, 136–40, 169
Celestine, bishop of Rome, 62
Cicero, 2, 9, 80, 153
Clair, Joseph, ix, 146, 171
Claudius, emperor, 118
Constantine, emperor, 11, 14–22, 35–36, 50, 63–64, 67–68, 109–10, 139, 156, 166
Constantius II, emperor, 19, 22, 29
Corsaro, Francesco, 24–25, 171
Curbelié, Philippe, 155, 171
Cyprian, bishop of Carthage, 163

Darius, Roman statesman, 155
Decian persecution, 163
Defensores civitatum, 40–41, 122
Demetrias, daughter of Juliana, 89–90, 92
Diocletian, emperor, 22, 40
Dioscorus, student, 95–96
Dodaro, Robert, ix, 1, 78, 119, 125–29, 150, 172
Donatism, 3–5, 33, 39–40, 49–52, 62, 66–67, 70–75, 83–85, 102–6, 132–41, 144, 151, 158, 167
  Augustine's offer to reconcile with, 139–40

origins of initial schism, 12–13, 19, 81–82, 109–10, 134, 137–39
subsequent schisms, 84–85
Donatus, 168
Drake, H. A. 70–71, 172
Dupont, Anthony, 85, 172

Eck, Werner, 38, 172
Ernesti, Jörg, 34, 173
Eugenius, emperor, 24–27
Eusebius Pamphili, bishop of Caesarea (Palestine) and historian, 17–18
Eusebius, Roman statesman, 132–33
Eustochius, jurist, 67–69
Eutropius, Roman statesman, 12–13

Faustinus, would-be Christian, 110–11
Faustus, Manichaean orator, 47–48
Felix, bishop of Apthungi, 15
Ferraro, Guiseppe, 76, 173
Flavianus, Roman statesman and historian, 25
Fraïsse, Anne, 107, 173
Frigidus, battle of, 24–27

Gaiseric, Vandal commander, 161–62
Gaudemet, Jean, 64–65, 173
Gaudentius, Donatus bishop of Timgad, 76
Gaumer, Matthew Alan, 85, 173
Gebbia, Clara, 64, 67, 69–70, 173
Gildo, African commander, 12–13
Gratian, emperor, 17, 28, 41
Gregory, Eric, ix, 1, 125, 173

Hahn, Joannes, 32, 173
Hanson, R. P. C., 29–30, 173
Heraclian, Roman consul, 141
Heraclius, bishop-designate of Hippo, 73–74
Hercules, statue of (Carthage), 154–55
Hesychius, bishop of Salona, 157

Index

Höffe, Otfried, 145, 154, 159, 174
Hollingworth, Miles, ix, 129, 174
Honoratus, bishop of Thiave, 163–64
Honorius, emperor, 11–12, 20, 33, 53, 72, 110, 119, 141, 161
    and church courts, 39–40, 64–65
    edicts against slavery, 26, 68–69
Horn, Christoph, 2, 130, 145, 174
Hugoniot, Christophe, 52, 69, 121, 143, 174

Jacques, François, 122, 174
Johnson, Kristin Deede, ix
Jovinian, emperor, 17
Julian, bishop of Eclanum, 94, 105, 148
Julian, emperor, 16–18, 29, 57
Juliana, mother of Demetrias, 89–90, 92
Justina, empress, 23, 71

Kah, Marianne, 120, 174

Lamirande Émilien, 50–51, 175
Lamoreaux, John, 64, 175
Lancel, Serge, 57, 67, 120, 175
Lee, Gregory, ix
Lepelley, Claude, 37, 57, 67, 70, 112, 142, 175–76
Leppin, Helmut, 29, 33, 176
Lettieri, Gaetano, 13, 176
Licinius, emperor, 22
Lizzi, Rita, 41, 176

MacMullen, Ramsay, 121, 176
Mandouze, André, 76, 176
Mani, 46, 49
Manichees and Manichaeism, 7–8, 46–49, 75, 96, 100–103
Marcellinus, tribune, 39, 51, 125–27, 132–44, 150–53, 158, 163, 167
Marinus, Roman commander, 141
Markus, Robert, 20, 26, 166, 176
Mathewes, Charles, ix, 1, 6, 77, 128, 131, 145, 176

Mathews, John, 34
Maximianus, deacon, 84
Maximus, emperor, 23–24, 26
Mclynn, Neil, 23, 97, 144, 156, 176–77
Melania, ascetic and philanthropist, 59
Miltiades, bishop of Rome, 15
Moreau, Madelaine 144, 148–49, 177

Nauroy, Gérard, 23
Nectarius of Calama, statesman, 53–58, 79, 151–53
Nicaea, council of (325), 74, 161
    Nicene Christology, 22–24, 28–29
Nisulo, Timo, 105, 177

Optatus, Donatist bishop of Thamugadi, 12–13

Pagans and paganism, 3, 21–28, 33, 38, 42, 52–58, 62, 79–81, 98, 108, 113, 152–53
    Augustine on pagan deities, 19, 109
    Augustine's overtures to, 119–22, 131–32
    revivals of, 25–26, 57
Parrish, John, 124, 177
Paulinus, bishop of Nola, 99
Pelagians and Pelagianism, 3–6, 33, 51–52, 88–106, 143–44, 164–65
    alleged optimism of, 5, 66, 71, 92–95, 99, 158
    Augustine's dossier of Pelagian errors, 99
Pelagius, 5, 20, 51, 89–91, 99–100, 144
Perreau-Saussine, Emile, 20, 177
Petilian, Donatist bishop of Cirta, 140
Petit, Jean-François, 83, 177
Piccolo, Gaetano, 100, 177
Pinianus, ascetic and philanthropist, 59–60
Plato and Platonism, 100–101, 107

Index

Plotinus, 107
Ployd, Adam, 105–6, 177
Porphyry, 107
Possidius, bishop of Calama, 1, 37–39, 53, 58, 65, 73, 169
Praetextatus, Roman statesman, 26
Proculianus, Donatist bishop of Hippo, 52, 132–33
Prudentius, poet, 26–29, 169,

Raikas, Kauko, 67, 177
Rapp, Claudia, 40–41, 177
Rebillard, Eric, 57, 146, 177–78
Ribreau, Mickaël, 113, 178
Romanianus, Augustine's patron, 107
Rome
    African bishops' appeals to, 61–63
    sack of (410), 18, 21, 34, 53, 157, 161, 165–66
Rufinus of Aquieia, historian, 26

Salamito, Jean-Marie, 4, 35, 90, 104, 178
Sallust, 9, 123
Salvian of Marseilles, 121
Severus, bishop of Milevis, 73
Shaw, Brent, 76, 178
Silvanus, bishop of Summa, 60
Simplicianus, bishop of Milan, 101
Smith, James K. A., 127, 178
Socrates, 107
Sozomen, historian, 32, 170
Stilicho, Roman commander, 33, 133
Symmachus, Roman statesman, 25, 117

Synesius, bishop of Ptolemais, 33, 170

Themistius, Roman orator, 28–29, 170
Theodosius, emperor, 4, 11, 17–18, 26–35, 41, 71, 141, 153
    consolidation of power, 23–26
    and paganism, 21, 53, 119–20, 156–57, 166
Tornau, Christian, 96, 102, 178
Tuliere, André, 32–33, 178

Valens, emperor, 23, 114, 157
Valentinian I, emperor, 17, 26
Valentinian II, emperor, 23–25, 71
Valentinian III, emperor, 161
Valerius, bishop of Hippo, 37–38, 73–74
Vandals (in Africa), 11, 110, 155, 161–65
Victor, bishop of Vita, 162, 170
Vismara, Giulio, 70, 179
Volusianus, proconsul, 125, 150

Ward-Perkins, Bryan, 120, 162, 179
Weissenberg, Timo, 130–31, 155, 179
Wetzel, James, ix, 155, 179
Wordsworth, William, 115, 179

Zeno, 98
Zocca, Elena, 52, 179
Zosimus, historian, 22, 28, 170

www.ingramcontent.com/pod-product-compliance
Lightning Source LLC
Chambersburg PA
CBHW031433150426
43191CB00006B/488